PRIDE AND GLORY

The Cimarron and Northwestern Railway Company

PRIDE AND GLORY

The Cimarron and Northwestern Railway Company

Tucker Baker
Matthew Hauser
Trevor Lombardi

Dedication

To the loggers and railroaders who lived and died along the Cimarron and Northwestern Railway and the Continental Tie and Lumber Company of Colfax County, New Mexico.
Gone, but not forgotten.

Cover design and front cover image: Trevor Lombardi
Back cover image: Raton Museum, Raton, New Mexico
Interior design, typesetting, and editing: Steve Lewis
Eagle Trail Press, Apache Junction, Arizona.

Library of Congress Control Number: 2021947088
ISBN: 978-0-9974267-5-5

Contents

Introduction

In the remote reaches of Colfax County, New Mexico, an old and long abandoned logging railroad is being rebuilt on its original grade by hand according to the 1907 methods used to construct the line. Abandoned for almost a hundred years, the Cimarron and Northwestern Railway (C&N) is coming back to life, not to haul timber down North Poñil Canyon to the village of Cimarron, but to educate young people on the history of logging and railroading in the American southwest. The current operation, run solely for educational purposes by the Boy Scouts of America at its high adventure base, Philmont Scout Ranch, is distant in both time and appearance from its historical predecessor. But to the Scouts and staff involved in preserving and interpreting this piece of history, the Cimarron and Northwestern is the 'Pride and Glory' of the canyon.

To the loggers and railroaders of days gone by, the C&N was indeed a major force as employer, land developer, timber harvester, transportation provider, sawmill builder, company store purveyor, and much more. In its own day the Cimarron and Northwestern Railway was a life-changing factor for those who worked and lived along its route.

The railroad and its parent timber company, the Continental Tie and Lumber Company (CT&L), have a deep and rich history in the surrounding region and in the lives of the people it impacted. The C&N may seem only as a minor factor in the larger northeastern New Mexico story, but never has the complete history of the company and associated personal biographies been fully examined and shared in precise detail and historical comparison. Granted, the history of northeastern New Mexico is a small microcosm of southwestern history, but in Colfax County alone ancient dwellings and petroglyphs dot the same canyon country where wagons traversed the Santa Fe Trail and later railroaders laid tracks. Fur trappers and gold miners plied the same Sangre de Cristo mountains and hills where Boy Scouts would later enjoy "Scouting Paradise" on backpacking treks. Cattle ranchers, fruit orchard growers, and land barons would enjoy vast ranches where prior bitter legal feuds over land ownership would descend into dark bloodshed across the whole region. It is becoming apparent that the C&N played a more significant role in this larger story that one might think upon first glance.[1]

While this book will focus on the timber lands and railroad companies, these companies consisted of people. People shaped and led these companies and the companies in turn impacted both land and people. The individual stories of the people involved with and impacted by the Cimarron and Northwestern Railway and the Continental Tie and Lumber Company are just as complex and colorful as the history and landscape in which they lived. The stories of Theodore A. Schomburg, Henry G. Frankenburger, A.G. Allen, John C. Osgood, Thomas W. Schomburg, Bert Pratt, Charles S. Wood, Guy H. Palmes, Margaret Ward, Alex McElroy, Gretchen Sammis, Robert Mahn, Edward and Mary Troutman, Waite Phillips, John Troy, and many others will be shared here as they relate to the Cimarron and Northwestern story.

Not to be forgotten are the loggers, engineers, firemen, teamsters, track workers, bridge carpenters, sawmillers, sawyers, mule skinners, and many others who accomplished the physical work. We do not know all their names and backgrounds, but explorations of historic accounts and photographs can shed light on their daily lives and how they interacted with the land. Their stories are as important and compelling as those of the timbermen who caused such profound change upon the land.

It must be noted here that any history written about a small railroad and its timber enterprises which ended in 1938 will no doubt miss some details, information, or events. The history given here is an attempt to piece together known portions of the whole into a cohesive

1 Several prominent publications provide a wealth of historical information and are excellent sources for additional reading. See Bromley's *The Last Train to Leave Cimarron, New Mexico: Why the Trains Left Cimarron*, Lamm and the Cimarron Historical Society's "*A Brief History of the Village of Cimarron*," Murphy's *Philmont: A History of New Mexico's Cimarron Country*, Pearson's *The Maxwell Land Grant*, and Zimmer and Lewis' *It Happened in the Cimarron Country*.

account with a foundation in primary historical sources from the period. Oral history, secondary historical writings, and local interpretation have played a prominent role in keeping the memory of these operations alive and perhaps this book will spur further confirmation or clarification of these accounts or shed new light on currently unknown people and events. The authors will certainly rejoice to revise or update this work should new information and artifacts become available that broadens the rich history of these companies. Join us as we delve into the fascinating and complex story of the people, places, events, and impact of the Cimarron and Northwestern Railway Company of New Mexico.

The Time Before Railroads

The land of Colfax County, New Mexico, and the Cimarron and Northwestern Railway is a region where the topography is as diverse, varied, and rich as its history and heritage. The highway welcome signs in Cimarron state it plainly, "Where the Rockies meet the Plains." The eastern portion of the county is predominantly grasslands where the Great Plains begin their ascent to meet the western half dominated by the Sangre de Cristo range of the Rocky Mountains. Spanish for "Blood of Christ," the red, pink, and brown hues illuminate the canyons and mountainsides in the setting sun.

The cool mountain waters of the Rayado, Cimarron, Canadian, and Poñil rivers commence in the high country and wind down to the plains to join the greater Canadian River watershed just southwest of nearby Springer, New Mexico. These mountain lands abound with bear, mountain lion, rabbit, marmot, raccoon, deer, elk, and trout, in their valleys, canyons, creeks, and meadows. The terra firma is conducive to the growth of corn, beans, squash, sunflowers, and of course, tremendous stands of timber ranging from piñon pine and scrub oak to Ponderosa pine, quaking aspen, and Douglas fir.

Prominent geological features such as Cimarron Canyon, Baldy Mountain, the Tooth of Time, Black Mountain, Urraca Mesa, and Wilson Mesa owe their origin to earthly forces at work before humans set foot in the area. The grasslands provide a wide home to grazing animals such as bison and cattle. These topographical conditions for life, animal husbandry, commercial harvesting, and later recreation have brought people to this region for centuries.

The canyon lands and mountain parks, where the Cimarron and Northwestern Railway would have sawmills and loggers fanning out across the countryside, had been home to a variety of people in the prior centuries. Today, almost all the land touched by the C&N and the CT&L is now located on present-day Philmont Scout Ranch and a unit of the Carson National Forest known as the Valle Vidal, Spanish for "Valley of Life." Events throughout human history have profoundly affected the land that is the focal point of this book.

The North, Middle, and South Poñil Canyons are the three main tributaries feeding the greater Poñil Canyon north of Cimarron. These canyons abounded with both human and animal life in prior centuries. Today they are only occupied for a few months during Philmont's summer season, yet large numbers of people pass through on Philmont treks or while hiking the public lands of the Valle Vidal. "Poñil" is used as a term for both the rounded shrub plant (also known as Apache Plume) with white rose-like flowers that proliferate in these drainages, as well as for a specific group of indigenous people that lived in the same area from 1100-1200 AD.

Evidence of these people was already noticeable during the heyday of the C&N, as many intricate petroglyphs line the walls of North Poñil Canyon near modern day Indian Writings Camp, a backcountry

Petroglyph panel near Indian Writings camp in North Poñil Canyon at Philmont Scout Ranch.

National Scouting Museum Collection, Cimarron, New Mexico.

Photo of Jicarilla Apache village taken in the 1870s.

Library of Congress Prints and Photographs Division, Curtis Collection, LC-USZ62-48376.

camp staffed seasonally by Philmont Scout Ranch. Later archaeological digs on both Philmont and the adjoining Chase Ranch have documented rock dwellings made in cliff overhangs and excavated pit and slab houses from this period, all having the C&N's tracks traversing directly through or adjacent to these archaeological sites.

By the time the Spanish began exerting considerable influence in northeastern New Mexico in the late 18th century, the indigenous peoples they knew in the area to be later traversed by the C&N were the Jicarilla Apache and the Ute. These tribes had sought the protection of the high-country mountains and timber, where they could escape from their traditional foes, the Comanche of the plains. These tribes would witness tremendous change over the next 200 years, as a bloody civil war would give birth to Mexican independence from Spain in 1821, with further upheaval during the Mexican-American War from 1846 to 1848. Periodic conflict with various government armies would eventually remove them from their familial lands by the close of the 19th century.[1]

The twenty-year period from 1840-1860 would significantly influence the entire trajectory of northeastern New Mexico and directly contributed to the conditions that would enable the creation and successful operation of the C&N and CT&L. The principal event was the deeding of one massive contiguous tract of land full of plains, mead-

1 Archaeological information on the Poñil Canyon: Bogan, *Let the Coyotes Howl*; Zimmer and Lewis 15-17; Murphy, *Philmont: A History*, 11-19, 25-26; and Gunnerson, "Chase Ranch."

ows, mountains, timber, and later-discovered precious minerals to individual ownership. Seeking to provide economic development and opportunity in the region, Mexican governor Manuel Armijo deeded this tract to Charles Hipolyte Trotier and Department of New Mexico secretary Guadalupe Miranda following their petition for the land in 1841. Trotier was a French Canadian by birth and origin, former fur trader, and successful Taos merchant and store owner. "Carlos Beaubien" was his preferred name upon settling in New Mexico in 1823, and history denotes him primarily by this surname. Beaubien's partnership with influential Mexican Guadalupe Miranda would secure what became known as the "Beaubien-Miranda Land Grant," defined by traditional boundaries that may seem somewhat vague by today's standards.

Other enterprising New Mexico foreigners such as Charles Bent and Ceran St. Vrain were enlisted by Beaubien to help colonize and develop the land. Meanwhile, Beaubien's son-in-law, Lucien Bonaparte Maxwell, and frontiersman Christopher "Kit" Carson assisted in establishing a permanent ranch called 'Rayado' on the creek of the same name at the south end of the grant along the bustling Mountain Route of the Santa Fe Trail. The Mexican-American War decimated Miranda financially, politically, and socially, and he would retreat from New Mexico altogether. After Beaubien's death in 1864, Lucien Maxwell was able to consolidate his title and ownership in the land grant by purchasing Miranda's portion and that of Beaubien's heirs. This second crystallizing event would create the well-known "Maxwell Land Grant" and provide a small feudal empire for Maxwell. When Maxwell sold his huge holdings to British investors organized as the Maxwell Land Grant and Railway Company in 1870, the vast tract was owned by one single individual.[2]

A combination of factors stifled quick economic expansion and serious exploitation of the vast virgin timber on the grant in the period immediately following Maxwell's sale, including a lack of efficient transportation, the remoteness of facilities for processing natural resources, legal disputes which instigated rampant violence known as the Colfax County War, and single corporate ownership of most of the timber. The primary transportation modes for mass commodity movements in mid-19th century America revolved around navigable waterways and livestock-powered wagons. While the Rayado, Cimarron, and Canadian Rivers provide sources of water for northeastern New Mexico, none

2 Zimmer and Lewis, 45-52; Murphy, *Philmont: A History*, 49-51, 58, 73.

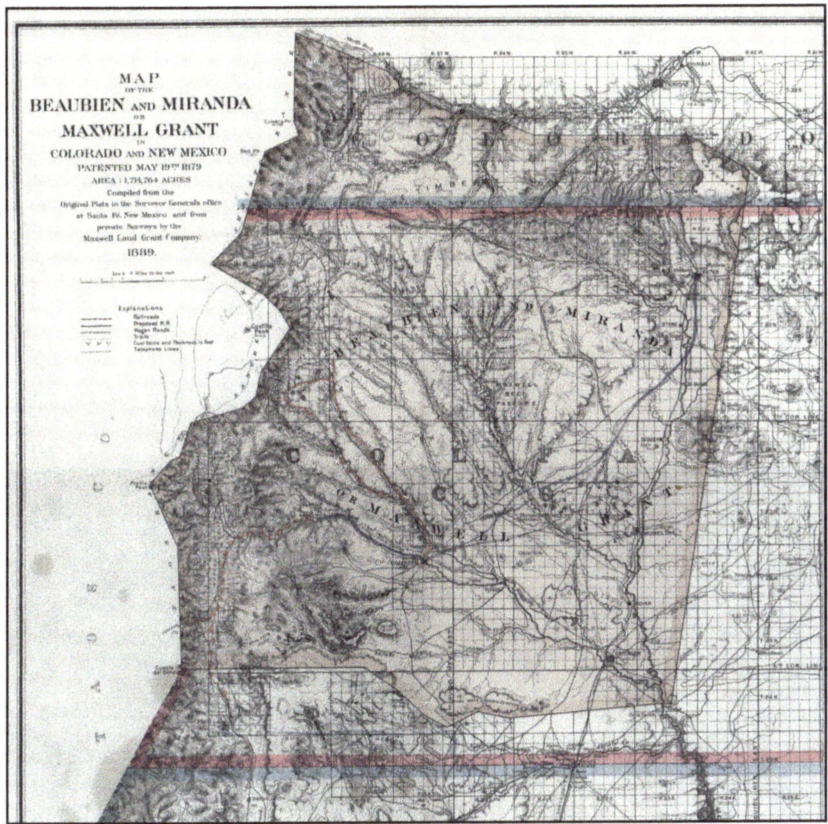

"Map of the Beaubien and Miranda Grant or Maxwell Grant in Colorado and New Mexico," 1889, as annotated by Theodore A. Schomburg with solid blue line for the St. Louis, Rocky Mountain, and Pacific Railway, solid red line for active Cimarron and Northwestern Railway track, and dotted red line for future railroad tracks.

T.A. Schomburg Collection MSS 747, File Folder 48. History Colorado Center.

are close to being navigable with adequate depth, width, and gradient for any type of commercial marine vessels. While wagon freighters and mule trains certainly became famous on the Santa Fe Trail that traveled through Cimarron, the town that Maxwell founded as his ranch headquarters on the Cimarron River at the entrance to Cimarron Canyon, they simply could not move the sheer tonnage of timber products needed to make a profit over long distances.

The answer would be in the coming railroads, not just in this pocket of New Mexico, but they would be indispensable across the American West. The Maxwell Land Grant and Railway Company had planned to bring rail service to Cimarron and the entire region to service newfound gold fields in the Moreno Valley and Baldy Mountain districts.

Baldy Town, Elizabethtown, Ute Park, and short-lived Virginia City all sprang up in response to the discovery of gold in the area, but the movement away from hard-rock mining to hydraulic placer mining ended the initial push for rail service to the region. Placer mining produced smaller amounts of gold dust and nuggets as the transportation product, instead of large and heavy quantities of raw ore from hard-rock mining which required transportation to a far-off smelter. Maxwell himself had been involved in limited timber harvesting and sawmilling in conjunction with a small gold stamp mill to process the raw ore on Ute Creek before his sale, but the lack of railroads would hamper large-scale timbering.[3]

Furthermore, complications arose with Maxwell's title to and management of his land grant which would prove burdensome to the Maxwell Land Grant and Railway Company. Originating in the vague boundary definitions in the Beaubien-Miranda Grant, the exact territory of Maxwell's holdings was questioned, both upon his survey and sale of the grant in 1870 and by the people Maxwell allowed to live upon his land. The first challenge to the land title was that it exceeded the legal limits for Mexican colonization grants. A second challenge stemmed from Maxwell's practice of being what might be considered a feudal landlord: allowing people to live on his land based on handshake agreements in exchange for tithing a portion of their crop or livestock herd to Maxwell as payment. The third challenge was brought by squatters, which were common throughout such large geographic tracts during the era of homesteading.

Maxwell's land management practices led to numerous people claiming a right to their holdings based on alleged handshake agreements and also via land improvements made under the 1862 Homestead Act. When the company demanded that the squatters either prove title to their claim, pay up, or leave, the ensuing violence of the Colfax County War would last until the US Supreme Court case *United States v. Maxwell Land Grant Company* was decided on April 18, 1887, which confirmed the Maxwell Land Grant Company's title to roughly two million acres in northeastern New Mexico and southeastern Colorado.

Many were actively involved in the bloodshed during this time, and nearby geographical landmarks would be named for the slain. Factions supporting the company, often backed by law enforcement, were opposed by the squatters, supported by 'squatters clubs,' circuit preachers,

3 Bromley, 15-16; Pearson, 45-46.

Settlers and log cabin on the Maxwell Land Grant.
Aztec Mill Museum Collection, Cimarron, New Mexico.

and gunslingers, who fought desperately over evictions. Deputy Sheriff George W. Cook was "ambushed" in North Poñil Canyon in 1888 at a confluence with another canyon which now bears his name, "Cook Canyon."

While returning from services in nearby Elizabethtown, anti-grant Methodist preacher Franklin J. Tolby would be murdered in Cimarron Canyon, and eventually Tolby Peak and the Methodist church in Cimarron would memorialize his name. Fellow preacher Oscar P. McMains would take up the cause for Tolby and the settlers until the final US Supreme Court decision came down.

The origin of many historical place names have been verified, but there are some which remain uncertain at the time of this writing. The naming of Metcalf Canyon, which would later give rise to the C&N station stop, is one of these. Multiple sources list the same event taking place at the confluence of the North Poñil, Metcalf, and Cook Canyons: a deputy sheriff was ambushed and shot. Most agree that George Cook was ambushed, rather than a deputy named Metcalf. The name for Metcalf Canyon likely came from the well-known regional proprietor of a toll gate in Emory Gap on the New Mexico-Colorado border approximately 45 miles east of Raton, New Mexico. Basil "Uncle Bill" Metcalf ran a toll gate in the aptly named Tollgate Canyon from approximately 1873 to 1885. A modern historical marker identifies him as the most well-known Metcalf in the region.[4]

The final reason for slow economic growth on the land grant relates to property ownership and right-of-way. When a landowner's title is unclear or challenged, securing a right-of-way, which is the legal right to build, own, maintain, and access a railroad on another's land, is extraordinarily difficult, making railroading building unlikely. Although many railroads into the Cimarron country were planned by investors, speculators, and the Maxwell Land Grant and Railway Company itself, the legal fight and local violence were deterrents to promoting the area.

"Cimarron," the namesake town of the C&N, comes from the traditional Spanish word for "wild," and during that time the area was too wild and risky for development. Only after the final US Supreme Court decision was handed down did firm control and development of the grant proceed on a large scale. In the meantime the old growth forest would continue to grow, waiting until the next generation of timbermen and railroaders placed it in their sights.

4 Colfax County War: Zimmer & Lewis, 52-54; Murphy, *Philmont*, 116-120. Death of Tolby: Murphy, *Philmont*, 118-119. Death of Deputy Sheriff Metcalf: Murphy, *Philmont*, 171. For a complete review of the Maxwell Land Grant and the related companies by similar names, see Keleher's *The Maxwell Land Grant* and Pearson's *The Maxwell Land Grant*. Deputy Sheriff George Cook: Pearson, 133-139. Basil Bill Metcalf: Taylor, Morris F. *Basil (Bill Metcalf) and His Toll Gate*.

Theodore Schomburg, Railroad Fever, and Catskill Logging

By the late 19th century, development of the Maxwell Land Grant had finally come into focus after the end of the dark Colfax County War. The residents of the area were committed to working with the resources and geography of the land as well as working with the dominant Maxwell Land Grant Company. Cattle and sheep ranching operations developed, both large and small, and prominent family ranches came into being during this period, including the Chase, Heck, Dawson, French, Vermejo, Springer, and Abreu. Many of these same ranchers would also lead the produce industry with orchards of apples, pears, peaches, plums, and cherries which were shipped across the country as the region became well-known for its fruit-growing. Gold mining continued in the Elizabethtown and Baldy areas with the Aztec, Montezuma, French Henry, Deep Tunnel, Black Horse, Legal Tender, and Mystic Lode mines delving ever deeper into the earth. Hydraulic and placer mining also continued in these same areas. It was into this world that the primary character in the Cimarron and Northwestern Railway story would arrive on the scene.[1]

Theodore Schomburg

Theodore A. Schomburg would eventually see the promised railroads and industry in the Cimarron area, and he and other industrialists like him would be the ones to bring these economic dreams to fruition. His story is inextricably linked to the C&N.

---

1 Economic conditions paraphrased from Murphy, *Philmont: A History*, 165.

Theodore Schomburg himself has a history as compelling and intriguing as that of the Cimarron and Northwestern Railway. Researching this gentleman was complicated by the fact that Schomburg's last name appears misspelled in many accounts. His and his wife's tombstone in the Fairmont Cemetery in Raton, New Mexico, bear the proper spelling of "SCHOMBURG." Other inaccurate spellings seen in the historical record are "Schomberg," "Shomberg," and "T.E. Schomberg." Furthermore, Theodore's son Thomas, who would succeed his father in certain business enterprises, was often erroneously named as the only 'Schomburg' involved with the C&N and the CT&L. Thomas would indeed steer the direction of these firms before their dissolution, but he was sent by his father to run them only after they had been in operation for many years.

Born July 8, 1864, at Staten Island, New York, Theodore Schomburg had lived in four totally different worlds before he was eighteen. His family moved to Dusseldorf, Germany, in 1868 after the death of his mother, and in 1872 the family moved again to England where his father began work in the London office of the Maxwell Land Grant Company (MLG Co). In 1881, a 17-year-old Schomburg crossed the Atlantic to the United States to work as an office boy for the Cimarron office of the Maxwell Land Grant Company, using a letter of introduction from MLG Co president Frank R. Sherwin. He would quickly grow in both responsibilities at work and in valuable business connections as he progressed from office boy, to clerk, chief clerk, and assistant superintendent.

The year 1891 saw him married to Lulu Whigham, daughter of Harry Whigham, his supervisor and New Mexico manager of the MLG Co, and a few years later Schomburg himself became superintendent for the large land grant company. One might ponder such a life moving in a short time frame from the heart of New York City to old-world Germany, to the European metropolis of London, and finally to what may have seemed the Wild West in remote northeastern New Mexico by the late 19th century.[2]

However intriguing Theodore Schomburg's early life may have been, his position as superintendent for the MLG Co brought him intimate knowledge of the people, natural resources, and potential for development of the area. This experience would prepare him for his

2 Pearson, *Maxwell Land Grant*, 177; Murphy, *New Mexico Railroader*, Vol 6, No 11, "The Cimarron and Northwestern: Historic Railroad of Northern New Mexico," pg. 2.

eventual control not only of the C&N Ry and CT&L, but of timber, mining, railroad, finance, and varied commercial interests throughout the southwest. These enterprises would make him one of the most prominent businessmen and timbermen in the region, and the local newspapers consistently mentioned his comings and goings.

At the time of his death in January 1929 he was involved with the Pagosa Lumber Company of Dulce, New Mexico, the Feather River Lumber Company of Plumas County, California, the Trinchera Timber Company of Russell, Colorado, the Montoro Mining Company of Arizona, the Rio Grande Lumber Company of New Mexico, the Trinidad State Bank of Trinidad, Colorado, the Pitkin Trading Company of Colorado, the First National Bank of Denver, the Natural Food Operating Company of Colorado, along with personal land holdings in Mexico and charitable causes such as the Albuquerque Children's Home and Hospital. He is the namesake for Schomburg Canyon northeast of Dawson, New Mexico, and the Schomberg Station siding on the Atchison, Topeka, and Santa Fe Railway (AT&SF) mainline between the New Mexico towns of Raton and Maxwell. Amtrak's Southwest Chief, a direct descendant of the same train on the AT&SF,

Theodore A. Schomburg with his wife, Lulu, and two of their three children.

T.A. Schomburg family portrait, circa 1900-1908. Accession #85.1.23, History Colorado Center.

still passes this siding today.[3]

Theodore Schomburg's life was typical of late 19th century success stories, yet unique in its circumstances and enterprises. Theodore and Lulu would have three children: Marie, Thomas, and Dorothy. Thomas would follow in his father's footsteps into the successful timber enterprises Theodore would build. Mr. and Mrs. T.A. Schomburg would eventually move from Raton, New Mexico, to Trinidad, Colorado, and finally to Denver, Colorado, where they built a large and comfortable house for the period.

Financial success allowed Theodore to maintain a hobby that would prove critical in archiving many aspects of his own personal life, as well as the life and times of the late 19th and early 20th centuries. Schomburg became an avid photographer. Archived in the T.A. Schomburg Collection at the History Colorado Center in Denver, many of the photos he took revolved around pleasure trips, picnics, friends, family, his home, and his children. Compared to personal and pleasure-outing pictures, only a handful could be classified as business-related. In several photos he is seen with a time-release cord for self-portrait photography. He enjoyed capturing mountainous landscapes in both Colorado and New Mexico, and many are images of the Maxwell Land Grant and present-day Carson National Forest.

In one of his letters to a fellow MLG Co official, he mentioned getting a telephoto lens which he was eager to use, a lens that would prove handy for landscape details on the large-format cameras he owned. Places in the photos include various ranches, the towns of Taos, Raton, Trinidad, and Cimarron, as well as landscapes probably taken in present-day Valle Vidal in New Mexico and the Stonewall Valley of Colorado. A few photos dealt with business interests, such as an early oil well drilling operation powered by a steam engine, and the wreck of Pagosa Lumber Co locomotive #70. Unfortunately, very few images include the CT&L Co or the C&N Railway. Later photographers, primarily Edward and Mary Troutman, would capture photos showing

3 The T.A. Schomburg Collection Guide lists Theodore's various enterprises in succinct fashion: T. A. Schomburg Collection, MSS.747, History Colorado Center. For Albuquerque Children's Home, see *Albuquerque Morning Journal,* December 16, 1917, and February 8, 1920. For "Schomberg Station," see Department of the Interior, US Geological Survey, Topographic Map, "Raton, New Mexico; Colorado,"1954. The location had apparently changed names because a 1915 USGS map shows only "Schomberg." See Department of the Interior, US Geological Survey, Topographic map, Koehler Quadrangle, 1915. New Mexico Historical Topographic Maps, Perry-Castañeda Library Map Collection, University of Texas at Austin.

Early T.A. Schomburg photo: "Stag Picnic, Sugarite, 1887." Clockwise from left: Charles Springer reclining, two unidentified Maxwell Land Grant Company men, Frank Springer reclining in the back, Francis Clutton seated at center, Harry Whigham, Joe Schroeder looking at Whigham, and Theodore A. Schomburg using a self-timer cord to take the group portrait. Schomburg was in his sixth year working for the Maxwell Land Grant Company. Four years later in 1891, Schomburg would marry Harry Whigham's daughter, Lulu.

New Mexico State University Library, Archives and Special Collections.

what we know today of CT&L and C&N operations.[4]

Theodore Schomburg was in a unique situation during his years working for the Maxwell Land Grant Company. His son Thomas would later recall, "At one time, my father was the only man who worked for the Maxwell Land Grant Company who went to every area of the grant. [He] was friendly with the squatters and would not be shot on site, except for the Stonewall country."

One artifact created by this well-traveled superintendent is the 1893 pocket map of the Maxwell Land Grant in the T.A. Schomburg Collection. A well-known map to historical researchers of the grant, Schomburg's copy had been carefully cut into approximately 4-by-

4 Much of Theodore and Thomas' biographies come from an interview with Thomas conducted by historian Lawrence Murphy. See Schomburg, Thomas W, Interviewed by Lawrence Murphy at Denver, Colorado, June 9, 1964, National Scouting Museum; T.A. Schomburg's photographic prowess: Photograph Study Prints, T. A. Schomburg Collection, MSS.747, History Colorado Center; Telephoto lens reference: File Folder 3, Correspondence 4/19/1898 – 6/13/1907, T.A. Schomburg Collection, History Colorado Center. Landscape photography recognition: Based upon the authors' backcountry experiences in both Colorado and New Mexico and the notes from the Schomburg Study Prints with the T.A. Schomburg Collection.

T.A. Schomburg taking a group photo using a self-timer cord.
From left to right: Theodore Schomburg, Jan Van Houten,
Lulu Whigham Schomburg, and Colonel Harry Whigham, Lulu's father.
T.A. Schomburg Collection, PH.605, Photo #117, History Colorado Center.

4-inch sections, glued to light fabric, and then skillfully folded into a leather-bound pocketbook. This converted his large wall map into a portable travel resource for use during his management activities. Well-worn, the pocket map had certainly seen many years of use. One incident in Schomburg's travels was a serious 1894 stagecoach accident near Meeker, Colorado, with Jan Van Houten and Charles Springer where Schomburg broke his collarbone. The accident occurred on the Meeker-Craig stagecoach line, an area in northwestern Colorado a full 400 miles from Cimarron, New Mexico. Van Houten served as a key leader of the Maxwell Land Grant Company and later the St. Louis, Rocky Mountain, and Pacific Company. Charles Springer was a local rancher, political leader, attorney, and brother to influential New Mexico attorney Frank Springer.

Theodore maintained organized letter books throughout his time with the MLG Co and many entries recount taxes paid on ranches sold to settlers, finances of the MLG Co, and efforts to deal with squatters during the Colfax County War. While timbermen in most cases were

T.A. Schomburg photo using self-timer cord with daughters Marie and Dorothy and son Thomas.

T.A. Schomburg Collection, PH.605, Photo #111. History Colorado Center.

mainly financiers in their company roles, Theodore was intimately familiar with the land he would later cut for lumber to be used throughout the southwest. From the earliest phase of his career he was dealing with landowners, squatters, finances, and timber rights. His letters and correspondence show his attention to detail and his articulate communication. These experiences with the day-to-day operations, economics, logistics, and legalities of the property would prepare him to build a vast timber empire.[5]

Railroad Fever

When young Theodore Schomburg arrived in 1881 to begin work for the Maxwell Land Grant Company, he stepped into a world being forever changed by the dynamics of railroading. The MLG Co from its beginning had worked tirelessly to bring a railroad to the area. Earlier

5 Quote from Thomas: Schomburg, Thomas W, Interviewed by Lawrence Murphy at Denver, Colorado, June 9, 1964; Pocket map: File Folder 48, T.A. Schomburg Collection, History Colorado Center; 1894 stagecoach accident: *The Meeker Herald.* (Meeker, Colo.), 01 Sept. 1894; Superintendent correspondence: File Folders 1-4, T.A. Schomburg Collection, History Colorado Center.

maps from the time of Maxwell's land sale in 1870 show several proposed rail lines, including a route surveyed by William Jackson Palmer, formerly of the Kansas Pacific Railroad. Palmer would eventually start his own railroad, the Denver & Rio Grande (D&RG), a line he envisioned to stretch from Denver south to Mexico City through El Paso, Texas. His 1867 survey recommended the route through Raton Pass into New Mexico, yet the Atchison, Topeka, & Santa Fe Railway (AT&SF) also had plans to enter New Mexico along the Mountain Route of the Santa Fe Trail.

Both lines had built into the vicinity of the southern Colorado town of Trinidad, and the race came to a head in February 1879 as Raton Pass literally had room for only one railroad right-of-way. Foreshadowing the events that would occur during the Colorado Railroad Wars a few years later, competing teams of railroad graders and hired gunslingers came together in a fight for the vital right-of-way. 'Uncle Dick' Wootton, operating his famous toll road through Raton Pass pass, supported the AT&SF, thus ensuring the Raton Pass route for the AT&SF. The AT&SF would reach Santa Fe in 1880 by a branch line off their main line. Later that same year the D&RG would enter New Mexico farther to the west by heading south from Antonito, Colorado, to Española, New Mexico. In 1887 the Texas, Santa Fe, and Northern Railroad built north from Santa Fe to Española, thereby linking Santa Fe to the D&RG system. The entire route from Antonito to Santa Fe would come under the D&RG in 1895 and would be known as "The Chili Line."[6]

Other railroad schemes were also proposed, including the Cimarron & Rio Grande railroad to extend west through Cimarron Canyon, swing through the Elizabethtown-Baldy mining areas, and then proceed to the coveted destinations of Taos and Santa Fe, New Mexico. Projected, proposed, but ultimately never-built railroad schemes litter American history, and the Cimarron and Rio Grande was no exception to this pattern.

The year 1902 saw the Cimarron and Taos Valley Railroad surveyed from Maxwell to Farmington, New Mexico, but nothing was ever built. In 1903 Schomburg himself received a prospectus for the Raton and Elizabethtown Railway that would have bypassed Cimarron and traveled near the Ring family ranch, essentially following the Cerrososo

6 Raton Pass struggle: Pearson, 80-81; AT&SF reaching Santa Fe: Myrick, *New Mexico's Railroads,* 7; D&RG connection to Santa Fe: Myrick, *New Mexico's Railroads,* 117.

1867 photograph taken during the first railroad survey into New Mexico, looking south from Raton Pass.

Boston Public Library, *Photographs of the American West,* Alexander Gardner plate #53.

Canyon wagon road to Elizabethtown. Even after rail service eventually came to Cimarron and the C&N Ry was in full operation in 1908, H.S. Wanamaker arrived in Cimarron to solicit stock purchases and bonds to build the Mountain, Valley, and Plains Railroad from Dallas, Texas, to Cimarron, a snake oil scheme that never materialized.[7]

The industry that developed in the 1880s and 1890s in southern Colorado and from the emergence of the AT&SF in New Mexico would later alter the course for Superintendent Schomburg and the MLG Co. After winning the railroad race into New Mexico, the AT&SF established their division point at Raton, a town they built near the abandoned stagecoach station of Willow Springs on the New

7 Early railroad projections on the MLG: "Map of the Maxwell Land Grant situated in the territories of Colorado and New Mexico. USA. Showing the Projected Railways, 1870," Fray Angelico Chavez History Library, New Mexico History Museum, 78.9 F1870; Cimarron and Taos Valley RR: Myrick, David F. *New Mexico's Railroads: A Historical Survey*, 160; T. A. Schomburg Collection, MSS.747, History Colorado Center, File Folder 10, Raton and Elizabethtown Railway Prospectus, 1903; MV&P RR: Bromley, 49-51.

Mexico side of Raton Pass. The AT&SF also established the town of Springer, New Mexico, named for the prominent attorney and MLG Co leader Frank Springer who represented the MLG Co in the famous US Supreme Court case.

The AT&SF and the MLG Co would partner to form the Raton Coal and Coke Company in 1880 to begin extensive coal mining in the rich fields surrounding Raton.[8] Coal was needed for steam locomotives and steam engines in various industries, including what would become the dominant Colorado Fuel and Iron Company (CF&I) founded in 1892. Coal mining would proliferate in southern Colorado and mines would be served by both the D&RG and another railroad (through reorganizations) that would later be an important timber customer and transporter, the Denver, Texas and Fort Worth (DT&FW).

The DT&FW ran south from Denver to Trinidad, then turned east toward Clayton, New Mexico, before heading to Fort Worth, Texas. DT&FW branch lines would extend to various canyons and resource-rich areas to supply commodity traffic for the line, one of these being a branch extending from Trinidad up the Purgatoire River Valley to Martinsen, located in Longs Canyon on the Colorado portion of the MLG. Expanding railroads, growing towns and communities throughout the southwest, and coal mines all demanded more timber, and now the MLG Co could exploit that opportunity.

Catskill Logging

Logging and sawmills in and around short-lived Catskill, west of Raton, New Mexico, would be the first of many large-scale timber enterprises on the Maxwell Land Grant. This operation would set the stage for later logging based on railroad logistics, and it brought together the characters that eventually would form the large timber companies. The operation at Catskill laid the groundwork for the Continental Tie and Lumber Company and the Cimarron and Northwestern Railway.

In 1890 the MLG Co persuaded the DT&FW railroad to build a branch 15½ miles from their line at Martinsen, Colorado, to the Canadian River in New Mexico, in addition to 16 miles along the river (known then as the Red River). The MLG Co contributed in-kind finances by giving the right-of-way, all timber needed for construction, and one-half interest in prospective town sites. The deal struck between

8 For Raton Coal and Coke Company and founding of Raton, see Pearson, 81-82; DT&FW: Schomburg, Thomas W. Interviewed by Lawrence Murphy in Denver, Colorado, June [illegible], [illegible].

McAlpine sawmill at Catskill, New Mexico.

Arthur Johnson Memorial Library Collection, Raton, New Mexico.

the railroad and the MLG Co held that construction of the 16 miles along the Canadian River would not begin until the grant company had secured timber contracts that would have an output of at least 20,000 board feet of timber a day, thereby guaranteeing sufficient traffic to repay the railroad's investment.

The timber contracts were secured in the summer of 1890 to place sawmills along the branch line. Railroad construction started, and MLG Co manager M.P. Pels laid out the townsite of Catskill, a name suggested by DT&FW general manager C.F. Meek. Catskill would grow quickly as a lumber town with multiple mills and timber operations contracted with the MLG Co for 25 million board feet of lumber annually. A.C. Drake would construct many large brick beehive-shaped ovens in Catskill that would heat treetops and limbs into charcoal. Two sets of ovens, one group of ten and another group of fourteen, were directly positioned on rail sidings to load the charcoal into outbound boxcars. More permanent than the portable sawmills in use along the river, these large brick ovens remain standing to this day. Catskill would boast many homes, two hotels, restaurants and saloons, a baseball team, and even a women's eleven-piece brass band. Timbering on a large scale had finally arrived and royalties from the timber companies made Catskill a financial success for the Maxwell

Beehive charcoal ovens at Catskill, New Mexico.

Raton Museum Collection, Raton, New Mexico.

Land Grant Company.[9]

The first few years of Catskill were indeed successful, but depletion of nearby timber stands, a national economic depression, and an unwise agreement with the railroad would lead to financial problems by the turn of the century. The DT&FW would be absorbed into the Union Pacific Railroad system becoming the Union Pacific, Denver, and Gulf Railway (UPD&G) in 1890. With economic depression in 1897 and most of the near-at-hand timber already harvested, outbound carloads began decreasing on the UPD&G. Each timber operation was using livestock-powered wagons to skid raw logs to the mills, since the railroad did not participate in direct rail logging but was only obligated to transport milled lumber products from the area.

Railroad traffic had decreased so much that UPD&G officials were quite vocal to the MLG Co about the minimal traffic from Catskill, with only the Newton Lumber Company shipping carloads. As the railroad track aged, the route to Catskill was becoming expensive to maintain and operate. Expensive railroading can lead to reduced track maintenance and that is what happened along the UPD&G's trackage around Catskill. Superintendent Theodore Schomburg even noted in a letter to the New Mexico Lumber Company that the UPD&G might abandon the trackage along the river, leaving Catskill as the lone ship-

9 Pearson, 165-167; Zimmer and Lewis, 123-126.

Community event at Catskill, New Mexico, c.1893.

Raton Museum Collection, Raton, New Mexico.

ping point on the line and dramatically increasing the cost to sawmillers such as New Mexico Lumber.

However, by 1899 the railroad was in the hands of the Colorado and Southern Railway (C&S), itself a new entity created from several bankrupt railroads, including the UPD&G. The C&S showed no interest in maintaining the high-cost branch as the trackage deteriorated, and since traffic was less than what the MLG Co had promised, the C&S abandoned the branch in January of 1902. The MLG Co had contributed financing again and again in both cash and timber supplies for initial track construction and subsequent branch extensions, but now the MLG Co was content to let Catskill fade away. When the railroad was abandoned, so too was Catskill and only a few people remained in the area. Catskill logging died in twelve short years with the town being abandoned in 1902.[10]

The lessons learned in Catskill would eventually be implemented in future logging and railroading operations carried out on the Maxwell Land Grant. New timber companies would be on their own for transporting raw timber to their sawmills and any railroad construction would be at the carrier's own expense. The MLG Co would certainly grant the right-of-way for a railroad, but never again would the grant company willingly make large financial contributions to fund a short-

10 Pearson, 241-242; Zimmer and Lewis, 126.

term railroad branch. At this time attention was focused on railroads to connect the existing communities in timber areas, such as Ute Park and Poñil Park, and new town sites were not spearheaded by the MLG Co.

Several long-term timber companies and timbermen were launched by Catskill logging. William H. Deleker, who would later join Schomburg as an incorporator of the Continental Tie and Lumber Company, was involved with logging around Catskill. Deleker and Schomburg would again partner as part of the Feather River Lumber Company in California. John C. Osgood's Maxwell Timber Company would take over the business formerly handled by the Richard Dunn Tie and Timber Company making hand-hewn ties, mine props, poles, posts, and cordwood. The approaching fate of J.C. Osgood and his Colorado Fuel and Iron Company would play a central role in launching the Cimarron and Northwestern Railway. Catskill logging was Osgood's first timber foray into the Maxwell Land Grant and the next chapter of logging by Osgood would close the curtain on the first phase of the C&N story.

The Rocky Mountain Timber Company

At the turn of the century, Theodore Schomburg and John C. Osgood were poised to further exploit the best remaining timber stands of the Maxwell Land Grant. However, it would be Osgood's failure that would create the opportunity for Schomburg to start the Continental Tie and Lumber Company and the Cimarron and Northwestern Railway. Were it not for Osgood's management of the timber and the financial issues of the Colorado Fuel and Iron Company, the C&N railway might never have existed.

After the 1887 US Supreme Court decision in favor of the Maxwell Land Grant, the grant company further exerted its now full legal right to the title of its land regarding squatters and the management of the vast natural resources on the grant. As mentioned by Thomas Schomburg in his interview with Larry Murphy in 1964, the Colorado portion of the grant, particularly the Stonewall Valley, was a hotbed of anti-grant sentiment and settlers refused to cooperate by legally purchasing or leasing land or respecting timber rights. With squatters cutting timber illegally, the development of the Colorado portion of the grant stalled. Theodore Schomburg set to work to settle the issue in 1899:

> E.A. [sic] Schomburg of Raton, New Mexico, Superintendent of the Maxwell Land Grant Company, says in reference to the evictions now determined on: "All this talk about a thousand families being rendered homeless through the efforts of our company is pure nonsense. In the whole Colorado portion of the grant there are not more than 300 squatters, including men, women, and children and it is

Settlers in front of the Shouse General Store, Stonewall, Colorado, c.1890. O.P. McMains stands near the horses with his hand on the wagon-wheel.

Trinidad Collection: CHS.X4316, History Colorado Center.

> not the intention of the company to oppress them in any manner whatsoever. The truth of the matter is, though, that a large number of these squatters make their livelihood by cutting our timber and selling it, and we propose to put a stop to that if we can. Any settler on the Colorado portion of the grant who will give proper guarantees not to destroy our timber land and who is willing to recognize our title by buying or leasing, has nothing to fear at all; but it is a case where patience has ceased to be a virtue and if they will not quit their depredations and recognize our title they will have to move off, every one of them, if it takes the whole force of the United States government to put them off.[1]

Indeed, it took nearly the full force of the US government to rectify the Stonewall situation. In the same interview with Murphy, Thomas noted that his father had the US Marshal in Denver come to the Stonewall Valley to alert squatters of the grant company's intentions and the US Supreme Court verdict. Thomas recalled that when the marshal met with the squatters, the convincing argument was that if they did not cooperate with the grant company but continued to be hostile, the next visitors in the valley would be the United States Army. The Stone-

1 *The Silver Lance.* (Crystal, Colorado). Chronicling America: Historic American Newspapers. Lib. of Congress. 06 Oct. 1899.

wall settlers were convinced and eventually worked with both the grant company and Superintendent Schomburg.

With the Colorado portion of the grant rendered more peaceful regarding the timber rights and squatters, Osgood's growing Colorado Fuel and Iron Company took a keen interest in the area as a CF&I subsidiary, the Colorado and Wyoming Railroad, extended up the Purgatoire River to tap timber and coal resources. Theodore Schomburg was key in steering the sale of the Colorado portion of the Maxwell Land Grant to CF&I, along with the exclusive timber rights on the whole grant to Osgood's newly formed Rocky Mountain Timber Company.

On March 1, 1901, the Rocky Mountain Timber Company was given a twenty-year contract for all timber on both the New Mexico and Colorado portions of the Maxwell Land Grant. One important stipulation of the contract was that a railroad must be built through San Francisco Pass to Poñil Park within five years. In exchange for his services, Schomburg was named vice president and general manager of the Rocky Mountain Timber Company and received forty percent of the stock in the venture. Leaving his position as superintendent with the MLG Co, Schomburg now focused his efforts on timber stands, the company sawmill in Weston, Colorado, on the Colorado and Wyoming Railroad (C&W), and managing outbound lumber shipments over the C&W and C&S.

Schomburg's departure from MLG Co may simply have been to better his business opportunities, but perhaps Schomburg saw the apparent writing on the wall for the MLG Co. A few years later in 1907, a twenty-year recap report on the state of the Maxwell Land Grant Company would conclude that there was no financial hope in the company directly managing the land's resources and assets. Land sales would be the only solution and Schomburg, having intimate knowledge of the situation and having witnessed the financial issues the company constantly encountered, may have opted to join the Rocky Mountain Timber Company to avoid another potential bankruptcy mess.[2]

The railroad connection to Poñil Park would be the key to Osgood's failure, Schomburg's success, and the goal of the Maxwell Land Grant

2 For land sale to CF&I, see T.A. Schomburg Collection, File Folder 3, Correspondence 1897-1901. For Rocky Mountain Timber Company, see T.A. Schomburg Collection, File Folder 4, Letter, T.A. Schomburg to J. Hearne, August 30, 1904; and File Folder 105, Letter, Rocky Mountain Timber Company to Maxwell Land Grant Company, April 15, 1902. For the Maxwell Land Grant Company report, see T.A. Schomburg Collection, File Folder 5, "History of the Administration of the Maxwell Land Grant 1887-1907."

Company. Poñil Park was a small community that existed for decades prior to the large-scale timbering being planned by the Rocky Mountain Timber Company. But logging would forever change the community, and it would become a centralized town before disappearing altogether once the logging operations ceased. The exact area included in Poñil Park varied depending on the source, but the main village was located at the confluence of North Poñil Canyon and Lowery Canyon, now known as Seally Canyon, approximately twenty-two miles north of Cimarron, seven miles south of Van Bremmer Park, and fourteen miles southwest of Vermejo Park. Census records and newspapers would include ranches as far away as the Rich Ranch in Middle Poñil Canyon, but the grant company was focused on Poñil Park proper near the canyon confluence.

In certain sources and maps, Poñil Park is also listed as Livingston or the Livingston Ranch. One example is a 1910 Maxwell Land Grant Company document that confirmed the Continental Tie and Lumber Company's fulfillment of its railroad agreement, and it specifically mentions Poñil Park being known as the Livingston Ranch area. In correspondence with one of this work's authors, the Forest Service archaeologist for the district that includes Poñil Park reported that the Livingston family indeed had a ranch in the area and references have been made to the cemetery as the "Livingston Family Cemetery." The term "park" refers to the wide open area near the canyon confluence as compared to the steep and narrow canyon further to the south. Many places referred to as "parks" would become sawmill and timber camp sites for the CT&L along the C&N Ry line. Poñil Park should not be confused with the location then and now known as "Poñil," which was situated at the confluence of the South and Middle Poñil Canyons. That location was also known as "Five Points" because five canyons intersected there, and in the early 1940s it functioned as the base camp and operational headquarters for Philturn Rocky Mountain Scout Camp, the direct predecessor of Philmont Scout Ranch.[3]

The logging industry would forever change Poñil Park. At first predominately consisting of farmers and ranchers, the *Las Vegas Gazette*

3 Poñil Park Census records: Department of Commerce and Labor, Bureau of the Census. Thirteenth Census of the United States: 1910 – Population. Ponil Precinct 26, Colfax County, New Mexico; For Livingston-Ponil Park, see "Agreement between the Maxwell Land Grant Company and the Continental Tie and Lumber Company" dated May 20, 1910, T.A. Schomburg Collection, File Folder 22; Carrie Leven, Assistant East Zone Archaeologist, Questa Ranger District, Email to Tucker Baker, July 16, 2020; For Five-Points, Poñil, and Philturn history see Murphy, *Philmont: A History*, 210.

Poñil Park originally consisted of scattered ranches and isolated family farmsteads.
Steve Lewis Collection.

reported in 1868 that "Mr. Hendricks who lives in the Poñil park [sic] raised 30 tons of potatoes this year," and in 1891 the *Santa Fe Daily New Mexican* noted, "A colony of Kansas farmers have selected lands in Poñil Park, Colfax County, and will locate there." Its remote location did not shield the area from violence as the *Santa Fe Daily New Mexican* related in 1890 that "Mr. Tandy of the Poñil park, visited Raton Wednesday. A few days ago some evil-doers of that neighborhood burned his house and effects to the ground." Despite this incident, 1902 population figures listed 83 inhabitants of Poñil Park, compared to Cimarron (pop. 363), Catskill (pop. 638), and Poñil (pop. 31).

Poñil Park was indeed small in 1902, but it was an established community in the sense that it had existed (albeit unincorporated) for some time before the railroad arrived. Located in the heart of virgin timber country on the New Mexico side of the grant, the MLG Co hoped to grow the community without being directly involved in the planning and development of the town site. Timber estimates and hand-drawn maps from 1902 underscored the prime position Poñil Park enjoyed servicing the surrounding area's timber to the tune of thousands of ties, props, and millions of board feet of commercial lumber. The primary issue was getting a railroad there.[4]

The difficulty of constructing a railroad to Poñil Park and Osgood's management of the Rocky Mountain Timber Company led to his failure to meet the specified contract clause for retaining Maxwell Land Grant timber rights. Theodore Schomburg was concerned about both issues during his time as vice president and general manager of Osgood's timber outfit in Weston. In a lengthy August 30, 1904, letter to Rocky Mountain Timber Company President J. Hearne, Schomburg recaps Osgood's failure to build a railroad to Poñil Park, notes that this failure means the timber contract with the MLG Co will be cancelled by 1906, which was the end of the five-year window to reach Poñil Park by rail, and that all money made from timber cutting on the New Mexico portion of the grant must be returned to the MLG Company. Schomburg heavily criticized Osgood for running Rocky Mtn Timber as a "department of Colorado Fuel and Iron" with conservative cutting primarily geared for CF&I mines instead of exploiting growing timber demand in the region. Furthermore, Schomburg had planned for the company "to be more extensive in our timber operations" and was none too pleased when cutting on the Colorado portion of the grant was stopped entirely at the behest of CF&I interests. Always having an eye for current and future business, Schomburg included estimates and maps of timber remaining on the Colorado and New Mexico portions of the Maxwell Land Grant.[5]

To this end, Schomburg wrote Albert A. Miller, another timberman in Denver, on September 13, 1904, detailing the various rail routes to Poñil Park with maps featuring hand-drawn route surveys, timber stands, track grade, prospective construction costs, and potential profit margins based on assumed shipping rates. In a tactic often repeated by Schomburg, he annotated copies of various Maxwell Land Grant maps with railroad routes and resource-rich areas to back up his letters' contentions. The three options were all based on the current railroads in the area.

The first route was a connection to the AT&SF at Dover, New Mex-

---

4 All newspaper quotes from Chronicling America: Historic American Newspapers. Lib. of Congress: *Las Vegas Gazette.* (Las Vegas, N.M.), 26 Oct. 1878.; *Santa Fe Daily New Mexican.* (Santa Fe, N.M.), 19 April 1890 and 22 Aug. 1891; For 1902 population numbers, see *Albuquerque Daily Citizen.* (Albuquerque, N.M.), 22 March 1902; T.A. Schomburg Collection, File Folder 16, Hand-drawn timber estimate maps. "Tp 29 N – R 17 E," "Tp 30 N – R 17 E."

5 TA Schomburg Collection, File Folder 4, Letter, T.A. Schomburg to J. Hearne, August 30, 1904; File Folder 50, Map of Rocky Mountain Timber Company timber estimates.

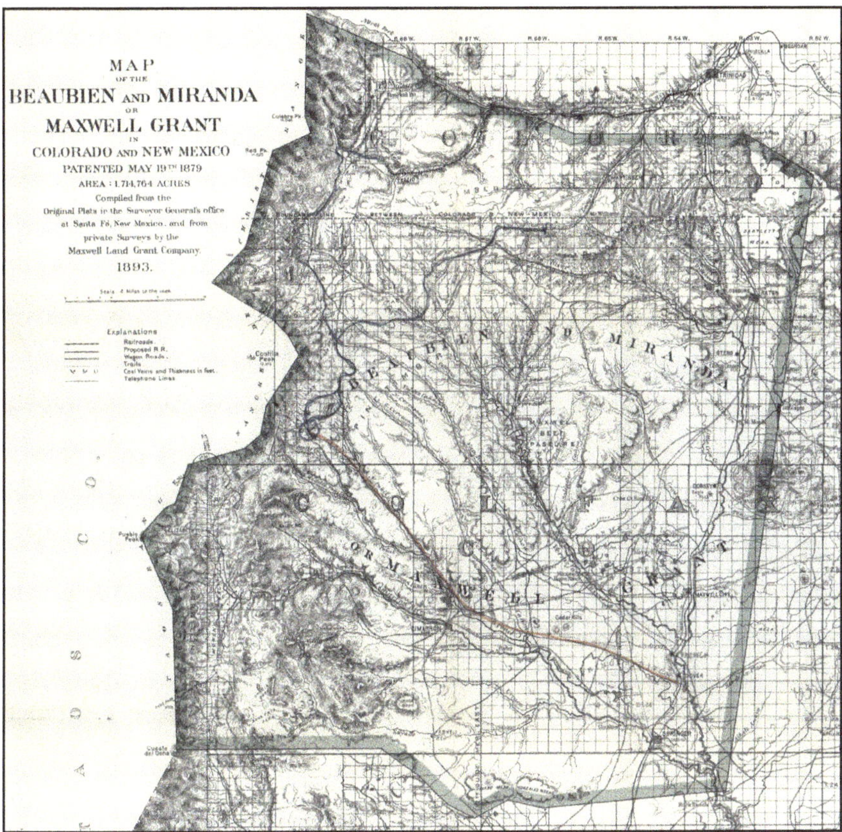

"Map of the Beaubien and Miranda Grant or Maxwell Grant in Colorado and New Mexico," 1893, annotated by T.A. Schomburg, showing three railroad options to Poñil Park before the arrival of the St. Louis, Rocky Mountain, & Pacific Railway. Two northern route options in blue; southern option in red.

T.A. Schomburg Collection MSS 747, File Folder 48. History Colorado Center.

ico, just north of Maxwell, running northwest through Cimarron and up the North Poñil Canyon. The other routes came south from Colorado through San Francisco Pass, which was considered the best entry point based on previous rail surveys for Catskill. The second option was a connection with the Colorado and Southern at Pels, Colorado, a station on the former UPD&G / C&S trackage to Catskill. The third option was a connection with the Colorado and Wyoming Railroad at Weston, Colorado, proceeding almost due south to Poñil Park.

Schomburg did not discuss which company would organize or run the prospective railroad, but his language makes it clear he is laying the groundwork for another outfit to take over where Osgood failed, and he is anticipating Miller could be a potential investor. Schomburg would follow up with Miller in another letter on February 9th, 1905, relating how building a railroad to Poñil Park was necessary to secure a new, long-term timber contract with the Maxwell Land Grant Company.[6]

Long before Osgood officially witnessed the Maxwell Land Grant timber contract cancelled by the grant company, Schomburg was organizing his own timber company and a related railroad outfit. The Poñil Park railroad failure was probably the least of Osgood's concerns during the brief time the Rocky Mountain Timber Company held the Maxwell Land Grant Company timber contract. Osgood needed financing at CF&I and in 1902 he brought in George Jay Gould, son of infamous railroad baron Jay Gould, and the younger Gould would bring in John D. Rockefeller. By 1904, Rockefeller and Gould had engineered a corporate takeover of the Colorado Fuel and Iron Company and the self-made founder John C. Osgood was pushed out. The Maxwell Land Grant Company would cancel the Rocky Mountain Timber Company contract by 1906 and that legal action rang down the curtain on the first act of large-scale timbering on the grant. The Continental Tie and Lumber Company and its Cimarron and Northwestern Railway would take center stage in the next act.

---

6 All from TA Schomburg Collection: File Folder 4, Letter, T.A. Schomburg to A.A. Miller, September 13, 1904; File Folder 48, "Map of the Beaubien and Miranda Grant or Maxwell Grant in Colorado and New Mexico, 1889," as annotated by Theodore A. Schomburg; File Folder 4, Letter, T.A. Schomburg to A.A. Miller, February 9, 1905

Birth of a Short Line

Development, Fundraising, and Formation

While J.C. Osgood and the Rocky Mountain Timber Company failed to capitalize on their opportunity, Theodore Schomburg was constantly in motion to seize upon the prospect of logging the remaining timber on the Maxwell Land Grant. Approaching his former company, Schomburg was able to secure timber rights on the entire New Mexico portion of the Maxwell Land Grant in a contract signed April 1, 1904. The contract and a later agreement in 1908 would spell out the conditions for Schomburg that would include a stumpage fee and the construction of a railroad to Poñil Park. The railroad could be standard or narrow gauge, connected with a currently operating railroad, and while San Francisco Pass was listed as the railroad point of entry from Colorado, this route was not required.

Schomburg then maneuvered to recruit investors to form a timber company to conduct the logging, as he would assign his option in the contract to this newly formed timber outfit. His manifold correspondence to Colorado timbermen such as Albert A. Miller and William H. Deleker during his time with the Rocky Mountain Timber Company and his connections from his superintendent days at the MLG Co would pay off as Schomburg did indeed secure the needed company investment. The Continental Tie and Lumber Company was formed in October 1905:

> The Continental Tie and Lumber Company. The incorporators are T.A. Schomburg, D.C. Beaman, Albert A. Miller, W.H. Deleker,

> all of Denver, Colorado. The objects for which this company was formed are the manufacture of and purchase and sale of all kinds of timber and lumber; the erection of mills, treating plants and other establishments necessary to carry on such business; the acquisition of lands; the construction and operation of railroads, tramways, and wagon roads, for the transportation of material and products incidental to such business; to do a general bonding business. The capital stock is $250,000 divided into 2,500 shares at $100 each. The number of directors shall be four and those who will manage the business of the company for the first year are the incorporators. The term of existence is 50 years and the principal place of business is at Raton, Colfax County, New Mexico, with C.N. Blackwell named as agent.[1]

Deleker was financially involved in logging outfits in and around Catskill, associated with the Rocky Mountain Timber Company, and would later join Schomburg as an investor in the Feather River Lumber Company in Plumas County, California. D.C. Beaman was general counsel for the Colorado Fuel and Iron Company and also knew Schomburg from the Rocky Mountain Timber Company. Another financial backer was Frank Springer. Several years prior, Schomburg had assisted Springer with preparing the brief for the Maxwell Land Grant Company's case before the US Supreme Court. Springer would return the favor by financially backing the incorporation of the CT&L Co.[2]

After incorporating the Continental Tie and Lumber Company, the next move by Schomburg was to locate a rail route to Poñil Park, attract enough additional investment to construct the railroad, and begin logging and sawmilling operations. All three of these efforts were made infinitely easier when more railroads arrived in Colfax County, coal mining accelerated, and many new communities developed.

In 1901 rancher John Dawson sold his ranch located between Cimarron and Raton to the Dawson Fuel Company. The ranch would become the site of the coal mining town of Dawson, New Mexico, and

---

1 Incorporation announcement from *Santa Fe New Mexican.* (Santa Fe, N.M.), 25 Oct. 1905. Chronicling America: Historic American Newspapers. Lib. of Congress.

2 Maxwell Land Grant Company Records, MSS 147, Box 8, File Folder 6, Center for Southwest Research: Contract between Maxwell Land Grant Company and Theodore Schomburg, April 1, 1904; Agreement between Maxwell Land Grant Company and Continental Tie and Lumber Company dated January 31, 1908; For Deleker and Springer's investing in the CT&L Co, see Murphy, *Philmont: A History,* 169. For D.C. Beaman background, see *Santa Fe New Mexican.* (Santa Fe, N.M.), 01 June 1907. Chronicling America: Historic American Newspapers. Lib. of Congress. Thomas Schomburg would note in his 1964 recorded interview with Lawrence Murphy that his father Theodore helped Frank Springer prepare the brief for the Supreme Court case: Schomburg, Thomas W. Interviewed by Lawrence Murphy at Denver, Colorado, June 9, 1964. For a complete biography of Frank Springer, see David Caffey's *Frank Springer & New Mexico*

the Dawson Railway was soon constructed to connect Dawson with Tucumcari, New Mexico, 132 miles to the southeast, which provided connections with the Chicago, Rock Island, and Pacific Railroad and the El Paso and Northeastern. In 1906 Phelps Dodge purchased the Dawson Fuel Company (which would be operated by their subsidiary, the Stag Canyon Fuel Company), and they merged the Dawson Railway into their subsidiary El Paso and Southwestern Railroad. Dawson would grow to 2,200 residents in 1905, and the extensive coal mining and construction would create more demand for timber products the Continental Tie and Lumber was geared to supply.[3]

The second railroad to enter the area would be even more important to C&N history. The St. Louis, Rocky Mountain, and Pacific Company and their subsidiary St. Louis, Rocky Mountain, and Pacific Railway would be a complementary business to enable the success of the CT&L, the C&N, and it would even indirectly influence the name of Schomburg's planned railroad.

St. Louis, Rocky Mountain, and Pacific engine No. 105 at the Cimarron depot.

Aztec Mill Museum Collection, Cimarron, New Mexico.

Formed in 1902 by St. Louis investors Thomas Harlan, Henry Koehler, Hugo Koehler, and Max Koehler, as well as Charles Springer, Frank Springer, and Jan Van Houten, the St. Louis, Rocky Mountain,

3 For rancher John Dawson and the Dawson Railway, see Myrick, *New Mexico's Railroads*, 84-85, 91-92; and Bromley, 26. For town of Dawson, see Zimmer and Lewis, 183-192.

and Pacific Company controlled over 500,000 acres of bituminous coal fields in the greater Raton area, operated mines at Brilliant, Koehler, and Van Houten, and had coke ovens at Gardiner. The St. Louis industrialists had grand plans to reach Taos, Farmington, and perhaps even the Pacific coast if financing and opportunity was secured, but the railway was primarily geared to open more markets for their coal and coke operations.

The St. Louis, Rocky Mountain, and Pacific Railway was formed in 1905 with construction continuing into 1906. On December 10, 1906, the first regularly scheduled train of the Rocky Mountain Route rolled into Cimarron from Raton, and by 1907 the railroad was operating 105 miles of track. The western terminus was located at Ute Park, a small station on Ute Creek directly south of the Baldy Mountain gold mining district, with the line moving east through Cimarron Canyon to Cimarron. From there the tracks advanced northeast toward Raton, the site of the AT&SF connection. South of Raton at Clifton House one line went into Raton while another ran to the eastern terminus at Des Moines, New Mexico. Des Moines was the connection with the Colorado and Southern Railroad on their mainline from Denver to Fort Worth. An at-grade railroad crossing was located

St. Louis, Rocky Mountain, and Pacific railroad shops in Cimarron.

Raton Museum Collection, Raton, New Mexico.

at Colfax (roughly halfway between Cimarron and Raton) and since the El Paso and Southwestern Railroad (former Dawson Railway) held prior right-of-way, the newly installed gates were normally left open to the EP&SW and closed against the StLRM&P. This meant that StLRM&P trains would have to stop to open the gate, move the train through, and stop again to let the gate man back on board.

The Springers and Van Houten influenced the decision for the division point and shops to be located at Cimarron. A five-bay brick roundhouse, machine shop, car shop, turning wye, two story station, livestock pens, and a yard were built much to the delight of the *Cimarron News and Press* which touted the high quality of the facilities. The coal was marketed as "Swastika Coal and Coke," using an indigenous people's symbol not yet tainted in later years by the Nazis. The railroad was also known as the "Swastika Route" since each railcar and locomotive was adorned with the company logo, a swastika inside a circle with the words "Rocky Mountain Route."[4]

The arrival of the St. Louis, Rocky Mountain, and Pacific Railway changed everything for the Continental Tie and Lumber Company, and the changes were decidedly in favor of the logging enterprise. Christopher N. Blackwell, a Raton businessman and cashier at the First National Bank of Raton, was involved with the formation of the Rocky Mountain Route and also served as agent for the Continental Tie and Lumber Company in Raton. First National Bank of Raton served as the depository for the AT&SF Ry, the StLRM&P Company, and the StLRM&P Ry.[5] This connection would be the first of many close ties between these companies, as the Rocky Mountain Route would be the outbound carrier from Cimarron for CT&L lumber products. The growing coal mines in the area, new towns, and expanding railroads would also demand more ties, mine props, telegraph and telephone poles, and commercial lumber from saw timber. Northeastern New Mexico was rapidly expanding and developing, leading to more inter-

4 Henry Koehler, Jr. Prospectus: St. Louis Rocky Mountain and Pacific Company. May 10, 1905. Aztec Mill Museum, Cimarron, NM; For St. Louis, Rocky Mtn, and Pacific Railway history, see Pearson, 207-209; Bromley 31-38; Zimmer and Lewis, 137-141; Myrick, *New Mexico's Railroads*, 160-162; Murphy, *Philmont: A History*, 165-168. For route map and overview, see "St Louis, Rocky Mountain, and Pacific Railway: The Scenic Route of New Mexico," Reprinted brochure, Railroad Club of New Mexico, 1962; and *The Railway Age*, Vol. 43, January 1 to June 30, 1907, 677. For Rocky Mtn shops, see *Cimarron News and Press* (Cimarron, N.M.) 23 May 1907. Chronicling America: Historic American Newspapers. Lib. Of Congress.

5 Blackwell's role in the StLRM&P: Bromley, 26. First National Bank of Raton: *The Cimarron News and Press*. (Cimarron, N.M.), 14 March 1907. Chronicling America: Historic American Newspapers. Lib. of Congress.

est and investment in Schomburg's operations. Even the prospectus for the St. Louis, Rocky Mountain, and Pacific Railway noted Schomburg's timber research and how beneficial his logging efforts would be for the new railway:

> Careful estimates of the amount of standing timber on the eastern slope of the Rocky Mountain range absolutely tributary to the St Louis, Rocky Mountain, and Pacific Company, and inaccessible to other lines, by Mr. T.A. Schomburg, Vice-President of the Rocky Mountain Timber Company, a large concern operating in Colorado, are as follows: Saw timber, 1,000,000,000 feet; Railroad Ties, 18,000,000; Mine Material, a vast amount , certainly enough to supply the growing demands of the market for forty or fifty years. Still further forests of great extent on the Western slope of the Taos Range will become accessible if the railroad line is extended to Farmington.[6]

Opportunity was knocking for Schomburg and he continued to recruit potential investors and to research potential railroad routes to Poñil Park. Tucked into a file folder pertaining to the New Mexico and Western Railway and the Eagle Nest Dam in the T.A Schomburg Collection is an undated and unaddressed document that outlines Schomburg's labors at that time. Its contents clearly triangulate its date to the period between CT&L formation and the incorporation of C&N Ry, and it follows a pattern remarkably similar to Schomburg's earlier efforts to attract investors. The document discusses three routes to Poñil Park with the first branching off the Colorado and Southern at Pels, Colorado, including an elevation map from Pels to Poñil Park. The elevation map details the extreme elevation changes across Longs Canyon and a local unnamed summit, and the considerable work needed to reach Van Bremmer Park, an area just north of Poñil Park. The second route originated on the Colorado and Wyoming Railroad at Weston, Colorado, and proceeded southward similar to the first route. The final route was described as an "extension" of the St. Louis, Rocky Mountain, and Pacific Railway proceeding northwest up Poñil Canyon from Cimarron.

The advantages and disadvantages of each route were discussed. The two routes originating in Colorado would see empty trains heading downhill into the timberlands and loaded trains coming up the grade, which was an inefficient method of operation. Schomburg noted his

6 Henry Koehler, Jr. Prospectus: St. Louis Rocky Mountain and Pacific Company. May 10, 1905, pg. 19.

Poñil Canyon as it appeared before railway construction.

Aztec Mill Museum Collection, Cimarron, New Mexico.

preference for the "St. Louis extension" as the construction costs would be lower due to not having to descend into deep mountain drainages, empty trains could proceed up in elevation into the timberlands, then return down the grade into Cimarron when loaded. The plan that would be selected for building the railroad for the Continental Tie and Lumber Company was to start at Cimarron on the Rocky Mountain Route and proceed northwest up Poñil Canyon. This led to choosing "Cimarron and Northwestern" as the name for the new railroad.[7]

With investors secured and a profitable route selected, the Cimarron and Northwestern Railway was incorporated on January 21, 1907, under the laws of the territory of New Mexico, and the first meeting of stockholders was held two days later on January 23. The company's lifespan was fifty years with $240,000 raised for acquiring equipment and for construction. $120,000 of common stock was sold and $120,000 of 7% two-year bonds were sold to the general public. The incorporators and major investors were the same as the Continental Tie and Lumber Company: Theodore A. Schomburg was chosen as president, Albert A. Miller as vice president, William H. Deleker as secretary-treasurer, and Henry G. Frankenburger as general manager. Schomburg held $90,000 of C&N stock (three-fourths of stock issued) and the CT&L held the remainder. The mortgage bonds were

7 Theodore Schomburg, undated and unaddressed document with elevation figures, File Folder 12, T.A. Schomburg Collection.

Henry G. Frankenburger and Manly Chase preside over the unveiling of a new headstone for Rev. Franklin J. Tolby in Cimarron Cemetery on June 29, 1913. Frankenburger is fourth from the right with hat in left hand.

Aztec Mill Museum Collection, Cimarron, New Mexico.

also guaranteed by the CT&L.[8]

Frankenburger would be the main manager, supervisor, local advisor, and point-of-contact for all Schomburg's enterprises in the Cimarron country. He did everything from serving as the railroad traffic manager, supervising daily operations for both the railroad and the timber company, collecting information and data for Schomburg, soliciting business for both companies, and anything else required by Schomburg's expanding commercial interests. Frankenburger would be one of the few people involved during the entire lifespan of the Cimarron and Northwestern Railway from incorporation to abandonment. At the time of C&N incorporation, Frankenburger was involved in cattle ranching and was living in Trinidad, Colorado, where Schomburg was then residing. An accomplished gardener, a devout Methodist, and an active Freemason, Frankenburger would become a pillar in the Cimarron community and a key decision-maker for the railroad. He and Manly Chase would even be the officiants at the unveiling of a

8 Murphy, Lawrence, *New Mexico Railroader*, Volume 6, No. 11, "The Cimarron and Northwestern: Historic Railroad of Northern New Mexico, Part I," November 1964, 3; Volume 6, No. 12, "The Cimarron and Northwestern: Historic Railroad of Northwestern New Mexico, Part II," December 1964, 2.

new gravestone marker for Rev. Tolby at Cimarron Cemetery in 1913.[9] Frankenburger would be the person to carry out the mission of the planned railroad. The purpose and scope of the Cimarron and Northwestern would be succinctly stated in Interstate Commerce Commission reports years later:

> The articles recite that the carrier was incorporated for the purposes of building, owning, and operating a standard-gauge single-track steam railroad extending from Cimarron in a general northwesterly direction to a point in Van Bremmer Park, N. Mex., a distance of about 36 miles. The principal incorporator was T.A. Schomburg, president of the Continental Tie and Lumber Company, which purchased the standing timber on lands of the Maxwell Land Grant Company. The Continental Tie and Lumber Company maintains control of the carrier through stock ownership. The general offices of both companies are at Cimarron, though the articles of incorporation name Raton, N. Mex., as the principal place of business of the carrier. The carrier is virtually a plant facility for the transportation of the lumber mill products of the Continental Tie and Lumber Company. To supply the mills and bring out lumber is the sole reason for the road's existence. When the timber is gone, the Continental Tie and Lumber Company, having no interest in the cut-over lands, intends to close the road and take up the rails.[10]

The Cimarron and Northwestern Railway would operate in concert with the Continental Tie and Lumber Company, and incorporation documents relate that the railroad was bound for Poñil Park and lands beyond, all the way to Van Bremmer Park to the north. Indeed, earlier timber evaluations showed dense stands of timber in Van Bremmer Park, and passing through Poñil Park would allow access to this timber to fulfill contractual obligations. But the purpose was clear from the start that the railroad was designed solely for timber hauling. Once the timber was cut out, the railroad would be abandoned.[11]

---

9 Tolby gravestone ceremony: MacDonald, Randall M., Gene Lamm, and Sara E. MacDonald. *Cimarron and Philmont*, 29; Frankenburger's garden noted for growing a 10-inch wide lemon: front page of *The Cimarron News and Cimarron Citizen*. (Cimarron, Colfax County, N.M.), 12 March 1914. Frankenburger also attended the regional Masonic leadership conference. This same newspaper edition would also note a certain Charles G. Cypher visiting Cimarron: *The Cimarron News and Cimarron Citizen*. (Cimarron, Colfax County, N.M.), 15 Oct. 1914.

10 Decisions of the Interstate Commerce Commission of the United States of America, Vol. 106, Valuation Reports. October 1925 – February 1926, pp 562.

11 Van Bremmer Park area timber estimates: File Folder 16, Hand-drawn timber estimate map, "Tp 30 N – R 17 E;" File Folder 50, Map of Rocky Mountain Timber Company timber estimates. T.A. Schomburg Collection. History Colorado Center.

Survey, Construction, and Communication

Schomburg and Frankenburger began moving quickly and several phases of construction overlapped considerably. The complete railroad right-of-way was secured almost overnight. With the bulk of the right-of-way on lands belonging to the Maxwell Land Grant Company, and since a railroad was required in order to meet the contractual obligation, securing the right-of-way was a given. On January 24, 1907, just three days after incorporation, Schomburg and Charles Springer signed an agreement to secure a 50-foot-wide railroad right-of-way through the Springer Ranch in Poñil Canyon north of Cimarron for $11,000. This agreement stipulated that the C&N would build ditches, right-of-way fences, and wagon road crossings. Charles Springer would in turn receive $550 in cash and an $11,000 C&N gold mortgage coupon as payment. This agreement mentions "that said right-of-way shall be substantially on the line of the Kelly survey as heretofore staked to the ground."

On April 30, 1907, for $5,000 the C&N secured a right-of-way under a similar set of conditions with Manly Mortimer Chase of the Chase Ranch. With the right-of-way secured, the selection of a surveyor would be the next major decision. A.G. Allen would take center stage as the chief engineer for the C&N Ry arriving in February 1907. Allen had experienced the full arc of an engineering career and this project is believed to be the final act of his well-traveled life. Just three years later in 1910 when the railroad was expanding, Allen's absence is conspicuous in the railway's records, as Guy H. Palmes would take up the role of chief engineer. A glowing testimonial of Allen was printed by the *Cimarron News and Press* on May 30, 1907, and the chief engineer's biography bore many parallels to Theodore Schomburg's trans-Atlantic life. "Mr. A.G. Allen, engineer in charge of the construction of the Cimarron and Northwestern, is an engineer of unquestioned ability and a man of interesting personality."

Allen was born in 1866 in Madras, East India, to a family of engineers. He was educated at Clifton College in Gloucestershire, England, and came to the United States in 1883 where he worked as an irrigation and hydraulic engineer in Nebraska, Colorado, and Idaho. His railroad career started in the following years as a bridge engineer and later division engineer of construction for the AT&SF Ry in eastern Oklahoma. In 1893, Allen joined the Grand Trunk Railway System in western Canada. His position would be to survey and locate the right-of-way "through dense country" with the help of "native guides" from the Hudson Bay Company. The article describes the arduous nature of this engineering work in a very remote part of Canada, "to explore, compile maps and make estimates for the building of a railroad through a block of five hundred miles of hitherto unexplored swamp and forest land, in the Hudson Bay country." The article states that Allen left the Grand Trunk in 1907 "on account of his health." It continues, "He took charge of the building of the Cimarron & Northwestern railroad on account of the exceptional conditions of the climate here, and is highly pleased with the locality." The same newspaper front page detailed Allen's story of a beloved and expensively tailored dress suit falling apart through ranch work in South Dakota. Fortunately, Allen's surveying of the C&N line would prove less traumatic to his raiment, and March 1907 found the surveyed route ready for grading.[12]

A myriad of contractors, companies, and various individuals were involved with the grading and actual construction of the railroad roadbed, fills, track, trestles, culverts, and bridges. As work progressed in 1907, persons involved with these construction efforts were much talked about in Cimarron, and the "Locals and Personals" illuminated more characters in the C&N story. The primary grading contract was let in April 1907 to the Whitescarver Construction Company of Trinidad, Colorado.

> The Whitescarver Construction Co. have taken the contract to build the twenty-two miles of railroad up Poñil Canyon for the Cimarron and Northwestern. They have already sub-let several miles of the work to an Oklahoma contractor.[13]

The news that the road would be twenty-two miles was a revelation, since that distance would only take the C&N to Poñil Park and not to Van Bremmer Park as originally reported. Grading subcontractors included the Maney Brothers of Oklahoma, Tim Curran and Jack Keefe of the partnership Curran & Keefe, John W. Shea, James Griffin, and

---

12 Memorandum of Agreement between Charles Springer and T.A. Schomburg, signed January 24, 1907, Chase Ranch Foundation, Cimarron, NM; Right of Way Deed, Manly M. Chase to the Cimarron and Northwestern Railway Co., April 30, 1907, Raton Museum; A.G. Allen as chief engineer: Murphy, *New Mexico Railroader,* Volume 6, No. 12. "The Cimarron and Northwestern: Historic Railroad of Northern New Mexico, Part II," December 1964, 4-5; A.G. Allen article: *The Cimarron News and Press.* (Cimarron, N.M.), 30 May 1907.

13 Quote from *The Cimarron News and Press.* (Cimarron, N.M.), 4 April 1907. Grading contract and construction announcement: *The Railway Age*, Vol. 43, January 1 to June 30, 1907, The Wilson Company, Chicago, 1907, pg. 717, Google Books; *Raton Range* (Raton, N.M.) 6 April 1907, Arthur Johnson Memorial Library.

Grading crew in Poñil Canyon near the Chase Ranch.

New Mexico State University Library, Archives and Special Collections.

others. The Maney Brothers had George S. Foster in charge of their outfit and L.M. Rideout was noted in the press as resigning his position with the Maney Brothers in August 1907 after many months of hard work completing his five-mile grading contract.[14] Daily notes on the C&N were common journalistic occurrences. The March 21st *Cimarron News and Press* is a good example:

> W.S. Ward Jr and R.S. Zeiger, both of Denver, Colo., at present with the location party of the Cimarron and Northwestern in Poñil Canyon, were into the dance Saturday night. [...] Chief Engineer A.G. Allen, of the Cimarron and Northwestern drove down from the camp Sunday. Mr Allen was formerly assistant chief on the Grand Trunk, probably one of the most difficult pieces of engineering in the world.[15]

The April 4th edition of the *Cimarron News and Press* reported that

14 Confirmed subcontractors are listed here from *The Cimarron News and Press*. (Cimarron, N.M.). Chronicling America: Historic American Newspapers. Lib. of Congress. Maney Brothers: 05 Sept. 1907; Curran & Keefe: 14 March 1907; John W. Shea: 05 Sept. 1907; L.M. Rideout: 11 April 1907, 08 Aug. 1907, and 13 June 1907. James Griffin: *Santa Fe New Mexican*. (Santa Fe, N.M.), 26 Dec. 1907.

15 *Cimarron News and Press* (Cimarron, N.M.) 21 March 1907. Chronicling America: Historic American Newspapers. Lib. Of Congress..

Charles Lowther was a member of Allen's engineering outfit and that Charles W. Bridges was hired as bridge and building foreman for the C&N.

Bridges had formerly been the bridge foreman for the StLRM&P Ry and had his hands full building a multitude of bridges, trestles, and structures for the C&N. April 11th brought even more news with O.B. Bishop moving his family to Poñil Park to farm the old Livingston Ranch. L.M. Rideout was the first subcontractor to get dirt moving and his outfit was camped at the end of mile marker one. Rideout's livestock escaped from the Cimarron corrals while he awaited tents, tools, and other supplies to arrive. T.J. Collier of Oxford, Mississippi, joined his brother S.J. Collier as members of the engineering party for the C&N.

The worst news was that CT&L's Ute Creek sawmill burned to the ground from a boiler fire, claiming 365 feet of belts for machinery, but sparing 900 logs in the yard. Despite this piece of bad news, W.C. Campbell, who had been a rodman for over a year with the StLRM&P Ry surveying crew, returned in March 1907 from his home in east Missouri to take a position as a rodman with the C&N surveying corps. In a statement that rings true with many inhabitants of northeastern New Mexico, Campbell remarked "there was a fascination about this country that gets into a man's blood and brings him back."[16]

The construction of the C&N crystallized in May 1907 and a series of news articles provided remarkable insight into the railroad and timber operations. The May 23rd edition leads off with the headline, "Tapping the Wonderful Lumber Reserves of Colfax County."

> Magnitude of the Lumber Industry in the Country Just Now Being Opened by the Cimarron & Northwestern Railroad
>
> The building of the Cimarron & Northwestern railroad is being rushed with all possible speed these days, and the favorable weather is giving the contractors a very satisfied feeling. Seven miles of the grade have been completed, and a dozen miles of telephone poles have been set, preparatory to stringing the wire. [...]
>
> The opening of this railroad will open to commerce one of the richest

16 Quote on survey party and A.G. Allen from 21 March 1907 edition, Charles Lowther and Charles W. Bridges mentioned on 4 April 1907, and remaining information from 11 April 1907. *The Cimarron News and Press.* (Cimarron, N.M.). Bridges and bridge building foreman: *Raton Range* (Raton, NM), 30 March 1907. W.C. Campbell returning as rodman: *Raton Range* (Raton, NM), 30 March 1907.

fruit and agricultural districts in the world. Thousands upon thousands of acres of fertile valleys and parks lie along the right-of-way of this new road, and these will be opened for practical farming for the first time when the railroad is completed.

But primarily, the building of the Cimarron and Northwestern is for the purpose of opening the vast reserves of timber which remain untouched in the thirty miles of country to be tapped. The road will be standard gauge for twenty-two miles from Cimarron, and the upper portion, through the rougher country, will be narrow gauge.

An immense amount of preparatory work has already been done in the forests along the railroads, and as rapidly as men can be secured they are being sent to the lumber camps. The Continental Tie & Lumber company, who owns the timber on this immense tract, find that good labor is a scarce commodity, and are now paying the highest wages ever known in the history of the lumber industry. Tie makers are particularly scarce, and the company finds that it is necessary to teach raw hands this branch of the work, usually at considerable loss to the company. A tie maker is paid at the rate of 12 cents per tie in the camps of this company, and a good workman can turn out about forty ties per day. In 1902 the lumber companies in this section were at the rate of 8 cents per tie. During the next three years the price increased to 10 cents, and this year an additional advance has been made. The cheaper of common labor is paid at the rate of 20 cents an hour, while a cog man can earn $2.50 per day at com-

Timber crew hand-hewing railroad ties with a broadaxe.

Library of Congress Prints and Photographs Division: LC-DIG-fsa-8a28887

mon work. Loggers are paid $3.50 per day and are in demand and drivers of single teams in the woods are receiving $75 and $80 per month. The lumber camps are under splendid regulations, and are desirable fields for laborers of all classes. It is hardly probable that the demand for men in this district will be supplied for years to come, as the company has extensive plans for the future.

At present the Cimarron Canon Mill of the Continental Tie and Timber company [sic] supplies the Gate City Lumber company at Raton. The product of the Dean Canon mill goes to the Cimarron Lumber company and to the St. Louis, Rocky Mountain, & Pacific railroad. A large quantity of ties have been shipped to Cheyenne, Wyoming, for the Colorado & Southern railroad company recently.

The new mills which will be put in operation along the line of the new railroad will greatly increase the lumber output of the country. A mill with a capacity of fifty thousand feet per day will be erected in Hart Canyon. One at the mouth of the Celly [Seally Canyon, also known as Lowery Canyon at that time] will have a capacity of one hundred thousand feet, every twenty-four hours, as will also one at Metcalf. The Cook Canon Mill will turn out twenty-five thousand feet per day. The mills will all be operated by steam plants, the coal for which will be mined along the right-of-way of the C & N. W.

These days when lumber is cash in the bank are in direct contrast to the early days of the lumber industry in the country. Even at as late a date as the building of the Catskill railroad, lumber was only worth $8.25 on the cars at Catskill. Now it is worth more than one hundred per cent more. Now the lumber industry is one of the most important of this prosperous section, and will employ large amount of labor in the next few years, all at good wages.

C. & N.W. RAILROAD WILL TAP EXTENSIVE COAL FIELDS

The building of the C. &. N.W. Railroad from Cimarron to Van Bremmer will tap twelve miles of the best coal in the southwest. The coal up this canon is the same as all the coal being worked by the St. L., R.M. & P., and the Dawson Fuel Co., in this county, and lies in three immense veins, easy of access, and of the best quality coking coal. There is virtually no limit to the quantity of coal in these hills, and it is believed that as the demand for fuel increase, these fields will be developed. For the present the C. & N. W. railroad will mine coal for their own use and for the use of the Continental tie and Timber company in their big mills.[17]

The sawmill estimates bore a handsome projection of 275,000 board feet of timber milled a day, certainly a stable business for both the CT&L and the C&N. Immediately opposite this glowing forecast for timbering was an article focused on the Rocky Mountain's communication means: "A Railroad That Uses Both the Telephone and the Telegraph." Both the C&N and the Rocky Mountain utilized telephones as key parts of their operations.

Another important factor that was noted involves the coal resources along the C&N. The early timber mills in the area burned wood scraps and non-marketable lumber for fuel to run steam plants, but just as new technology such as the telephone changed the industry, so too would bountiful local coal resources. As noted in the article, the new mills would use coal from mines near the railroad and with the operation rostering ten gondolas ("coal cars" as seen in the historical record), fuel deliveries would be common occurrences on this line.[18] While unconfirmed, the closest coal mine to the trackage may have been the Chase Ranch mine located about one mile north of the Chase Ranch headquarters. Other nearby mines may have supplied coal for the mills along the route.

Significant industrial coal mining operations would not occur along the C&N, but Theodore Schomburg did attempt to encourage subsequent development of these resources. A June 16, 1908, letter to Senator W.A. Clark of New York had Schomburg trying to convince Clark to haul coal over the C&N Ry by building a railroad branch extension from Poñil Park. Ostensibly, this was aimed at soliciting support and funds for such an enterprise, but Schomburg's suggestion did not come to fruition.[19]

The May 4th edition of the *Raton Range* trumpeted that railroad construction would be complete by September 1907, aided by a new technology installed at Metcalf specifically for use in the construction: the telephone. The railway telephone at Metcalf, the fruit and ranch lands of the Chase and French ranches, timbering operations, and warehouse construction would be prominently featured in the local

---

17 *The Cimarron News and Press*. (Cimarron, N.M.), 23 May 1907. Chronicling America: Historic American Newspapers. Lib. of Congress.

18 Ten gondola cars: *Moody's Manual of Railroads and Corporation Securities*. United States: Moody Manual Company, 1915, 265.

19 Letter, T.A. Schomburg to Senator W.A. Clark, June 16, 1908. File Folder 4, T.A. Schomburg Collection.

Metcalf, New Mexico. Telephone poles are shown near the track, and wires are visible running to the larger building.

Aztec Mill Museum Collection, Cimarron, New Mexico.

newspapers. The headline from the May 30, 1907 *Cimarron News and Press* touts:

> CONSTRUCTION WORK IS BEING PUSHED
> Curves and Grades Will be Eliminated in Ascent Up Poñil Canon
> 1400 Feet Climb in Twenty-Two Miles
>
> About the busiest place in Colfax County just now, is up in Poñil Canon, along the right-of-way of the new Cimarron & Northwestern railway. In this canon, so rich in historic interest, abounding in the beauties of mountain and valley, forest and stream, so close to the heart of nature, is just now being enacted one of the most important chapters in the history of the great southwest.
>
> Within a stone's throw of the ancient dwelling-place of Kit Carson, is being stored the bridge material for half a hundred bridges which the railroad will require, to eliminate as much as possible curves and grades, in the ascent up Poñil Canon. All through the famous French and Chase ranches are camps of railroad graders, and further up the canon are corps of engineers and camps of lumbermen the former completing the surveys and placing the grade stakes and the latter getting out the ties and building materials for the road, out of the virgin forests of the upper canon.
>
> The Cimarron and Northwestern railway leaves the St. Louis, Rocky Mountain & Pacific railway at the eastern edge of the Cimarron

townsite, where they have more than twenty-five acres of station grounds. Here is already built a large warehouse, 50x100 feet, for the storage of grain, provisions, etc., for the various camps, and here are being graded more than a mile and a half of side tracks. These tracks are placed just the proper distance apart so that a double pile of lumber may be placed between, and here will be located the storage yards of the Continental Tie and Lumber company. The station grounds and lumber yards are on a slight elevation, and constitute a most handsome site for the purpose. The grading for the yards is well along and will be virtually completed ere the end of this week, ready for tracking. Leaving the station grounds the new road will enter the famous French ranch by a slight grade, crossing the French irrigating ditch system by a two-span bridge. In mile two, occurs the heaviest fill on the entire line, a fill of four thousand yards. From this point the railroad enters the Chase ranch, cutting off a corner of the famous Chase orchard, where it was necessary to cut down about thirty elegant bearing apple trees, about seventeen years old. After passing the Chase orchard the road hugs the sides of the canon, avoiding the rich agricultural lands, and crossing and re-crossing the Poñil river many times. In fact, in the twenty-two miles of the road it will require fifty-one bridges, in addition to a number of channel changes, where the waters of Poñil will be diverted from the old course and the railroad built in their place. The engineering work in the building of the Cimarron & Northwestern is what is termed light mountain work, and when the road is completed will stand as one of the neatest achievements in railroad building in the southwest. In the twenty-two miles of road there is a climb of one thousand four hundred feet, and the maximum grade is two per cent. The heavy traffic,

A typical creek crossing, with handcar and crew on the bridge.

Aztec Mill Museum Collection, Cimarron, New Mexico.

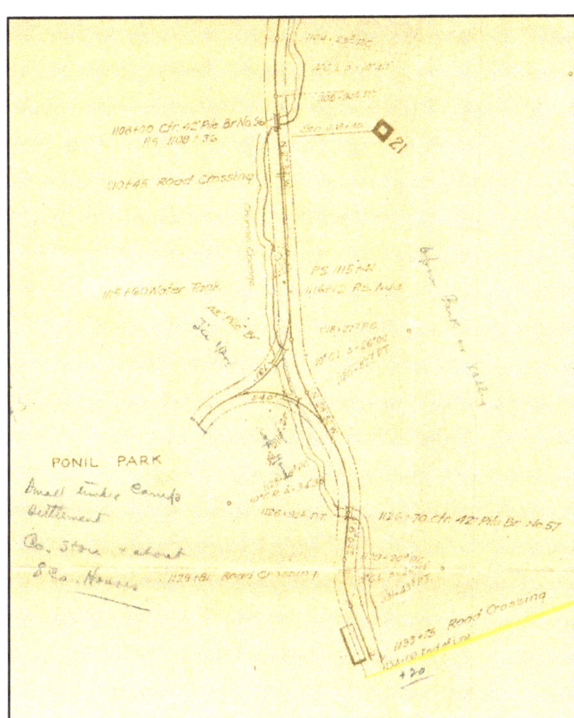

C&N survey plat of the terminus at Poñil Park. Details are shown locating the water tank, tie yard, bridges, and the wye that stretched across Poñil Creek. Pencil notes indicate a company store and about eight existing houses at the timber camp. Notation at bottom reads, "End of Line."

Palmes, Guy H. "Right of Way and Track Map Cimarron and Northwestern Railway," Sheet 6. May 20,1917. United States National Archives and Records Administration, College Park, MD.

of course, will all be downhill, and the capacity of the road will only be limited by the abilities of the engine to hold the load back on the down run. One engine can safely handle forty loaded cars. The bridges are all designed for 100-ton engines, and the rolling stock and road bed will be the best ever used in this character of work.

In the management of the railroad are among the most progressive business men of the southwest, and their method of building railroads is somewhat of an innovation. For instance, Mr. T.A. Schomburg, who is in charge of the road, has ordered the construction of a telephone line, not only to the construction camps along the line, but also to the camps of the locating engineers, many miles in advance of the graders. Ordinarily, these camps have no communication with each other or with the grading camps and headquarters, and as a consequence much valuable time is lost, and much expense is incurred in maintaining messenger service. The Cimarron & Northwestern engineers and surveyors may communicate with each other and with the general offices of the road, in Trinidad, by telephone, at any time, and graders, bridge men, construction men, and all may be directed either from the general offices or from the office of the engineer in charge.

Another feature which will facilitate the building of the road is the ease with which material is procured. The securing of material and especially timber, has usually been one of the greatest drawbacks in modern railroad building. The material for the Cimarron & Northwestern was all purchased before even the grading contracts were let, and as a consequence immense quantities of it are arriving daily now, and by the time the grade is ready it will all be on the ground, ready for use.

One great advantage which the new road had was the fact that the right-of-way lays through the immense timber reserves of the Continental Tie and Lumber company, who immediately set a number of men at work getting out the necessary materials. Bridge pilings, telephone poles, bridge timbers and ties are being cut on the sides of the upper Poñil canon and slid down the roadway ready for use. The sides of the cannon for miles are lined with this material, ready for use. On account of the size and strength of the bridges, the stringers are all being cut in Dean canon, and delivered to the Kit Carson supply yards.

Mr. C.A. Bridges [sic. Read: Charles W. Bridges], who is in charge of the bridge construction of the road has a pile driver and a force of men at work now in the upper canon, and has the piles driven for a number of bridges. Mr. Bridges has been connected with bridge construction work on the Santa Fe, Rock Island, D & R.G., and the St. Louis, Rocky Mountain & Pacific, and will give the new line excellent bridge structures.

In the building of mountain railroads the danger of washouts and slides must be taken into consideration, and the engineer in charge has planned and is executing a practical system of flood ditches and culverts which will thoroughly protect the roadbed from these dangers, and handle the flood waters from immense drainages traversed by the road. [...]

BIG WAREHOUSE COMPLETE

The new warehouse of the Cimarron & Northwestern, just east of town was completed last week and this week the St. Louis, Rocky Mountain & Pacific track gang is at work building tracks into the house, so that supplies can be unloaded there. There is a large quantity of building material along the line now, awaiting a storage place, and a large number of ties have already been unloaded at the junc-

Completed track high above the creek where it would be protected from washouts.

Aztec Mill Museum Collection, Cimarron, New Mexico.

tion of the Cimarron & Northwestern and the Rocky Mountain.[20]

The efforts of Schomburg and Frankenburger in advance planning, communication, and rapid action were paying dividends and their labors were noticed in the community. This was not a hastily nor crudely constructed logging railroad with ties simply laid about on the ground. The Cimarron and Northwestern Railway, as recounted by Thomas Schomburg years later, "could handle loads, much heavier loads, heavier locomotives, than the company had. It was an ICC road, Interstate Commerce Commission road, and had to abide by all rules of inspection, maintenance of way, and all that. So, it was really a first-class railroad, what we call a short line or an industrial railroad."[21] Indeed, Schomburg's rail and lumber operation in Cimarron was a busy, prolific, large-scale enterprise.

As predicted by the press, track construction commenced in June 1907 in Cimarron heading northwest, and B.B. Baker, former roadmaster on the StLRM&P, was hired as roadmaster that same month. As noted in previous newspaper accounts, the road was built as standard

20 *Raton Range* (Raton, NM), 4 May 1907, Arthur Johnson Memorial Library; *The Cimarron News and Press.* (Cimarron, N.M.), 30 May 1907. Chronicling America: Historic American Newspapers. Lib. of Congress.

21 Schomburg, Thomas W. Interviewed by Lawrence Murphy at Denver, Colorado, June 9, 1964.

Section crew enjoying a break at an adobe ruin near the Chase Ranch.
Aztec Mill Museum Collection, Cimarron, New Mexico.

gauge, meaning the rails were 56½ inches (4ft 8½ in) apart. Narrow gauge track was originally planned going north from Poñil Park, and it was even surveyed and staked out in June 1907, but it was never implemented. Narrow gauge, especially 3-foot gauge, was quite common in New Mexico and Colorado as narrower track meant reduced costs for smaller and cheaper crossties and the ability to navigate tight curves in the mountains. Apparently a lack of financing and legal conflicts over timber rights north of Poñil Park were factors that prevented the planned dual-gauge trackage.

Being a standard gauge railroad afforded the C&N many advantages. Inbound railcars of supplies, equipment, livestock, machinery, and so forth could be taken directly into the backcountry sites, sawmills, and timber camps along the route. Final products destined for outbound shipment did not need to be transferred in Cimarron from narrow to standard gauge railcars and vice versa. In fact, Thomas Schomburg stated that if a large order of ties, mine props, or poles was needed by the StLRM&P or the AT&SF Ry, the C&N would take the Rocky Mountain or Santa Fe cars directly to the backcountry loading sites and simply interchange the loaded cars in Cimarron for final transit and delivery.

The rails used were a mix between 52 pounds-per-yard and 56 pounds-per-yard, meaning each 3-foot segment of rail would weigh 52 or 56 pounds. Thus, a 30-foot rail segment, known as a 'stick' or 'panel' of rail, would weigh 520 pounds or 560 pounds. The rail was manufactured in 1886 by the Joliet Company in Joliet, Illinois, and similar to much of the C&N equipment, was second-hand and found new life as 'relay' steel on the C&N. The relay steel would be more than able to handle the weight and stresses of the C&N's equipment and the rail poundage used was another example of the well-constructed and well-organized operation. While most of the rail was sold off after abandonment in 1930, an old and long-discarded cattle gap near the historic Rich Ranch (also known as "Rich Cabins") was discovered in 2014, comprised entirely of 1886 rail with Joliet inscription marks still clearly visible. Two sticks are now proudly on display at modern-day Metcalf Station.

All the ties utilized were hand-hewn ties from along the C&N route, many of them 'rough cut' ties, meaning only the top and bottom were hewn flat and the sides left naturally rounded and normally unpeeled. Tie plates were likely not used on the main line and sidings; however, tie plates may have been inserted in sensitive or high-traffic areas such as switches, shop tracks, and tight curves. Historic photos of the line in operation suggest that all tracks were dirt ballasted.[22]

There was no shortage of incidents and happenings during construction in 1907. History may not reveal whether these events contributed to why it took six months to construct only twenty-two miles of track, but they provide more character to the railroad's story. As the original September completion date came and went, Hiram Christensen was brought in as another grading contractor. Roadmaster Baker oversaw a colorful crowd of construction workers, as shown by newspaper accounts from June 1907: "Some of the construction camps on the Cimarron & Northwestern paid off the boys, making things lively in and about Cimarron."

Apart from railroad and sawmill construction, the CT&L Co was

22 Track construction commences: *The Cimarron News and Press.* (Cimarron, N.M.), 13 June 1907.; Survey stakes for broad and narrow gauge completed: *Raton Range* (Raton, NM), 7 June 1907; B.B. Baker as roadmaster: *Raton Range* (Raton, NM), 14 September 1907; Boxcars in the backcountry: Schomburg, Thomas W. Interviewed by Lawrence Murphy at Denver, Colorado, June 9, 1964; Rail weight: Murphy, *New Mexico Railroader,* Vol 6, No 11, "The Cimarron and Northwestern: Historic Railroad of Northern New Mexico," 5; and "Continental Tie and Lumber Co. Inventory," March 8, 1938, Maxwell Land Grant Company Records (MSS 147), Center for Southwest Research.

also engaged in building various office and residential structures. The CT&L Co would construct company housing for managers and supervisors wherever they had a large concentration of employees. The October 24 edition of the *Cimarron News and Press* mentions this additional residential construction along with additional notes:

> The Continental Tie and Lumber company is building four dwelling houses just west of its new planning mill. [...] A.G. Allen, chief engineer of the Cimarron & Northwestern railroad, came in Monday evening from Trinidad, bringing with him eight men to work on the bridges on the above line. [...] George S. Foster, agent for Maney Brothers, left for Trinidad Tuesday morning. Mr. Foster is trying to find two cars of oats which he has bought and paid for and which stalled somewhere on the line of the Santa Fe railroad. The oats are very much needed here and should have arrived two weeks ago.

No fuel for the livestock meant major problems for the graders working on the route, but each week brought progress and more supplies. October brought seven carloads of steel rails, ten railroad flatcars, and rapid track construction. It would be in October that the railroad's sole locomotive would arrive, bearing the auspicious #1, and noted in the local press as arriving from the Southern Iron & Equipment Company in Atlanta, Georgia. Also in October, the contractor was finishing up the Continental Tie and Lumber Company planer mill with two carloads of mill machinery that arrived and more to follow. November brought the large boilers and the associated parts for the planer mill powerhouse in Cimarron.[23]

By the close of 1907, Schomburg managed and marketed his business enterprises from Denver with frequent business trips to Cimarron and correspondence with Frankenburger in Cimarron. General Manager Frankenburger supervised daily operations and assignments from Schomburg. Chief engineer Allen oversaw the survey crews, engineering, and physical routing of the railroad right-of-way. Allen and Frankenburger handled the formal filing of the located line at the Colfax County courthouse on Deed Book #31 in 1907. Bridge Foreman Bridges built bridges and trestles in a multitude of locations along the

---

23 Hiram Christensen as grading contractor: *Raton Range* (Raton, NM), 21 September 1907; Colorful crowd: *The Cimarron News and Press.* (Cimarron, N.M.), 20 June 1907; Allen, Fulton, houses, steel rails, and flatcars: *The Cimarron News and Press.* (Cimarron, N.M.), 24 Oct. 1907; Locomotive #1 arrival and planer mill being finished: *Raton Range* (Raton, NM) 19 October 1907; Powerhouse boilers arrive: *Raton Range*, (Raton, NM), 2 November 1907; *Santa Fe New Mexican.* (Santa Fe, N.M.), 26 Dec. 1907.

View of the combined two-story CT&L and C&N office building in the Cimarron yard. The ties on the yard track are all hand hewn.

New Mexico State University Library, Archives and Special Collections.

line with a railroad pile driver. Roadmaster Baker supervised railroad track construction and even the *Santa Fe Daily New Mexican* noted how the C&N was nearing completion in December 1907.[24]

Completion and Costs

The Cimarron and Northwestern Railway was completed in January 1908 and much press was given both to this new railroad and the growing potential of Colfax County. "Cimarron Has Splendid Prospects" was the trumpeting headline in the *Santa Fe Daily New Mexican*:

> Last week the last spike was driven by Chief Engineer A. G. Allen, for the Cimarron and Northwestern Railway which, starting from Cimarron, follows Poñil cañon to the great lumber forests of Poñil Park. The railway has been in process of construction since last February and is 22 miles in length. The roadbed is excellent and there are over sixty-five bridges. This railway was built especially for the use of the Continental Tie and Lumber company to exploit their immense timber holdings in the Poñil district. There is lumber in sight for a quarter of a century within easy reach of the terminus of this road.[25]

The specific date of completion and when the first train ran have been difficult to determine. The ICC Valuation Docket from 1926 lists the road as completed on January 1, 1908, yet the *Santa Fe New Mexi-*

24 Copy of "Cimarron and Northwestern Railway, Located Line," Deed Book #31, 1907, Colfax County, New Mexico, Raton Museum.

25 *Santa Fe New Mexican*. (Santa Fe, N.M.), 15 Jan. 1908. Chronicling America: Historic American Newspapers. Lib. of Congress.

can on January 15, 1908, noted that the road was finished "last week." Secondary sources list either January 6 or January 7 as the completion date, so the sources converge on completion being the first week of January 1908. Train operations would start shortly thereafter. The mill facilities were ready and enough timber had been felled for the first trainload.[26]

The completed right-of-way was top-notch engineering and the term 'light mountain work' accurately assessed the route. Subsequent 1917 trackage on right-of-way maps signed by then C&N engineer Guy Palmes and General Manage Henry Frankenburger confirm the hard efforts to open the line. Comprised of six separate map sheets, all right-of-way deeds and legal instruments, township and range lines, topographical illustrations of creek crossings, hand-written pencil notes, station stops, and more are listed in precise detail for the trackage directly owned by the railroad from Cimarron to Poñil Park.[27] The four-track yard and mill facilities in Cimarron were situated east of the present-day junction of highways 64 and 58 and south of Poñil Creek. The modern-day highway junction is about the exact point where the C&N connected with the StLRM&P Ry.

Leaving Cimarron and crossing the French Ranch irrigation system, the railroad hugged the west side of Poñil Canyon and crossed the mouth of Dean Canyon at mile post 3.5. This milepost would become a station stop with a siding to spot cars for shipments to and from F.R. Burnett's Dean Canyon mill and the Chase Ranch. Copious hand-written pencil notes of "pinon pine," "scrub oak," "mine props," and "orchard – apple" litter the maps and illuminate the topography, resources, and precise location of the railroad route.

The "orchard – apple" note refers to another colorful story in the railroad's history. Thirty Chase Ranch apple trees, roughly seventeen years old and at peak production, had to be felled to clear the right-of-way. Oral tradition holds that Manly M. Chase, whose apples won a gold medal at the 1893 Chicago World's Fair, made the railroad pay

26 Murphy lists the completion date as January 6, 1908: Murphy, *New Mexico Railroader*, Vol 6, No 11, "The Cimarron and Northwestern: Historic Railroad of Northern New Mexico," 5. The ICC in one of its valuation dockets lists the completion date as January 1, 1908: Decisions of the Interstate Commerce Commission of the United States of America, Vol. 106, Valuation Reports. October 1925 – February 1926, 562. Pearson writes the first train rolled on January 6, 1908: Pearson, *The Maxwell Land Grant*, 243.

27 Palmes, Guy H. "Right of Way and Track Map Cimarron and Northwestern Railway." May 20,1917. Sheet #1. United States National Archives and Records Administration, College Park, MD. The whole route is detailed on 6 sheets with a small overall route depiction on the first sheet.

Chase Ranch apple orchard where thirty trees were felled to make way for the rails.

Aztec Mill Museum Collection, Cimarron, New Mexico.

top dollar for each fruit tree felled.[28]

Continuing past Dean Canyon, the roadbed was a tight fit between the west Poñil Canyon wall and the Poñil River in the stretch directly opposite the Chase Ranch headquarters. Two Poñil Creek channel changes were completed at mileposts 4.75 and 5.05 before departing the Chase Ranch tract. Beyond the Chase Ranch and into the North Poñil Canyon, the creek crossings increased in frequency, with as many as nine or ten per mile. The confluence of the North Poñil Canyon and Poñil Canyon, known today as "6-Mile Gate," was denoted on map sheet #3 and on later public timetables as "South Poñil."[29] At mile marker 6.75, the railroad roadbed crossed over the creek to the east side of Poñil Canyon and allowed for a gradual right hand curve into the North Poñil Canyon at mile marker 7 with the curve taking the

28 Chase Ranch Apple Orchard and the C&N: Bromley, 45; *The Cimarron News and Press.* (Cimarron, N.M.), 30 May 1907; Murphy, *Philmont: A History,* 169. For an overview of the Colfax County fruit tree industry, see Zimmer and Lewis, 143-148. Right of way notes from Palmes, "Right of Way and Track Map Cimarron and Northwestern Railway," May 20, 1917, Sheet #2. F.R. Burnett mill: Maxwell Land Grant Company Timber Royalties Due, October 1907, November 1907, December 1907, January 1908, Maxwell Land Grant Company Records. MSS 147, Box 8, File Folder 6, Continental Tie and Lumber Company.

29 "6-Mile Gate" gets its name from the fact that there is a Philmont road gate at this location. State Road 204, the main road through Poñil Canyon, is a public road from Highway 64 all the way to the Elliot Barker State Wildlife Management Area. This gate is 6 miles from Highway 64, hence the name, "6-Mile Gate."

View of C&N trackage in North Poñil Canyon near Philmont's Indian Writings camp. Troutman took the photograph standing in rock cut #2 looking northwest across the trestle and track going through rock cut #3.

Aztec Mill Museum Collection, Cimarron, New Mexico.

roadbed to the west side of the North Poñil Canyon.

At South Poñil, a small siding was located along with the notes "sec. house & W.T." identifying a maintenance section crew house, likely for storage of tools and track materials. The next two miles were in the narrowest portion of North Poñil Canyon and a cut was dynamited out of the canyon wall at mile post 8, measuring approximately 40 feet long, 20 feet wide, and 20 feet deep. The course of the creek had to be rerouted for the south bridge approach and two pile bent trestles bounded the rock cut on either side. It is not known today if the graders, train crew, or section crew members were aware that this rock cut exposed a *hadrosaur* track on the underside of an overhang where the tracks went through the cut. Several decades later, a confirmed *T-Rex* track would be located just about 100 yards across the creek from the rock cut. Dinosaurs roamed this area well before the iron horse of the canyon steamed along steel rails. The present-day road, a direct descendent of the wagon road the railroad crossed as many times as the Poñil Creek, still utilizes this rock cut as a part of its route.[30]

After milepost 9, the North Poñil Canyon gradually increases in width. Creek channel changes were still needed in places, and bridge

30 Right of way notes from Palmes, "Right of Way and Track Map Cimarron and Northwestern Railway, May 20, 1917, Sheet #3.

View today taken from the same angle as the Troutman photo (left) at rock cut #2 looking northwest to rock cut #3.

David O'Neill Collection, June 2021.

crossings continued in abundance to reduce grades and curves where possible. Between mileposts 10 and 11 the railroad goes through modern-day Indian Writings, a Philmont backcountry camp. Near mile 10 the rail bed passed directly through what are now archaeological sites containing excavated post and slab houses from the Poñil and Jicarilla Apache peoples. Petroglyphs adorn the canyon walls in multiple locations only a few hundred feet from where the C&N laid tracks and ran daily trains.

Between miles 11 and 12, a second and third rock cut were dynamited out of the canyon walls. The second was the largest on the route being approximately 70 feet long, 30 feet wide, and 30 feet deep. The rock blasted out was used to build the 120ft long approach fill and bridge abutment to the cut on the south side. On the north side, an immediate creek crossing mandated another pile bent trestle. One-hundred yards after clearing this trestle, the smallest rock cut was traversed, this one being only 20 feet long, 10 feet deep, and 20 feet wide. The modern road uses the third rock cut, but not the second, which wraps around to the north of it to cross the creek at a lower elevation. The third rock cut is home to an inscription on the inside wall near where the track would have run, but not an indigenous petroglyph. It is the handiwork of Shorty Murray, a cowboy for the Chase Ranch and later Waite Phillips' Philmont Ranch. He carved "Shorty Murray, Jan 1921," perhaps the date the railroad removed the rails and gave way to cowboys on horseback tending cattle herds.[31]

Beyond mile 12 the canyon widens even further, and creek crossings were reduced as the grade ran over a gently sloping canyon floor. At mile 14, "METCALF" is the station listed at the confluence of the Metcalf Canyon and North Poñil Canyon. Notes for Metcalf read "small valley or 'park,'" "sec. house," and "N.S." A note of "portable sawmill" is listed at the confluence of Cook Canyon and the North Poñil, located immediately north of the Metcalf-North Poñil junction. Two sawmills were in this vicinity, one in Metcalf Canyon and one in Cook Canyon, leading to the growth of a small community and another siding.

From miles 14 to 21, no further rock cuts were needed, but scores of creek channel changes and bridges were employed around the winding creek bends. Mile 21 was situated at the south end of Poñil Park with pencil notes of "open park or valley." After a creek crossing at mile 21 there was another siding and a water tank located on the main line shortly after the siding rejoined the main. Immediately after the water tank was the first switch for the turning wye, a triangle of track used to turn locomotives, and if built long enough it could turn entire trains around. The turning wye had the main line on the west side of the creek and the two legs crossed over the creek to the east side with two major trestles, one for each leg. Portions of this trestle complex remain to this day. The 'tail' of the wye, referring to the track segment after the second wye switch that allows the train or locomotive to reverse direction, was in a small side canyon near the Poñil Park cemetery.

Pencil notes include "tie yard" on the south side of the wye and "mine prop" yard on the north side of the wye. Underneath the station "PONIL PARK" are the notes "small timber camp settlement, Co. store and about 8 co. house." After the wye and a final creek crossing is a railcar loading dock located at the very terminus of the railroad. Two sawmills were in Poñil Park, one at the mouth of Lowery Canyon (Seally Canyon today) near mile 21 and one in Hart Canyon near the terminus of the line at mile 22.[32]

This describes the Cimarron and Northwestern Railway upon its

31 Right of way notes from Palmes, "Right of Way and Track Map Cimarron and Northwestern Railway, May 20, 1917, Sheet #3.

32 Right of way notes from Palmes, "Right of Way and Track Map Cimarron and Northwestern Railway, May 20, 1917, Sheets #4, #5, and #6.

Poñil Park in winter showing rail cars loaded with lumber.

Ardelle Koperski, 1917, National Scouting Museum Collection, Cimarron, New Mexico.

completion in 1908. The maximum grade was 2% and the maximum curvature was 12 degrees. Final construction costs were $235,216.13 covering engineering, land, grading, bridges trestles, culverts, ties, rails, other track material, tracklaying, surfacing, right-of-way fences, water and fuel stations, shops, engine houses, and other miscellaneous structures. Grading stands out at $73,006.93 perhaps due to the multiple rock cuts needed. Equipment expenditures included $7,436.00 for the sole second-hand 2-8-0 Baldwin locomotive, $15,499.00 for freight-train cars, and $743.00 for other items which brought the equipment total to $23,678.00. Adding general expenses of $6,292.77 covering interest, legal work, stationary, and other items, the grand total cost of building the Cimarron and Northwestern was $265,186.90. This figure put the railroad $25,186.90 over the initially raised funds of $240,000.[33]

At that time the C&N could not continue building the line into Van Bremmer Park as originally planned. It was difficult for Theodore Schomburg to raise the needed funds, since the final construction costs were $25,186.90 over budget. Pearson explains that the economic conditions of the time precluded raising additional funds:

> The railroad was completed just as the country was caught in the 1907 financial panic and the lumber market collapsed. Building operations, railroad construction, and improvements of all kinds were

33 Decisions of the Interstate Commerce Commission of the United States of America, Vol. 106, Valuation Reports. October 1925 – February 1926, pp 569.

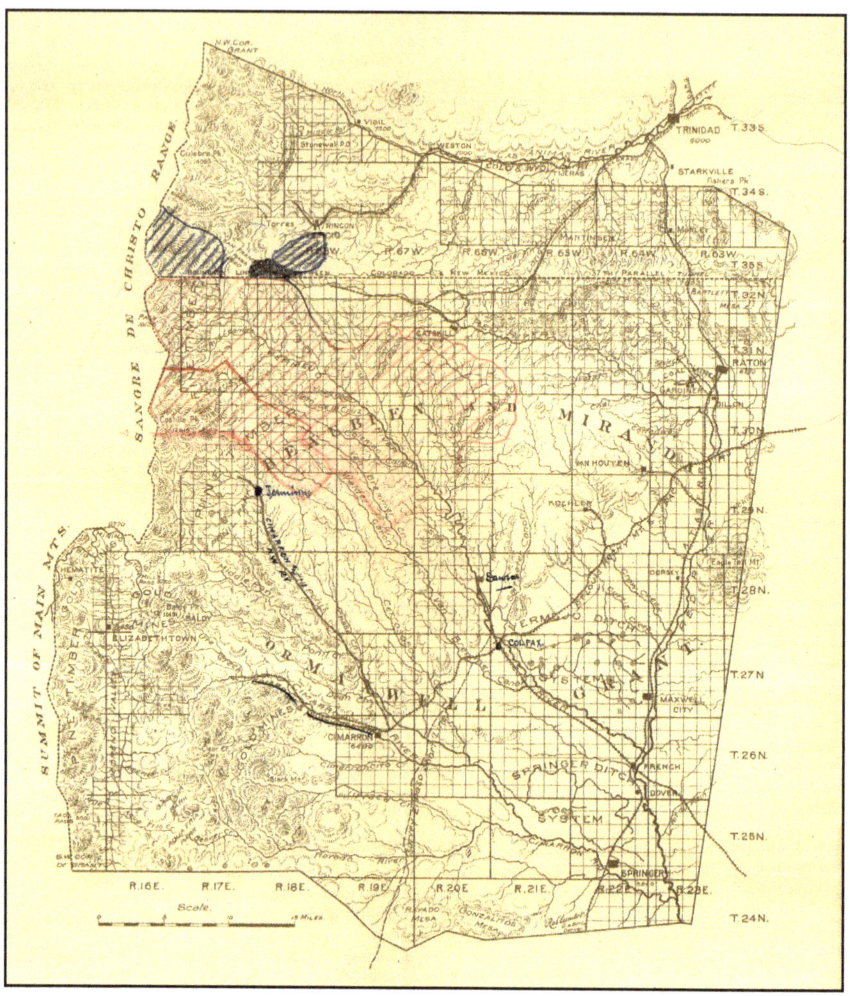

Maxwell Grant Map annotated by Theodore A. Schomburg showing timber stands in Van Bremmer & Vermejo Parks north of Poñil Park.

T.A. Schomburg Collection MSS 747, File Folder 48. History Colorado Center.

> suspended, mills were closed, and banks were failing over the nation.[34]

While Pearson is correct that the economy was especially hard-hit, there may have been other factors. Simply put, the C&N had already built to its existing capacity. One evidence of this is that C&N engine #1, the sole locomotive owned by the railroad, was a 66-ton engine which could not pull all forty flatcars and ten boxcars at once. The extra cars would be placed at backcountry sawmills and on various sid-

34 Pearson, 243.

ings for loading and unloading.

The Bartlett Case

There was a pressing legal issue that may have been a factor in dissuading the Cimarron and Northwestern from constructing the line north to Van Bremmer Park as originally planned. This involved a conflict over timber rights in the Van Bremmer Park and Vermejo Park areas. In the spring of 1907, as surveying and grading was progressing, with track construction for the C&N to begin soon, a lawsuit was filed regarding timber rights on the forty-thousand acres north of Poñil Park.

The case was filed by William H. Bartlett, owner of the land in question. *Maxwell Land Grant Company, John C. Osgood, and the Continental Tie and Lumber Company v. William H. Bartlett* was brought before Judge John R. McFie in Santa Fe. Familiar names represented the company, including David C. Beaman, Frank Springer, Charles A. Speiss, and A.C. McChesney. Bartlett was represented by attorneys George C. Merrick of Chicago, and R.E. Twitchell and A.A. Jones of Las Vegas, New Mexico. The question at issue was who owned the timber rights, and it reached back to Osgood's earlier timber venture and railroad construction failure. When the MLG Co gave Osgood the right to all the merchantable timber on the New Mexico portion of the grant in 1901, it hinged on Osgood fulfilling the railroad construction obligation within five years. Later in July 1902 the MLG Co sold 40,000 acres of land to Chicago grain dealer William Bartlett, but excluded the timber rights. Bartlett contended that the timber rights reverted to him after the cancellation of the Osgood-MLG Co contract. The case was predicted in the press to be "voluminous" and Judge McFie finally rendered his judgment almost a year and half later on November 9, 1909, in favor of the plaintiffs. The CT&L Co retained the timber rights on the questioned 40,000 acres with timber valued at $250,000, but the court case more than likely discouraged railroad expansion to the north of Poñil Park.[35]

Surprisingly, the overall historical relationship between Theodore Schomburg, Thomas Schomburg, the CT&L Co, and William Bartlett was rather friendly despite the court fight over timber rights. When the

35 All notes from Chronicling America: Historic American Newspapers. Lib. of Congress. Announcement of case: *Santa Fe New Mexican.* (Santa Fe, N.M.), 01 June 1907. History of case: *Santa Fe New Mexican.* (Santa Fe, N.M.), 04 June 1907. Final judgment: *Las Vegas Optic.* (East Las Vegas, N.M.), 05 Nov. 1909.

William H. Bartlett's *Casa Grande* mansion in Vermejo Park.

Stephen A. Zimmer Collection, Double Z Bar Ranch, Cimarron, New Mexico.

elder Schomburg was forming the Continental Tie and Lumber Company only a few years prior to the lawsuit, Schomburg offered Bartlett a one-fourth interest in the enterprise which he declined.

Theodore's son Thomas Schomburg would recount much of the Vermejo Park connection under Bartlett's ownership in his interview with Lawrence Murphy in 1964. Thomas would stay overnight when traveling from Colorado to the Poñil Park timber country, and he mentioned that "mother and father would be invited to stay a week" at Bartlett's lavish ranch headquarters. Furthermore, Thomas stated that Bartlett, "helped the company [CT&L Co] around 1909 in a very critical financial time." It is unclear whether this support involved dropping the court case rather than appealing the decision, or whether it included financial assistance after a devastating March 1909 fire in the lumber yard. The support could have very well been for the upcoming 1910 expansion the C&N and the CT&L Co were to undertake into the Bonito Canyon. Thomas recalls that the Schomburgs were close with William Bartlett until his death in 1918.[36]

36 For William Bartlett, T.A. Schomburg, and Vermejo Park history, see Laurie, Karen P. "History of Vermejo Park, New Mexico." *New Mexico Geological Society 27th Annual Fall Field Conference Guidebook*, pp 87-92, 1976. For Thomas Schomburg's remarks on Bartlett and Vermejo Park, see Schomburg, Thomas W. Interviewed by Lawrence Murphy at Denver, Colorado, June 9, 1964.

Equipment and Rolling Stock

The Cimarron and Northwestern Railway equipment and rolling stock roster was indicative of its nature both as a logging railroad and as a common carrier. The roster through the years included one steam locomotive, 39 flatcars, 4 boxcars, 10 coal gondolas, one caboose, and one pile driver. All of the rolling stock had been manufactured well before Theodore Schomburg ever conceived of building the line.

Locomotive #1

In October 1889, the Burnham, Parry, & Williams Company of the Baldwin Locomotive Works received an inquiry from the Western New York and Pennsylvania Railroad (WNY&P RR) for six consolidation type locomotives, each built to the same specifications. 'Consolidation' was a term that referred to a 2-8-0 locomotive wheel arrangement in Whyte Notation, which translated to 2 small leading wheels, 8 driving wheels, and 0 trailing wheels beneath the cab. The locomotives were numbered 163 through 168, and the engine that would eventually become the C&N's only locomotive would start her forty-year service life as WNY&P RR. No. 165.

Apparently, the Baldwin Locomotive Works was quite busy at this time since all six engines in this order were not built consecutively, as other orders were fulfilled between the construction of these engines. No. 163 marked the first engine of the group, so it was the first of the six engines to roll off the assembly line. For some unknown reason No. 165 was the second engine built instead of No. 164. No additional records can confirm the exact reason why this occurred. All locomotives underwent a trial on the boiler before they were completed and shipped from the factory. Construction probably started on No. 164 before No. 165, but perhaps the trial process took longer or other issues may have delayed its completion. Once any problems were resolved, the engine was finished, but this came well after No. 165 was completed. For whatever reason, No. 165 would be Baldwin's 10,568th locomotive built.[1]

Grossing 118,000 pounds in weight, equipped with 50¼ inch diameter driving wheels, built to burn soft coal, and sporting a wagon top boiler with cabs of yellow pine, these engines would have been considered relatively large and heavy for their time when compared to other locomotives built. They were typical examples of basic, all-purpose service locomotives commonly built by Baldwin and other locomotive manufacturers in the late 19th century. All six engines and their tenders left the Baldwin factory painted a dark green shade with WNY&P RR lettering. The boiler jackets were of planished steel, which was a chemically treated steel that would withstand the heat from the boiler without requiring paint. This type of boiler would have looked very dark, akin to bluing on gun barrels, and they were a common alternative to Russian Iron jackets which were also available options on Baldwin locomotives.

The Baldwin engineering specifications indicated that these engines came equipped with air brakes, but photographic evidence is inconclusive. If the engines left the factory with mounted air compressors and main reservoir tanks, they were installed on the engineer's side of the engine, opposite the side seen in known early photographs of the engines. Although they were new locomotives, they were built with the old-fashioned link and pin coupler system which matched the existing equipment on the railroad. They would not keep this feature for long since starting in 1892 and continuing into 1894, the WNY&P RR would upgrade all its equipment with more advanced and safer automatic couplers and the rolling stock would receive necessary air brake equipment. No. 165 was completed in January 1890 and arrived by

1 "Baldwin Locomotive Works engine specifications, 1869-1938," Series 2, Volume 17, pg. 143, DeGolyer Library, Southern Methodist University, Dallas, Texas. Web; Baldwin Locomotive Works, Index of Companies, Construction Numbers from May 1889 to July 1896, Nos. 10000 – 14999, Page 65, DeGolyer Library, SMU. The Whyte System is commonly used for classifying steam locomotive wheel arrangements in the United States.

Former Pennsylvania Railroad No. 6291, Baldwin builders No. 10568, newly arrived at the Southern Iron & Equipment Company in Atlanta, April 1907.

Southern Iron & Equipment Company Records, Archives Center, National Museum of American History, Smithsonian Institution.

rail at her new home in western New York state soon afterwards.[2]

These six engines would be the first ones purchased under the relatively new company name. The WNY&P RR's locomotive roster was mostly a carryover from its predecessor, the Buffalo, New York & Philadelphia, which primarily used American type (4-4-0) and ten-wheeler (4-6-0) locomotives. A handful of Consolidation locomotives were purchased for heavy freight service prior to the reorganization of the railroad into the WNY&P for the purpose of hauling longer and heavier freight trains. Lumber, coal, crude oil, and general merchandise were among the most typical commodities on this railroad, and the aging smaller engines were better suited for passenger and local freight services. Once No. 165 and her sisters arrived, they became the biggest and most powerful engines on the roster and were only surpassed in tractive effort by another group of Consolidations purchased the following year and another small group purchased in 1899.

2 Locomotive specification: "Baldwin Locomotive Works engine specifications, 1869-1938," Series 2, Volume 17, pg. 143, DeGolyer Library, SMU; Boiler jacket types: Graybeal, Johnny. Along the ET&WNC Volume II: *The Ten Wheelers*. Tarheel Press LLC, 2001. Pg. 123-124; Air brake system: see Pietrak, Paul V., Joseph G. Streamer, and James A. Van Brocklin, The History of the Western New York & Pennsylvania Railway Company and its Predecessor and Successors, Photo of WNY&P RR No. 163, pg. 2-20, "Excerpts from Annual Reports," pgs. 13-10, 13-13.

These engines were rated to produce just under 22,000 pounds of tractive effort with a 4.73 factor of adhesion, proving this engine design to be well balanced between available power and weight on the driving wheels. Therefore, these locomotives would have been particularly good for handling heavier than normal tonnages without too much slippage or the inability to start on unfavorable grades. With an average loaded freight car weighing around forty tons, these engines should have been able to pull up to 42 cars on straight and level track. It is unlikely that the grade along the Western New York & Pennsylvania was completely flat and perfectly straight, so these engines would probably have worked by themselves with somewhere between 20 to 30 loaded cars depending on ruling grade percentages. All six engines of this order would have been well-suited for all types of service on the WNY&P RR.[3]

On May 26, 1900, the ever-expanding Pennsylvania Railroad (PRR) agreed to take control of the Western New York & Pennsylvania Railroad and would eventually assume all operations along the line. Change would not come overnight, and the engines would continue to serve as they had in the previous decade. The engines could have been reassigned to new duties on different lines within the Pennsylvania Railroad system, but the biggest change for these engines came when they were renumbered and lettered for PRR. The former WNY&P No. 165 would be renumbered as PRR No. 6291. The exact date when the locomotive and her sisters were renumbered is unknown, but there was an effort on the PRR's part to complete the task for all locomotives on the former WNY&P's roster by 1903. In practical terms, it would take time for the Pennsylvania Railroad to assess the engines and renumber them based on their existing numbering and class designation system.

Baldwin classified these engines as 10-32E, based on Baldwin's classification system used for the construction of locomotives which helped determine part and design commonality. Most railroads had their own classification systems, and the Pennsylvania Railroad was no exception. The letter H was the assigned designation for Consolidation type locomotives. Because they had so many of these engines on the

---

3 Steam locomotives historically and today are referenced with the female pronoun. Completion and delivery of No. 165: Baldwin Locomotive Works, Index of Companies, Construction Numbers from May 1889 to July 1896, Nos. 10000 – 14999, Page 65; Baldwin Locomotive Works Engine Specifications, 1869-1938, DeGolyer Library, Volume 17, Page 143; Consolidation locomotive information from Steam Locomotive Dot Com, PRR: Class 163/H odd (Locobase 11648); Pietrak et al, "Motive Power and Service Facilities," pgs. 11-37, 11-38, "Excepts from Annual Reports," pgs. 13-7, 13-9.

roster, this designation was too broad by itself so the PRR went one step further to help distinguish the difference in engines. No. 6291 and her sisters were given the unique class designation of "163 H odd" which may have been the only identifying feature that carried over from their beginnings on the WNY&P RR.[4]

After 1900 the Pennsylvania Railroad's quest for expansion continued with more acquisitions and mergers until it became one of the dominant rail transportation sources in Pennsylvania, New York, and Maryland. It was at this time the PRR began several improvement projects that would make the railroad famous as "The Standard Railroad of the World." Beginning with consistent station architecture, this standardization effort would eventually work its way down to the engineering aspects of the railroad's motive power fleet. No. 6291 would be the first engine among her sisters that would no longer be needed, and she was sold in April 1907 to the Southern Iron & Equipment Company in Atlanta, Georgia.

The "163 H odd" engines did not fit the engine design standard that was becoming iconic to the PRR, but the exact reason for the sale was undocumented. Maybe there was not enough work to go around, and she could not handle the bigger and longer trains beginning to become more common after the turn of the century. Or perhaps it was just a rendezvous with destiny. Regardless of the reason, she started a new life in the used equipment dealership as SI&E No. 584. All her sisters would eventually be sold to Southern Iron & Equipment as the PRR phased out older motive power and favored engines of standard class designs. This would be the shortest chapter in this engine's life as she was purchased later that same year in August to begin a new service life on a different railroad that had just begun breaking ground in the mountains of the New Mexico territory of the Maxwell Land Grant.[5]

The first known photograph of SI&E No. 584 would show her newly acquired from the PRR. It seems as though SI&E was in a hurry to

---

4 Pennsylvania RR takes over the WNY&P RR: *The New York Times*. (New York, New York). The New York Times Time Machine, 27 May 1900; Renumbering and Class Information from: Baldwin Locomotive Works, Index of Companies, Construction Numbers from May 1889 to July 1896, Nos. 10000 – 14999, Page 65; and Steam Locomotive Dot Com, Class 163/H odd (Locobase 11648); Renumbering in 1903: Pietrak et al.

5 The Pennsy Modeler, Keystone Crossings Databases, All Time Steam Locomotive Roster. Class H, 6291; Baldwin Locomotive Works, Index of Companies, Construction Numbers from May 1889 to July 1896, Nos. 10000 – 14999, Page 65, DeGolyer Library; Southern Iron & Equipment Company Records, Archives Center, National Museum of American History, Smithsonian Institution.

Cimarron and Northwestern No. 1 at SI&E in Atlanta, Georgia, August 1907; refurbished, freshly painted, with side rods dropped for hauling.

Southern Iron & Equipment Company Records, Archives Center, National Museum of American History, Smithsonian Institution.

make her ready to sell, for they simply painted over her former number and "Pennsylvania" lettering on the tender, yet the original "from the factory" gold striping is still faintly distinguishable which makes it easy to assume she is still dark green in color. The SI&E took another picture of her in August before she was shipped to her new home in Cimarron.

The appearance of the engine is remarkable, compared to the earlier photo. Coal burning engines traditionally wore black paint to help hide the soot and cinders, and in this picture her tender, cab, and driving wheels show a dark yet somewhat glossy finish which may indicate the engine had been fully repainted as a condition of the sale. SI&E did in fact make a few other small changes before shipping the engine from Atlanta by replacing the cowcatcher and adding a front number plate to the smokebox. The connecting rods between the main driving wheels and the piston rods were removed which suggests she was transported dead in tow like a freight car, as opposed to being loaded on top of a flat car for transport.

This photo provides some additional details about the engine. First, it shows the original paint scheme of the Cimarron & Northwestern Railway. A common lettering format with the company name on the tender and the engine number was located both on the cab under the windows and on the sand dome of the engine. The most notable change is that her cab appears to have been replaced with another design with different doors and windows and a more rounded roof. The biggest difference is that her third set of driving wheels now have flanged tires in contrast to blind drivers as specified in the original design. A blind driver, one without flanges, is designed to sit on top of the rail without being guided by the rail. This picture shows the air compressor is missing from the engineer's side. Later photos show it mounted on the fireman's side. These changes imply that the engine underwent regular shopping and maintenance work during its service, or possibly these items were changed in Atlanta as a condition of the sale.

At this point in time the Interstate Commerce Commission (ICC) had not yet begun enforcing mandatory inspection and repair procedures on locomotives, so without any reliable shop records it is not known to what extent the engine experienced maintenance and repair work. One characteristic common to all steam locomotives was the essential need for good maintenance, and with the engine now seventeen years old, C&N No. 1 should have seen dozens of inspections and repairs. If SI&E was willing to repaint the locomotive to the customer's order, it is possible the company also gave the engine an overhaul before she shipped west.

Apparently, the engine needed the extra set of flanged driving wheels, but the second set remained blind so the engine could better handle curved track. The Baldwin builder's specifications did not call for a headlight, yet one is clearly seen in the photo. It is unlikely that she served on the WNY&P without one for any length of time. It is possible the railroad made their own unique headlights and they preferred to add their own design instead of having to reconfigure a new locomotive. A unique characteristic of C&N No. 1 was her simplicity as a modern locomotive which made alterations possible, yet she retained much of her original design throughout her entire service life.[6]

Flatcars, Boxcars, Caboose, and Pile Driver

As a logging railroad, flatcars, also known as platform cars, were more versatile than boxcars in the sense that they could handle raw logs, cut and stacked saw timber from backcountry mills, and various machinery and equipment as needed. Since the C&N was a common

6 Southern Iron & Equipment Company Records, Archives Center, National Museum of American History, Smithsonian Institution; Baldwin Locomotive Works Engine Specifications, 1869-1938, DeGolyer Library, Volume 17, Page 143.

C&N flatcars loaded with stacks of fresh-cut timber.

Aztec Mill Museum Collection, Cimarron, New Mexico.

carrier, the flatcars were required to have brakes and official ICC lettering. The C&N could not have home-built log cars without brakes that were common on other logging operations, especially in the southern United States. The flatcars were 34 feet long, had a capacity of 50,000 lbs., stenciled with car numbers 100 through 139, and "C&N Ry" marked on the sides. These flatcars were wooden-framed and topped with wood decking which allowed for loading freshly cut logs in triangular piles or bundled stacks of rough-cut lumber. Most surviving pictures of the flatcars in service show two piles of logs chained to the flatcars, while others show rough cut boards stacked high between set vertical posts.

Flatcar 108, along with another flatcar, carried a load different from the rest. It carried the company's only pile driver. It appears the company modified two flatcars with a boiler suitable for a steam tractor and a steam donkey engine to make an effective pile driver. Flatcar 108 carried both pieces and was further modified with a chain driven mechanism allowing for self-propulsion, which meant it could work independently and not require C&N No. 1 to move it while on a job. Consequently, it was only photographed sitting alone with the pile rigging structure folded back on top of the second flatcar. The C&N would have used the pile driver for trestle construction, but it is unknown whether this pile driver existed during the railroad's initial construction. The pile driver most certainly would have been quite busy

C&N flatcars carrying the pile driver and engine.

T.A. Schomburg Collection, MSS 747, F.32.782. History Colorado Center.

when the railroad later relocated the tracks up the South Poñil Canyon to the base of Wilson Mesa.[7]

The boxcars were obtained second-hand from other railroads, as historic photos show visible "Cotton Belt Route" heralds and logos, indicating a prior life on the St. Louis Southwestern Railroad, commonly known by its popular nickname, "the Cotton Belt." While not on the roster, but being pulled in interchange service, the photographic record shows El Paso and Southwestern livestock cars and AT&SF boxcars being pulled behind C&N trains. The stock cars were only used seasonally for livestock, so the remainder of the year they could be used like regular boxcars. Boxcars would carry inbound shipments to backcountry sites, such as machinery, supplies, or livestock feed, and outbound shipments such as mine props and cross ties.

According to all known photographic evidence, C&N No. 1 would routinely pull cuts of four flatcars together and might pull two cuts at one time with additional cars near the front of the train. Any more than ten or eleven total cars would have strained the engine's pulling ability on the steepest grades if all cars were fully loaded, but this railroad had an unusual and relatively flat grade for a mountain railroad. Gravity would still have naturally offered a helping hand in delivering a loaded train down the canyon toward Cimarron. The C&N railroaders quickly learned that they could transport more empty cars up the

7 T.A. Schomburg Collection, MSS 747, Neg. No F-32.782, History Colorado.

1920 photo of Margaret and Zenas Ward with the Chases in C&N caboose No.2 in Cimarron yard. Hand-hewn ties are seen in the foreground.

Chase Ranch Foundation.

canyon when needed, and then move more loaded tonnage than what she was rated for with the assistance of gravity on the trip back down to Cimarron.[8]

The Cimarron and Northwestern roster only carried one caboose on all known equipment rosters, but some evidence hints that either the caboose was re-lettered or that possibly two different cabooses were involved. The September 14, 1907, *Raton Range* reported, "The Cimarron & Northwestern caboose No. 001 has recently been repaired and repainted at the Rocky Mountain shops." All known photographs of any caboose on the C&N show Caboose No. 2 rather than No. 1. This could mean that perhaps the caboose was lettered 001 from its previous owner and repainted as No. 2, possibly to avoid confusion with locomotive No. 1, or perhaps some incident caused No. 1 to be removed from service and a new caboose procured.

For most of the railroad's history, a wooden caboose labeled Cimarron & Northwestern Caboose No. 2, which looked somewhat like a miniature baggage car, frequently rode directly behind the locomotive on each trip up and down the Poñil Canyon. Caboose No. 2 furnished the entirety of the daily passenger accommodations. A large side door allowed the caboose to transport parcels and packages in a small freight room. It contained a few seats for passengers, served as an office for the

8 Photograph of C&N train with a former Cotton Belt boxcar: "Log Train," Photographer, location and date unknown, likely Edward A. Troutman, Aztec Mill Museum, Cimarron, NM.

View of caboose #2 and boxcar with "Cotton Belt Route" herald.

Aztec Mill Museum Collection, Cimarron, New Mexico.

conductor, carried a large metal toolbox on the underframe, and the cupola gave a lookout for the train crew. Thomas Schomburg would describe passenger operations as follows: "We had a regular passenger tariff and handled passengers. We had a regular old caboose, had a part to hold passengers. [...] [Passengers were] mainly employees of the lumber company going back and forth from the timber and sawmill camps." Since boxcars and flatcars were being dropped off and picked up at intervals on both runs, having the caboose ride next to the tender made pickups and drop-offs quicker as the caboose was not constantly shuffled around.[9]

Service History

Once No. 1 arrived at Cimarron in October 1907, she would be put right to work with the new railroad and its other rolling equipment. It is not known when the locomotive was first fired in her new home, but fortunately for her the neighboring railroad, the St. Louis, Rocky Mountain & Pacific, had just finished building a new roundhouse and machine shop in Cimarron which offered the proper facilities for any final inspections or repairs before she would begin service.

Photographs and written records tell us that an operational pattern quickly emerged to indicate how the engine earned her keep on

9 *Raton Range* (Raton, NM), 14 Sept. 1907; Schomburg, Thomas W. Interviewed by Lawrence Murphy at Denver, Colorado, June 9, 1964.

the new railroad. She always pulled or pushed on the head end of the train. She never seemed to pull any of the flatcars directly behind the tender. In fact, every known picture of the engine shows mixed trains with either boxcars or stock cars first behind the caboose or tender followed by the flatcars. The most efficient operation would have called for C&N No. 1 to pull empty flatcars and boxcars uphill from Cimarron toward Poñil Park, then to switch these cars out for others which had been previously staged on sidings and loaded by the Continental Tie and Lumber Company workers.

In the category of "locomotive maintenance" there were many stories and insights into the operation of the railroad. In 1914 the local press shared a wealth of information on C&N No. 1 maintenance and repair. In April the train did not run "up to the mills on Monday" as No. 1 was "given a thorough overhauling" and returned to service on Tuesday. On July 2nd, the *Cimarron News and Citizen* reported that the engine was taken up to Raton for repair. The term used was "engineitis," which may have been a humorous way of describing a need for new flues and boiler work. The ICC standardized mandatory maintenance and repair work for all common carrier railroads in the United States by 1911. Flues had to be removed and inspected or replaced every four years of service and the boiler required a thorough inspection every five years. This work was difficult and expensive, so most railroads put it off until it was mandatory and essential. New Mexico had finally achieved statehood in 1912 so the railroad would hence-

View of St. Louis, Rocky Mountain, and Pacific roundhouse bay doors, machine shop, and power plant.

National Scouting Museum Collection, Cimarron, New Mexico.

forth be governed by all ICC regulations.

Careful examination of all known period photographs of this locomotive show her smokebox was either cut down to a shorter length or completely replaced at some point after her arrival in Cimarron. The front of the smokebox is much different from the original design, and other cosmetic features indicate the smokebox is nothing like the original. Replacing a smokebox would be a significant repair that could only be done in adequately equipped shops like those in Raton. Whether or not a local newspaper used the term "engineitis" to describe a specific type of repair is unknown, but another engine would have been leased as temporary power so the operations could continue. No other details describe the event, so it is not known which engine substituted for No. 1 at this time.

After the completion of this work, the engine was delivered from Raton by "Engineer Livingston," so engine No. 1 had run up and back from the Raton shops under her own power. This report is the first record of the engine's nickname, *Sally*. Apparently, she was very popular in Cimarron and considered to be the most trusted "employee" of the railroad. Unfortunately, later that same July the most trusted employee sustained a wreck. Upon returning from the mills at Ring and Bonito, "the tender completely turned over, caused by the spreading of rails on a soft roadbed. Engineer Jefferies sustained a sprained ankle in the accident, [...] The train did not arrive until a day or two later and is now again running on schedule, hauling down timber from the mills to be

New Year's Day wreck on the C&N, January 1, 1909.

New Mexico State University Library, Archives and Special Collections.

finished in the local mill." The train crew is fortunate nothing disastrous happened, as a sudden loss of water or an overturned locomotive could have led to a fatal boiler explosion. With regular operations resuming in a few days, the damage did not appear to be extensive.

However, Sally encountered her share of mishaps and accidents, as Garland Arnold, a Santa Fe engineer who worked the Las Vegas-Raton Division which included the old StLRM&P Ry, recalled to *Raton Range* reporter Charlie McCandless. Arnold referred to Sally as a "tea kettle" due to her light nature and mentioned that she derailed "off the main line" in the 1920s. Even with the locomotive out of service at multiple points in her service history, a report indicates that the lack of motive power did not stop this timber railroad from keeping lumber moving. In the New Mexico State Corporation Commission Annual Report for 1915, the commission had received a complaint that blocks of loaded flatcars were being moved down the C&N without the locomotive, with a brakeman manning the handbrake as the control on this movement. With the entirety of the grade from Poñil Park to Cimarron being 2% all downhill, it is possible that a team of strong men and livestock "kicked" the loaded cars down the grade with enough momentum to keep the "train" moving. Lumber had to move by all present means on the C&N.[10]

By 1910 the railroad reached its peak length of thirty-five miles with six station stops on its public timetable: Cimarron, Dean, South Poñil, Metcalf, Poñil Park, and Ring. The tracks extended further beyond Ring to the Bonito sawmill, but Bonito was omitted on the January 1915 timetable as public passenger service was not extended to Bonito. This timetable provides the best glimpse into the daily operations. Leaving at 7:30 AM from Cimarron, Sally with her mixed train would make stops at each point north on the line, arriving in Ring at 9:40 AM. Sally would average sixteen miles per hour between stops. However, the engine could reach top speeds possibly as high as 25 mph to allow sufficient time to take care of business at each stop while maintaining the schedule. The engine was not built for speed, but 25 mph could be easily achieved. After the stop in Ring, the engine and

10 Regulatory testing on locomotive boilers: Graybeal, pg. 22; C&N No. 1 out for overhaul: The *Cimarron News and Cimarron Citizen*. (Cimarron, Colfax County, N.M.), 16 April 1914; "Sally" taken to the Raton shops: Cimarron Print. Co. "*Cimarron News Citizen*, 07-02-1914." (1914); Tender overturns: Cimarron Print. Co. "*Cimarron News Citizen*, 07-23-1914." (1914); Garland Arnold recollections: "St. Louis, Rocky Mountain, and Pacific Train," Charlie McCandless; Train with no locomotive: *Fourth Annual Report of the State Corporation Commission of the State of New Mexico*, 1915, New Mexico State Corporation Commission.

CIMARRON & NORTHWESTERN RAILWAY.

T. A. SCHOMBURG, President, Denver, Colo. | H. K. HOLLOWAY, Sec'y & Treas., Denver, Colo.
H. W. ADAMS, Vice-President, Vermejo, N.M. | H. G. FRANKENBURGER, Gen. Mgr., Cimarron, N.M.
General Offices—Cimarron, N.M.

No. 2	Mls	*January*, 1915.	No. 1
		LEAVE] [ARRIVE	
†7 30 A M	0	Cimarron[1]	4 30 P M
7 45 »	4	Dean	4 10 »
8 00 »	8	South Ponil	3 50 »
8 30 »	15	Metcalf	3 20 »
9 00 »	22	Ponil Park	2 45 »
9 40 A M	26	Ring	†2 00 P M
		ARRIVE] [LEAVE	

Trains marked † run daily, except Sunday.

STANDARD—*Mountain time.*

CONNECTION.

[1] With Atchison, Topeka & Santa Fe Ry.

C&N timetable showing northbound schedule for train #2 and southbound schedule for train #1.

Official Guide of the Railways. United States: National Railway Publication Company. June 1916.

crew would have over four hours to wait until it would start the return trip to Cimarron.

Time was precious on any railroad, so with only one locomotive, they could not afford to have an engine sit idle for four hours. Not listed in the timetable is a schedule for exchanging empty freight cars (mostly flatcars) with those loaded on the sidings and spurs located along the line. No doubt the engine and her crew would have used the time between the scheduled run from Cimarron to Ring not only to service these sidings, but also the sawmills at Bonito and Poñil Park. With Sally being the only source of motive power for the railroad and the entire lumber company for that matter, it would have been the engine crew's responsibility to work efficiently to complete all the switching operations needed to keep the logging and lumber production operations going. With an hour and ten minutes up the canyon, 4 hours for switching on the north portion of the railroad, and an hour and a half on the return trip, plus time required to switch the yard in Cimarron, it would make for a full day of operation six days a week, Monday through Saturday.[11]

Sally attracted the attention of several visitors in Colfax County and found herself somewhat photogenic throughout her career in Cimarron. These snapshots not only capture her service in the Cimarron, Poñil, and Bonito Canyons, but also show how this lone locomotive changed during her service on the C&N. The earliest known photos show her working a log train at Ring, New Mexico, west of Poñil Park,

11 Timetable information: *Official Guide of the Railways,* National Railway Publication Company, June 1916, Cimarron and Northwestern Railway January 1915 public timetable.

Otto Perry's 1920 photo of Sally at work in Cimarron.
Denver Public Library, Special Collections, OP-6006.

and later shoving a mixed train at the Pratt and Wood sawmill located at Ring. These two pictures could not have been taken within a short period of time because Sally's tender has significantly faded from the first picture to the next. By contrast, the famous Caboose No. 2 appears to have been freshly painted between the photos.

In another picture Sally is seen at the Bonito sawmill, placing it between 1911 and 1916. This is the only time she was found without the caboose directly behind her tender while working north of Cimarron. Instead, she pulled a tank car. The tank car was likely there to provide additional water for the engine if shortages in water would not allow the crew to water the engine at the Poñil Park tank before heading back down the canyon.

Quite possibly the best picture of Sally was taken in 1920 by famed railroad photographer Otto Perry. Originally practicing his hobby on his days off as a mailman in Denver, Perry spent the majority of his career photographing steam at the height of its popularity, even documenting its demise in the 1950s. He captured Sally and her crew switching in the Cimarron lumber yard, providing tremendous detail of the engine by itself. The engine had been fitted with new tires, now with flanges on all eight driving wheels, indicating that the tight turns in the Poñil Canyon above the South Poñil station were not a problem for the engine. While the engine itself is not immaculate, she does appear to be well kept. This is also the first picture showing the new railroad paint scheme. Gone was the more western themed font of gold on the tender in favor of a simpler white lettering scheme. The paint job was not done with particular care as the old paint scheme is still visible under the new paint. Railroads typically repainted engines as needed when they were shopped for maintenance and repairs. It is possible that she was repainted during her visit to the Raton shops back in 1914. It is probable that she had made more than one trip to the Raton shops since then. The new paint scheme could have been applied at any one of those visits.

Although No. 1 always remained at the head end of the train as seen in all photos, curiously photographers seemed to catch her in a reverse movement, evident by the posture of the crew members or, in the case of Perry's photograph, by the steam leaking at the cylinders and the blurring on the right side of the driving wheels. Other notable details seen in Perry's picture include the styling of the headlight, her front number plate, and her whistle. This top lever whistle was definitely homemade in a railroad shop somewhere. It could have been the only feature of the engine that remained from her time on the Pennsylvania Railroad. Only those fortunate enough to work alongside Sally would know.[12]

The last known photograph of Sally provides almost as much contrast to Otto Perry's photograph as it does to earlier photos. Photographed on September 17, 1937, she is sitting cold and looking quite dilapidated, clearly showing that her service on the C&N had come to an end. We see yet more changes to the engine which helps tell the final chapter of her story. The second paint scheme on the tender remained, but the tender now has a kerosene lamp on the back. She never needed it in prior years, which begs the question as to why this feature would appear so late in her service life. It is unlikely the railroad decided to run it backwards during the return trip to Cimarron after the line was built up into the South Poñil. If the railroad did not want to turn the engine around, they would not have built a wye below Wilson Mesa. Perhaps it may have been added to comply with increasing ICC regulations for the period. Curiously, the light was an addition to the engine, yet the railroad did not install electric lighting on the engine indicating

12 Photos in order of reference: "Log Train Ring NM." Edward A Troutman, taken 1911-1916, Aztec Mill Museum Collection, Cimarron, NM; "Pratt and Wood's Sawmill." Probably Edward Troutman (based on plate carving), 1911-1916, taken at Pratt-Wood Mill in Ring, NM, Aztec Mill Museum Collection, Cimarron, NM; "CT&L Co Sawmill No. 3, Bonito N.Mex," Edward Troutman, 1911-1916, Bonito NM, David O'Neill Collection; Albi, Charles and William C. Jones. Otto Perry: *Master Railroad Photographer*. Johnson Publishing Company, 1982. Pg. 273.

One of the last known photos of Sally before she was sold.

National Scouting Museum Collection, Cimarron, New Mexico.

that the improvement was kept to a tighter budget which may have reflected the imminent end of the railroad's usefulness to the CT&L Co.

Another notable change to the engine is the addition of a second air compressor. For years she carried just the one compressor which must have been sufficient for operations in the North Poñil. The lone pump may not have been adequate for the slightly steeper grades in the South Poñil thus requiring another compressor so that the train brakes would work properly. It must have been a timely improvement because there are no reports of any runaway trains or wrecks that could have been caused by train brake problems. Another possibility for the second pump could have been to act as a backup to the first. Old Sally had aged 47 years in this picture, and it is not known if the first pump was original to the engine. Air pumps are appliances that can be exchanged with newer or overhauled models to make repairs quicker and easier. Instead of taking the time to fix an air pump which may have been gradually failing, perhaps the crews decided to add the second one to ensure the brake system did not fail completely while the locomotive was in route between destinations. The exact known reason remains a mystery, but it is yet another subtle alteration to the locomotive from the original configuration.[13]

This last photograph shows a rather inglorious end for such a fine locomotive that accomplished so much. From the time of her trial in 1890 to the railroad's abandonment in 1930, Sally had served for forty

13 Cimarron and Northwestern No. 1, Photographer unknown, September 17, 1937, Cimarron, NM, Dennis Hogan Collection; Photograph date from Roehm, Peter, "Taos and the Ghost Railroads of Philmont," 1955, 38, Box 7A, National Scouting Museum.

years in four different states for three different common carrier railroads. There is no telling the mileage this simple Baldwin locomotive accumulated in her career. Sally served faithfully to the end. What became of her remains somewhat of a mystery. According to Thomas Schomburg, she was sold to another firm in 1938 after a long sit in Cimarron. However, Thomas could not recall which company purchased the engine. Although it is not impossible that she found new life on another railroad, most likely she would have been purchased as a parts source or for scrap. The railcars were all obsolete in size and build and by 1930 most likely very worn from their years of service. As Thomas further concluded, these cars did not amount to much of anything, so they were probably scrapped in due time after the railroad's abandonment.[14] As for Sally, extraordinarily little remains of this locomotive besides photos and distant memories.

14 Schomburg, Thomas W. Interviewed by Lawrence Murphy at Denver, Colorado, June 9, 1964.

Operations in the Early Years

Timber and Logging Practices

The Continental Tie and Lumber Company, by virtue of its contract and agreements with the Maxwell Land Grant Company, controlled the direction of timbering in the area. They owned the timber rights, they had the technically superior mill at Cimarron, and they controlled the transportation outlet, the Cimarron and Northwestern Railway. This put the CT&L Co in the driver's seat regarding where it would establish mills and camps, where it would allow subcontractors to build their mills, which stands of timber would be worked in what sequence, and whether it would relinquish its timber rights to leave specific tracts to others.

Theodore Schomburg and Henry Frankenburger handled their strategic planning masterfully, but the men on the ground directing the day-to-day work were the timber foremen. "Timber Foreman" was the formal title, but the nicknames "woods boss" or "bull of the woods" were likely used by the foreman and the subordinate loggers. Leading this effort as CT&L Superintendent of Timber was Alex McElroy. Thomas Schomburg would fondly recall McElroy: "He was born and raised in that country and he could tell the biggest lies better than everyone I ever knew. He was a fine timber foreman. Red headed Irishman. He could tell the biggest yarns!" McElroy would later work as a timber foreman at Ute Park once the CT&L Co expanded operations there in the 1920s. Another intriguing individual was "Big Ike" Torrance, timber foreman at Poñil Park, who had 'fishing fever' according to Thomas. He recounted a story of how on one Saturday morning, Thomas took the daily C&N train north to Poñil Park and met up with Big Ike for a fishing trip. Ike had arranged for a team of horses to take the two to Shuree Ponds, a scenic lake area near Little Costilla Mountain approximately seven miles west of Poñil Park. Somehow novice fisherman Thomas Schomburg ended up with a full complement of fish while Big Ike hardly had a bite![1]

The timber the CT&L Co was harvesting had specific target markets. The predominant available timber in the region was Ponderosa pine, known to loggers such as McElroy and Torrance in that period as 'western yellow pine.' Pine was predominately used for commercial saw timber, fence posts, telegraph and telephone poles, and railroad ties. Commercial saw timber would refer to trees large enough to bring to a sawmill and cut into rough cut lumber for dimension stock (standard sizes). The second predominant tree was Douglas fir, known then as 'red spruce.' Douglas fir was in high demand as the CT&L Co began operations since mine props made from fir performed better than pine. Mine props were normally taken from the tops of large Douglas fir trees, left naturally rounded, sometimes not even peeled of their bark, and ranged from five to nine feet long with seven- or eight-inch tops.

When it came to conducting timber decisions, Thomas remarked in his 1964 interview with Lawrence Murphy that "Father [Theodore Schomburg] knew all the portions of the timber country very well. Timber foremen for the company would handle the portion of setting up camps or sawmills to work a stand of timber, and whether it would be for saw timber, props, or ties." And for assignments, "Timber foremen would assign 'prop men' certain areas to work mine props, same for saw timber, and hewn ties to the railroad." Interviewer Murphy would further describe life for mine prop crews: "Because of the delicacy with which props had to be handled, cutting crews were usually small, consisting of two or three men, or even a family, working together." Thomas made several important remarks regarding mine props which illuminate CT&L lumber sales at the onset of operations. First, the largest customer for mine props was the St. Louis, Rocky Mountain, and Pacific Company for their various coal mines near Raton. Second, if a large prop order was placed, Rocky Mountain boxcars

1 For logger terminology, see Barnett, James P., Lueck, Everett W. 2020. "Sawmill Towns: Work, Community life, and Industrial Development in the Pineywoods of Louisiana and the New South," 12-13; Schomburg, Thomas W. Interviewed by Lawrence Murphy at Denver, Colorado, June 9, 1964.

Mine props shown inside Dawson's Stag Canyon coal mine No. 1

Dawson Association Collection.

would be taken by the C&N Ry directly into the backcountry for loading and then transferred to the Rocky Mountain tracks in Cimarron for interline delivery. The same would be done for Santa Fe boxcars in later years, and mine props were the principal product in the early years before giving way to saw timber. Finally, the mine prop business was almost entirely for coal mining as the area's gold mines sourced timber near their claims as needed. A 1924 letter to J. Van Houten, Maxwell Land Grant Co president, tackled this subject. "Baldy mine people" were interested in cutting timber, but with the areas around their claims cut over, the CT&L Co felt that compensation was due only if timber outside the claims was cut.[2]

As the company name implied, railroad ties were another key product. At first all ties both for the C&N's construction and for general sale by the CT&L Co were hand-hewn ties and untreated. Later CT&L Co would move to sawed ties and chemical treatment for preservation, following the best practices in use at other tie manufacturers and suppliers. Major tie customers were the St. Louis, Rocky Mountain, and Pacific Railway, the Atchison, Topeka, and Santa Fe Railway, and the Colorado and Southern Railway.[3]

Loggers and teamsters were the ones physically doing the timber selection and felling. Teamsters drove livestock "teams" either with or without wagons. Loggers often worked in pairs or groups, sometimes even a family worked together. Once timber tracts were assigned, the first step in logging was tree selection. This was done by the "flathead"

2 Letter, CT&L Co to J. Van Houten, December 10, 1924. Maxwell Land Grant Company Records. MSS 147, Box 8, File Folder 6, Continental Tie and Lumber Company.

3 Schomburg, Thomas W. Interviewed by Lawrence Murphy at Denver, Colorado, June 9, 1964; Murphy, *New Mexico Railroader*, Vol 6, No 12, "The Cimarron and Northwestern: Historic Railroad of Northern New Mexico, Part II," pg. 4; Murphy, *Philmont: A History*, pg. 171

Timber crew sawing logs to length prior to loading on wagons.
Library of Congress Prints and Photographs Division: LC-USF33-012774-M4.

or "undercutter" who chose the tree, which direction to fell it based on lean, wind direction, and other factors in the area. The most economical way of cutting at that period was clear-cutting and 'high-grading' by taking the biggest and healthiest trees, leaving behind deformed or undesirable trees. Thomas Schomburg related that "each mill had its own area and, in each area, cutting was carried on in an orderly manner. All of it was on contract. Men were paid by the piece or linear foot when the material was delivered at the railroad. [...] Over the years we had several hundred working for the Continental Tie and Lumber Company."

After felling trees, removing the tops, and delimbing the log (performed by people known as "sawyers") the independent loggers, would transport the logs, called "skidding," either to a backcountry sawmill or a railroad loading site. Photos of these operations show skidding either using four-wheeled wagons or simply dragging timber on the ground with chains, choker setters on tongs, and harnesses by oxen, horses, or mules. Large machinery common on other large timber operations, such as American Log Loaders, McGiffert Log Loaders, Barnhart Loaders, Clyde Steam Skidders, cranes, and the like were not to be found in CT&L Co logging. Thomas also stated that the "two-wheeled wagon common in the Pacific Northwest" was not to be found in northern New Mexico logging.

The 'parbuckling' process was a common method for loading logs

Loading logs on a horse-drawn wagon using the parbuckling process.

Aztec Mill Museum Collection, Cimarron, New Mexico.

onto wagons. This involved stationing a four-wheeled wagon with the first axle cocked at an angle to the rest of the wagon (preventing it from rolling unexpectedly) and placing two large lumber pieces secured against the top of the wagon and the ground. Next, the felled tree was positioned at the base of the timbers with a rope or chain wrapped around and then leading to another draft animal. Finally, the other draft animal positioned on the opposite side of the wagon would pull the rope or chain, thereby dragging the log up the timbers and onto the wagon. Depending on the size of the timbers, photos show anywhere from a dozen to sixteen logs could be stacked on a wagon. Once loaded, the wagons were driven to the backcountry mills.[4]

Lumber Mills and Driving Wheels

At the time of the C&N's construction, numerous sawmills were in production both in Cimarron and the surrounding areas, and the opening of the C&N would lead to many more backcountry sawmills coming online. In late 1907 and early 1908, the MLG Co reported five mills paying timber royalties, although several were not near the C&N Ry route. First was the Maverick Park mill located on Maverick Creek, roughly two miles southwest of Ute Park. Run by W.J. Fulton, this mill

4 Barnett and Lueck, 12-15; Zimmer and Lewis, 151-152; Thomas Schomburg quotes: Schomburg, Thomas W. Interviewed by Lawrence Murphy at Denver, Colorado, June 9, 1964. Log wagon and parbuckling photos: Aztec Mill Museum Historic Photographs Collection, Cimarron, NM.

would transport milled timber to the StLRM&P Ry terminus at Ute Park for shipment. Fulton would be involved in an "anvil explosion" on July 4, 1907, losing his right thumb in the process. The accident bears no relation here, but the noteworthy event brought journalistic attention to warrant this note: "Mr. Fulton is a well-known sawmill man of Ute Park, and at the time of the accident was engaged in sawing timber for the Continental Tie and Lumber Company." With the CT&L controlling the timber rights, Fulton and other independent sawmillers were rough cutting timber and sending it to the CT&L planer mill in Cimarron for final processing into commercial lumber.

Second was F.R. Burnett's Mill in Dean Canyon, with a note that the mill was located over nine miles from the railway. The railroad would place a siding at milepost 3.5 on their route where Dean Canyon entered Poñil Canyon to spot cars for shipments to and from this mill and the nearby Chase Ranch. The third mill was W.H. Smith's in Dillon Canyon, again noted as over "9 miles from R'Y." With Dillon Canyon emptying into the plains immediately south of Raton, shipments would be hauled via wagon directly to either the StLRM&P Ry. or the AT&SF Ry. The fourth mill was E.T. Kearney's in Little Coal Canyon, also listed as "over nine miles from R'Y." The fifth gained the most with the opening of the C&N. Charles S. Wood's mill was in Hart Canyon immediately north of the terminus at Poñil Park,the newspapers reported him running at "full blast" once he secured more mill crew. Wood would indeed see success with the arrival of the railroad and would later partner with another lumberman, Bert Pratt, to open another sawmill once the railway expanded in later years.

Wood later partnered with Theodore Schomburg in many enterpris-

Debarking logs before milling.

Aztec Mill Museum Collection, Cimarron, New Mexico.

Railcar loading area at Poñil Park. *Top:* Lumber stacked on flatcars with C&N #1 at left billowing smoke. Teams of horses and wagons unloading logs in the foreground. *Bottom:* Loading platform with several loaded flatcars.

Ardelle Koperski, 1917. Richard Dorman Collection, Friends of the Cumbres & Toltec Scenic Railroad.

es, including as an incorporator with Schomburg in 1907 to form the Rio Grande Lumber Company in north-central New Mexico. Additional mills were also located in Cimarron Canyon supplying the Gate City Lumber Company in Raton and the Cimarron Lumber Company located directly on the StLRM&P Ry in west Cimarron. The Cimarron Lumber Company was principally backed by Charles Springer, and it was a substantial concern with a planer mill that created home furnishings, sashes, and doors, primarily geared toward residential lumber for the growing town.[5]

As noted in the press, a variety of new mills came into production following the completion of the C&N into the thick timber country. Two mills with a combined 125,000 board feet per day capacity would

5 W.J. Fulton's Maverick Park mill: *The Cimarron Citizen.* (Cimarron, N.M.), 03 June 1908. Fulton's July 4th accident: *The Cimarron News and Press.* (Cimarron, N.M.), 11 July 1907. For mills and timber royalties, see Maxwell Land Grant Company Timber Royalties Due, October 1907, November 1907, December 1907, January 1908, Maxwell Land Grant Company Records. MSS 147, Box 8, File Folder 6, Continental Tie and Lumber Company. For Cimarron Lumber Company, see Murphy, *Philmont: A History*, pg. 172; and Pearson, pg. 234. "Dean" is listed as a station stop on the 1916 and 1921 C&N Ry public timetables. See Official Guide of the Railways, National Railway Publication Company, June 1916, Cimarron and Northwestern Railway January 1915 public timetable; Ibid, June 1921, Cimarron and Northwestern Railway January 1921 public timetable. For Rio Grande Lumber Co. incorporators, see *Santa Fe New Mexican.* (Santa Fe, N.M.), 16 July 1907. C.S. Wood running his mill at "full blast," see *The Cimarron Citizen.* (Cimarron, N.M.), 15 April 1908.

CT&L planer mill (left) and powerhouse (right).

Aztec Mill Museum Collection, Cimarron, New Mexico.

be located in Metcalf at the confluence of the North Poñil, Metcalf, and Cook Canyons. Metcalf would feature a station stop, a siding, the direct single-wire telephone to company offices in Cimarron, and a small community dating back to an 1844 settlement by Charles Bent. Bert Pratt's 100,000 board feet capacity mill would be located at the opening of Metcalf Canyon while another "portable sawmill" of 25,000 board feet capacity is listed on the 1917 C&N Ry trackage map at the opening of Cook Canyon. At the terminus end, the Continental Tie and Lumber Co would open their own sawmill at the mouth of Seally Canyon in Poñil Park known as "Mill #2." Poñil Park would be similar to Metcalf in featuring a station stop and two mills with a combined 150,000 board feet capacity with Wood's Hart Canyon mill on the north end as the other. A total of 275,000 board feet of lumber could be milled in one twenty-four-hour period for the daily C&N train.[6]

Ultimately it would be the Continental Tie and Lumber Company's technically superior mill site in Cimarron that would control the flow of timber through the C&N Ry terminus there. The mill site would be known as "Mill #1" with Mill #2 situated at Poñil Park. Located in east Cimarron, the site would feature a four-track rail yard with ample space for a stack of lumber on each side, a planer mill, a box fac-

6 Sawmills, locations, and board feet capacity: *The Cimarron News and Press.* (Cimarron, N.M.), 23 May 1907. Chronicling America: Historic American Newspapers. Lib. of Congress. Charles Bent 1844 settlement preceding Metcalf: Rohrbacher, Charles "Rock," *Philmanac: A Trekker's Guide to the Philmont Backcountry*, Eighth Edition, 2020, pg. 153-155.

CT&L warehouse and company store in Cimarron.
Aztec Mill Museum Collection, Cimarron, New Mexico.

tory, the company office building, storage warehouse, company store, hay barn, locomotive engine house, and the interchange track with the StLRM&P Ry. Earnest Ludlum would be the first manager of the "big company store." Construction at the planer mill site began in 1907 and was completed in early 1908 as the C&N began operations. The *Albuquerque Journal* reported:

> The new railroad, the Cimarron and Northwestern is going to do much for the prosperity of this town. [...] Thirty-two men are employed in the shops here. The Continental Tie and Lumber Company has just finished its planning mill and box factory which employs sixty men. E.T. Johnson is superintendent. The building is 120 by 76 feet in dimensions, two stories high with the latest improved mill machinery and 160 horsepower boiler capacity.[7]

All the backcountry sawmills were single circular saw operations, cutting raw logs into rough lumber boards. The rough-cut lumber would be "shipped down green" (Thomas Schomburg) on the C&N to the planer mill in Cimarron. "Green" refers to cut lumber that has not been treated or seasoned. At Cimarron, two planer machines, a matcher, and a molding machine would trim the rough edges, finish the lumber smooth into its final cut state, after which it would be stacked in the yard for open air drying and seasoning. From there it

7 *Albuquerque Morning Journal.* (Albuquerque, N.M.), 03 Jan. 1908. Chronicling America: Historic American Newspapers. Lib. of Congress.

would be loaded onto boxcars at the in-house loading dock for interline delivery by the StLRM&P Ry.

The planer mill was powered by a separate powerhouse that included a 36" x 16" steam engine fed by two sixteen-foot boilers. The steam engine powered the line shaft that ran from the powerhouse to the planer mill. The planer mill was a two-story affair by design that allowed the line shaft to connect into the machines on the second floor. Individual leather belts would run from the line shaft on the first floor up to each machine on the second floor. The design of the second floor allowed for easier stacking and loading of lumber on outbound railcars. In both instances, the laborer is stacking down rather than stacking lumber upward or overhead.

Several company houses were located onsite, and historic photographs survive today of the office building and the company store. The office building was the combined Continental Tie and Lumber Company and Cimarron and Northwestern Railway offices. The first floor of the office was constructed of adobe, while the second was made of wood. The company store was a focal point of the site, as business was transacted there for passenger tickets, supplies, and company scrip. The building sported a siding from the StLRM&P and an unloading dock for inbound orders. Rounding out the site was a fire suppression system evidenced by the fire plugs seen in numerous historic photos.[8]

Early Railroad Operations

Railroad operations consisted of a daily mixed train. 'Mixed' refers to the fact that the train was a combination of freight and passenger traffic, rather than a dedicated passenger train or dedicated freight train. While no timetables from the early operating period have been located as of this writing, later timetables from 1915 and 1921 note that the daily mixed train ran 6 days a week, Monday through Saturday. As was common on railroads of the period, no trains operated regularly on Sundays. Both the 1915 and 1921 timetables show train #2, the northbound train, departing Cimarron at 7:30 in the morning with empty cars for spotting at loading points and mills. At 7:45 train

8 Thomas Schomburg quote: Schomburg, Thomas W. Interviewed by Lawrence Murphy at Denver, Colorado, June 9, 1964; For photos of the mill site, office building, company store, and yard, see Aztec Mill Museum Historic Photographs Collection, Cimarron, NM. CT&L Co inventories were taken in 1925 and 1938 and contributed to the description here. See Continental Tie and Lumber Company Inventory November 30, 1925, Continental Tie and Lumber Company Inventory, March 8, 1938, Maxwell Land Grant Company Records. MSS 147, Box 8, File Folder 6. Store manager: *The Cimarron News and Press.* (Cimarron, N.M.), 28 Feb. 1907

C&N flatcars loaded with logs at an undetermined siding location.

Aztec Mill Museum Collection, Cimarron, New Mexico.

#2 traversed four miles and arrived at the Dean siding. Milepost 8 at South Poñil was reached at 8:00 and the Metcalf station stop at 8:30. Train #2 pulled into the terminus at Poñil Park at 9:00 AM. Train #1 was the southbound train returning to Cimarron with loaded flatcars of rough-cut lumber and boxcars loaded with mine props and ties, arriving at Cimarron by 4:00 PM.

As the C&N extended in later years, the return time to Cimarron would be later, but the crew generally arrived in time to have supper at home. At any given time, the C&N would have boxcars and flatcars spotted at either its mill in Cimarron or at the backcountry mills and loading points. While other common carrier cars would be taken into the backcountry for final delivery or direct loading, C&N cars would not be used for interchange traffic and would only be used and spotted on C&N trackage. For regular operations, the C&N only operated one train each direction during daylight hours.[9]

Traffic over the line was dominated by timber movements. An occasional movement of coal cars was necessary from the on-line coal mine to the various backcountry sawmills, but the primary movement was either raw logs or rough-cut lumber on flatcars. Many photographs of operations feature raw logs stacked and chained down on the flatcars bound for a backcountry mill, often with one or two boxcars imme-

9 Timetable information: Official Guide of the Railways, National Railway Publication Company, June 1916, Cimarron and Northwestern Railway January 1915 public timetable; Ibid, June 1921, Cimarron and Northwestern Railway January 1921 public timetable. For passenger operations quote: Thomas Schomburg quote: Schomburg, Thomas W. Interviewed by Lawrence Murphy at Denver, Colorado, June 9, 1964.

diately behind the caboose. These photos indicate that a few empty flatcars would be spotted at sidings where loggers and teamsters could preload the cars from their wagons. This allowed the C&N to drop off the empties and pick up the loaded cars. The train operations were not involved in the actual logging of timber as was typical of some other logging railroads throughout the United States.

Since the train movements were limited to daily mixed trains, only a small group of employees was needed to crew the trains. More than likely, the first crew was able to handle the majority of train movements throughout the year, including any yard switching needed. Audrey Alpers collected train crew names in a 1994 recap of the Continental Tie and Lumber Company and the Cimarron and Northwestern Railway. The first crew consisted of engineer Jefferies, fireman Elias Martinez, and conductor Jesse Ashbaugh. When Jefferies was unavailable, Chas. Williams filled in as the engineer. When a third engineer was needed, Jesse Ashbaugh handled the train as engineer. Glen Sherwood as fireman and B. Atchison as conductor are also recounted by Alpers as backup train crew members.[10]

Other Railroad Business

The Cimarron and Northwestern Railway was primarily engaged in servicing the Continental Tie and Lumber Company and the related backcountry mills and operations connected to it. However, businessman Theodore Schomburg certainly attempted to attract and develop business where it could be profitably gained, including accommodating passengers and securing additional commodities. As previously mentioned, Schomburg attempted to interest W.A. Clark of New York in the possibility of building a railroad spur from Poñil Park to tap nearby coal veins and transport coal over the C&N. While that gambit proved unfruitful, the efforts to garner business from orchard growers proved to be more fruitful.

From the start of the Cimarron mill site, a box factory had been in operation to produce vegetable and fruit crates for the local orchard operations. Pears, cherries, plums, peaches, apples, and other produce were grown by ranchers Manly M. Chase, John B. Dawson, M.W. Mills, Jesus G. Abreu, M.E. Dane, George H. Webster, Jr. and even by the Farmer's Development Company in nearby Miami, New Mexico,

10 Alpers, Audrey, "The Continental Tie and Lumber Company and the Cimarron and Northwestern Railway," Cimarron Historical Society, June 5, 1994, Arthur Johnson Memorial Library,

Apples and apple crates from the Chase Ranch orchard of Manly M. Chase in Poñil Canyon.

Aztec Mill Museum Collection, Cimarron, New Mexico.

south of Cimarron. A "box estimator" from this period survives to this day and shows how this business contributed to the overall goals of the CT&L, as the company was very modern in production processes. An efficient and large-scale process allowed Frankenburger to solicit both box business and railroad shipments from Manly M. Chase in 1908:

> Relative to question of apple boxes, would say that we are pleased to quote you Standard Apple Boxes, knocked down, at 12 ½ cents each at our mill at Cimarron, or, we will deliver these to you in car loads of not less than 1000 boxes at Dean Canon siding, nailed sides and bottom, and tops loose, at 17 cents each, terms 30 days net. We quote you the latter price, thinking it possible that you might wish to pack some of your apples near Dean siding in order to make shipment from that point.

Just one year later, the Chases were shipping their apples to Texas and Colorado. In February 1909 the *Cimarron Citizen* reported that the Chases were filling large orders from Denver and west Texas and shipped three carloads in one day. Even produce growers in Colorado were interested in CT&L Co boxes, as Z.J. Fort with Celeryvale Farms contacted Theodore Schomburg with a large production order "of several carloads" for celery and onion crates. The Chases also shipped apples directly to Poñil Park on multiple occasions over the C&N. Boxes and crates were indeed part of the daily mill operations in addition to

Combined CT&L-C&N office building in the Cimarron yard.

Aztec Mill Museum Collection, Cimarron, New Mexico.

ties, props, poles, and lumber.[11]

The Bottom Line

The accounting figures for Theodore Schomburg's Cimarron operations certainly looked rosy at the onset of full operations. In a February 1, 1909, letter from Frankenburger to Schomburg, Frankenburger had taken Superintendent McElroy's timber estimates and projected millions of board feet of saw timber in various districts along the C&N route, and he identified the potential for hundreds of thousands of railroad ties and mine props. Using assumptions on shipping rates, returns on board feet of saw timber, and revenue from ties and props, Frankenburger estimated that a profit of $1,015,000 was possible in ten years of operation at half of the estimated timber amount.

As for the railway, the C&N was wholly owned by Schomburg and the CT&L through railway stock. A contract was set up to provide decent returns and balances for the C&N to allow payment of

11 Local fruit growers: Zimmer and Lewis, pg. 143-148. Box sale efforts: Letter, H.G. Frankenburger to M.M. Chase, July 29, 1908, National Scouting Museum; Chase shipping apples: *Cimarron Citizen*, No. 47, Wednesday, February 10, 1909, Village of Cimarron website; Celeryvale farms seeking boxes: Letter, Z.J. Fort to T.A. Schomburg, March 18, 1925, File Folder 108, T.A. Schomburg Collection. Various box estimators calculated by board feet from 1904 and 1928 are in File Folder 119, T.A. Schomburg Collection. Chase shipments: Cimarron and Northwestern Railway, Straight Bill of Lading, Chase Ranch to George H. Raeburn of Ponil Park, December 17, 1917, New Mexico State University Archives and Special Collections, Alpers Collection.

railroad construction debts. The April 1, 1907, contract between the CT&L and the C&N stipulated that the CT&L agreed to provide enough traffic for 3,600 cars annually and a $7 penalty per car under this agreed figure would be paid to the C&N if this obligation was not met. Despite the grand financial projections, timber production averaged only half of this contractual minimum and more than $111, 860 in penalty payments would be made to the C&N by June 30, 1916.[12]

The CT&L Co payments to the MLG Co for timber royalties display the up-and-down nature of the lumber market. Over $6,000 in royalty payments would be paid in 1907 which more than doubled to over $16,000 in 1908 at the onset of full lumber and railroad operations. The figure would continue to grow and 1910 saw the largest royalty paid to the MLG Co at $87,943.21. The returns for the Cimarron and Northwestern, however, did not grow at the same rate as the timber royalties for the CT&L Co. Net income in 1908 (January 1 to June 30) was -$50.61, $4,371.86 in 1909, and $4,544.86 in 1910. Revenue during these years ($33,067.90 in 1909 and $37,033.68 in 1910) did not fluctuate as dramatically as expenses ($20,730.94 in 1909 and $24,331.58 in 1910).[13]

A major conflagration in March 1909 struck the main Continental Tie and Lumber Company yard. Fire, the most common disaster to befall timber companies, did not spare the fledgling company. Reports on the fire came from all over the country with the Hernando, Mississippi, *Times-Promoter* writing that "The flames destroyed the planing mill, storage house and a large quantity of lumber. The loss is estimated at $70,000." The fire was front-page news for the March 29th *Albuquerque Citizen* and coverage on the fire illustrates both the blaze and key details on the CT&L:

> LUMBER PLANT AT CIMARRON WAS TOTALLY DESTROYED BY FIRE TODAY.
>
> One of the Largest Lumber Mills and Yards in the Southwest Caught Fire and all Efforts to Extinguish the Blaze Proved Unavailing --- Plant was Insured But Loss Will Probably be Half Million Dollars.

12 Timber and profit estimates: Letter, Frankenburger to T.A. Schomburg, February 1, 1909, "Estimate of Timber Controlled by CT&L Company," attachment, "Estimate of Timber – February 1, 1909." File Folder 17, T.A. Schomburg Collection, History Colorado Center. Contract and penalty payments: Murphy, *New Mexico Railroader*, Vol 6, No 12, "The Cimarron and Northwestern: Historic Railroad of Northern New Mexico, Part II," pg. 2.

13 Royalty payments from CT&L to MLG Co: Pearson, pg. 243. Revenue and expense for C&N Ry: I.C.C. Decision, Vol 106, pg. 570-571.

> Cimarron, N.M., March 29 - The mills, warehouses, shops and yards of the Continental Tie and Lumber company at this place are burning, and all efforts to stop the fire proved unavailing at a later hour this afternoon. The plant was one of the largest in the Southwest and the damage will be between $500,000 and $1,000,000.
>
> The fire originated from the sparks thrown out from an engine. It started in the mill and was discovered at 10:30 this morning, but by that time it had a good start. It has burned all day despite all the efforts to extinguish the blaze and it looks as though the entire plant and all the lumber stored will be consumed.
>
> There is usually half a million dollars' worth of lumber stored in the yards, the lumber being supplied from the company's mills along the Cimarron and Northwestern railroad. Several cars of lumber on the tracks are burning.
>
> The plant was well insured and the total loss cannot be told yet. It is probable, however, that it will exceed $500,000.

On the same day the *Las Vegas Optic* also carried the story, reporting fire losses at $500,000. Fortunately, later newspaper reports detailed a smaller final loss for the fire: "the loss [...] was from $12,000 to $15,000 and not half a million dollars as it was first reported. The damage was solely to the machinery and appliances of the planer mill and two cars of lumber which were scorched. The mill is a corrugated iron structure which kept the fire from spreading. The insurance is partial." The very next month machinery was purchased by the CT&L from a planer mill in Alamogordo, New Mexico, to replace what the fire had burned.[14]

The March 1909 fire, while a financial strain for the interrelated companies, did not diminish the ambition for continued expansion. By 1910, with multiple mills running at a production capacity of 285,000 board feet per day, the timber along the first twenty-two miles of the Cimarron and Northwestern was nearing exhaustion. The first phase had run its course, and a second phase of expansion was planned by Theodore Schomburg to extend the Cimarron and Northwestern Railway deeper into the thick timberlands of northern New Mexico.

14 All quotes from Chronicling America: Historic American Newspapers. Lib. of Congress: *Times-Promoter.* (Hernando, DeSoto County, Miss.), 08 April 1909; *Albuquerque Citizen.* (Albuquerque, N.M.), 29 March 1909; *Las Vegas Optic.* (East Las Vegas, N.M.), 29 March 1909; *Santa Fe New Mexican.* (Santa Fe, N.M.), 02 April 1909 and 12 April 1909.

Expansion to Ring and Bonito

The next phase of the Cimarron and Northwestern Railway was focused on reaching further into the timberlands controlled by the Continental Tie and Lumber Company, and it would involve continued development along the railway. Two years of daily sawmill capacity of 285,000 board feet of lumber began to deplete the timber stands located near the existing mills and the railroad. In order to solve this problem, new communities called Ring and Bonito would be born where new sawmills were built to process the region's more remote virgin timber. The remains of these expansions survive today in Forest Service roads, cemeteries, grave markers, tumble-down foundation stones, and various remnants of rusted metal lingering on the ground.

When the decision was reached to expand the railroad in late 1909, Theodore Schomburg and Henry Frankenburger acted quickly to survey a route so that construction could begin immediately. A.G. Allen had finally retired after construction of the original line, so a new surveyor and engineer was needed. Guy Harold Palmes would be that engineer and the next character in the C&N story. His correspondence with researcher Lawrence Murphy in 1964 succinctly captures the opening days of the C&N expansion. Palmes began work as a locating engineer, but this project was only the beginning of his career with the Schomburg enterprises in Cimarron. The story is as follows:

> As the first step in the construction of the new tracks, President Schomburg put an advertisement into a Denver newspaper soliciting a locating engineer. The man who answered that ad was Guy H. Palmes, who described what followed in his own words:

"I went to this office in the old Chamber of Commerce Bldg. in Denver and met, for the first time, that great builder of the West, Mr. T.A. Schomburg .... After visiting with Mr. Schomburg for an hour, he gave me an introduction to his manager, Mr. H.G. Frankenburger at Cimarron, New Mexico. Mr. Frankenburger told me he had asked Schomburg to send him an engineer, not a kid. He then said the contractor had destroyed the location stakes for a horseshoe curve just out of Ring. If I could relocate this curve I had a job. Well, I accepted the laughing challenge and I was with them just fifteen years as engineer of both the railway and lumber companies."

Despite his young appearance, Palmes had a good deal of experience in railroad and timber work. Born in Mississippi, Palmes' father had managed the Robinson Land and Lumber Company and its Chicora and Jackson Railroad in that state. Young Palmes attended Mississippi A&M College (now Mississippi State University) and graduated in civil engineering in 1908. He did survey work for the Chicora and Jackson and for the Yazoo Mississippi Levee District, before a malarial attack forced him to move to Denver. There he worked for the McArthur Pile and Foundation Company in surveying the Barker Meadow dam and reservoir in Middle Boulder Canyon, Colorado. He also surveyed a proposed electric railway line connecting Billings and Red Lodge in Montana before taking the Cimarron job.[1]

For the next fifteen years, Palmes would have a hand in all the railroad, wagon road, truck road, and engineering projects the CT&L and C&N undertook. He would fit well into the framework of the C&N, even hosting a wedding anniversary for his boss to celebrate the long marriage of Mr. and Mrs. Henry G. Frankenburger in 1914.[2]

Several factors influenced the direction and extent of the railroad expansion with Palmes as engineer. The lawsuit against William Bartlett was settled in November 1909, bringing clarity to the timber rights north of Poñil Park on William Bartlett's Vermejo Ranch, which included Van Bremmer Park. While the legal verdict favored Schomburg, the dispute more than likely discouraged the CT&L from conducting large-scale timber harvesting there in conjunction with the C&N, perhaps due to a détente reached with Bartlett. Thomas Schomburg, many years later, alluded to Bartlett helping the CT&L financially during a

1 Murphy, *New Mexico Railroader*, Vol 6, No 12, "The Cimarron and Northwestern: Historic Railroad of Northern New Mexico, Part II," pg. 4-5.

2 *The Cimarron News and Cimarron Citizen*. (Cimarron, Colfax County, N.M.), 15 Oct. 1914. Chronicling America: Historic American Newspapers. Lib. of Congress.

Ring, New Mexico, with Pratt & Wood sawmill (lower right).

Aztec Mill Museum Collection, Cimarron, New Mexico.

"very critical time" in 1909. This could have involved Bartlett helping to finance railroad construction if it would be built away from his ranch. Another possible factor may have been that timber estimates pointed toward a greater concentration of good timber, and thereby profits, in a southwestern direction from Poñil Park rather than to the north. All are potential factors that directed the railroad expansion west of Poñil Park through Lowery Canyon, known today as Seally Canyon. The C&N expansion plans were publicized in December 1909:

> It has been announced that the Cimarron & Northwestern railroad, in Colfax County, will be extended four miles at once. This new extension will be made up one of the canyons opening out into the Poñil and will be made for the purpose of getting timber of that country better. The contractor for the work has been let to H.K. Christensen, who completed the construction of the McCormick reservoir not long ago. The work will be begun at once and pushed as fast as possible.3

At the end of this four-mile extension would be the town of Ring, New Mexico, and that is where Palmes would take over to complete the double-S curve and the remainder of the railroad survey. The four-mile section was easy for Christensen, with no tremendous gradient changes

3 *Las Vegas Optic.* (East Las Vegas, N.M.), 03 Dec. 1909. Chronicling America: Historic American Newspapers. Lib. of Congress.

and only ten small trestles needed. No dynamite blasting was needed, and Seally Canyon does not have the sharp twists and curves that are seen in North Poñil Canyon. The remainder of track construction beyond Ring was more than likely handled directly by the CT&L Co or another railroad contractor.

The exact route and location of the full thirteen-mile railroad extension undertaken by the CT&L for the C&N in late 1909 and early 1910 beyond Poñil Park has been confirmed through the authors' personal reconnaissance of the railbed remains in this area. In addition, Thomas Schomburg's own personal statements on this subject, period maps showing the completed and operational trackage, and a professional geological examination of railbed remains using USGS one-meter LIDAR imagery also confirm the route. History, like science, is a changing study based upon currently available resources, and we are fortunate to have the latest research to draw upon.

An early route map of the C&N Ry by George R. Swain appeared in the December 1964 issue of the *New Mexico Railroader* which incorrectly showed the railroad going north out of Poñil Park, through the Forest Service designated site of Ring Place, the location of Timothy Ring's ranch, then proceeding due south past Ring Lake, Beatty Lakes, and ultimately to Bonito, forming a large U-shaped extension. The 1988 National Register of Historic Places Continuation Sheet for Ring

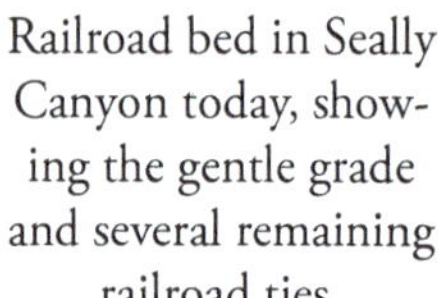

Railroad bed in Seally Canyon today, showing the gentle grade and several remaining railroad ties.

Steve Lewis Collection.

Place discusses the confusion about the railroad route between Ring (the town), Ring Place (the Timothy Ring ranch site), and Poñil Park.

Murphy questioned Thomas Schomburg on this very subject in their 1964 interview, confirming that the railroad went through Seally Canyon to reach Ring (the town and sawmill site) and did not go through the Ring ranch site (Ring Place). In addition, multiple period maps confirm the exact route taken in this extension and show the railroad entering Seally Canyon at Poñil Park, performing a well-executed double-S curve, and then terminating at Bonito camp in Bonito Canyon to the southwest of Poñil Park. The authors' own personal reconnaissance on the ground confirms that no railroad construction is evident north in the Ring Place area. We followed each portion of the remaining rail bed from Poñil Park through Seally Canyon to Ring Town, and then south to Bonito. Finally, a professional and certified geologist who has experience in historic railroad research completed a thorough examination of the geographic area using USGS one-meter LIDAR imagery to confirm the grading of the entire trackage of the C&N, including confirmation of the route through Seally Canyon and no evidence of railroad activity near Ring Place.[4]

The final railroad construction by Christensen, Palmes, and the CT&L was completed in the summer of 1910 and added thirteen operating miles of track for the C&N. The track was built in the name of the Continental Tie and Lumber Company and was thereby a private industry track. Through a verbal agreement between the companies, the C&N operated the line, while the CT&L owned and maintained the track. The track would not come under ICC common carrier service regulations, as did the twenty-two-mile C&N owned track from Cimarron to Poñil Park. Thus, no public timetables were required to be published.

A wye was already located at Poñil Park using the main line and two trestles over North Poñil Creek to form the two legs of the wye. Leaving Poñil Park, the extension departed from the main line a few hundred

4 The Ring Place National Register of Historic Places Continuation Sheet. Department of the Interior, National Park Service, National Register of Historic Places. NRIS # 88001054. July 19, 1988; Schomburg, Thomas W. Interviewed by Lawrence Murphy at Denver, Colorado, June 9, 1964; Maps mentioned: "Map Showing General Character of Lands Adjacent to the St. Louis, Rocky Mountain & Pacific Railway," T.A. Schomburg Collection, MSS 747, File Folder 48, History Colorado Center. "Map of the Beaubien and Miranda Grant or Maxwell Grant in Colorado and New Mexico, 1889," as annotated by Theodore A. Schomburg, T.A. Schomburg Collection MSS 747, File Folder 48, History Colorado Center; LIDAR research: Lueck, Everett. Certified Professional Geologist, The Woodlands, TX. Email and Letter to Tucker Baker with Google Earth KMZ file, April 25, 2020.

Pratt & Wood sawmill at Ring, New Mexico.
Loaded flatcars on one side (top); loaded train on the other side (bottom).
New Mexico State University Library, Archives and Special Collections.

feet from the southern switch of the wye, and it sharply curved westward into Seally Canyon. The rail line then remained south of Seally Canyon creek and squeezed through the steep and narrow gap through an igneous intrusion dike to enter what would become the community of Ring, New Mexico, four miles west of Poñil Park. At Ring, a sawmill siding was built to spot railcars for loading and unloading, and historic photographs document the sawmill siding and the whole area of Ring.

Beyond Ring, Palmes' engineering would play a pivotal role for the railroad to ascend out of Seally Canyon, up into the basin of the Beatty Lakes, and then to descend into the opening of Bonito Canyon. Palmes implemented the double-S curve to climb out of Seally Canyon so well that Forest Service Road #1914 would use the old railroad grade so it could efficiently travel to Beatty Lakes and the Iris Park camping area. FR-1914 is laid over the railbed from the west end of Ring to a point just south of Beatty Lakes, and from there the railbed enters the top of Bonito Canyon. The terminus, Bonito, was located about one mile north of Philmont's present-day Dan Beard camp and in a location in Bonito Canyon that allowed for CT&L Co Sawmill #3 and a turning wye to be built. Bonito would be on mile marker 35, which was thirteen miles by rail from Poñil Park.[5]

5 Lueck, Everett, Email and Letter to Tucker Baker with Google Earth KMZ File, April 25, 2020.

Interior, Pratt & Wood sawmill at Ring, New Mexico.

Aztec Mill Museum Collection, Cimarron, New Mexico.

Sawmill relocation and construction immediately followed the railroad expansion to locate mills more centrally in relation to the standing timber. Mill owners Bert Pratt and Charles S. Wood partnered to build a relatively modern and large sawmill at the new lumber town of Ring, New Mexico, located on the west end of Seally Canyon where the wagon road from Raton to Elizabethtown crossed the canyon. It is believed that Pratt and Wood relocated their old sawmills to put together the new mill at Ring, as references to the Pratt mill in Metcalf Canyon and Wood's mill in Poñil Park at the mouth of Hart Canyon cease after 1909. This would be logical since the motivation for expansion was due to depleted timber resources in the previous locations.

The 1917 C&N right-of-way map by Palmes shows a pencil mark noting "portable sawmill" at Metcalf near the mouth of Cook Canyon, but no mention is made of Pratt's Metcalf Canyon mill. The new Pratt-Wood mill was a considerable upgrade compared to prior backcountry sawmills and potentially received improvements over time. Historic photographs show an elevated sawmill, three large smokestacks from the boiler room burning coal or wood scraps for steam power, an interior of the mill floor lit by primitive light bulbs and wiring in perhaps a later installation, a large circular saw with a shotgun-feed carriage, a lengthy raised loading ramp adjacent to the railroad siding, and other

Loaded train at Pratt & Wood sawmill, Ring, New Mexico.

Aztec Mill Museum Collection, Cimarron, New Mexico.

machinery driven by leather or canvas belts attached to a main drive shaft underneath the mill floor.

These same photographs display the additional CT&L commissary opened at Ring, stock pens, wagon shops, and various shacks and houses for mill workers, loggers, and teamsters that line the surrounding valley. Expanding mills and logging camps meant new opportunities for the CT&L commissaries and inbound supplies were shipped from Cimarron over the daily C&N trains. James McGarvey would serve as commissary manager at Ring from 1912 until his death in 1915. He was buried elsewhere, but the Ring cemetery with many loggers, muleskinners, millwrights, and other lumber camp denizens survives to this day.

Postal records from the period list a post office at Ring, surprisingly referred to as "Poñil," but confirmed as the post office at Ring town as it was listed as the site of "Pratt & Woods, Mnfrs of native lumber and general store." Other postal customers enumerated show a physician by the name of Hale Barter and the farm implements purveyors of Lail and Wilkins. Coins of various private, non-circulating denominations (5, 10, and 25 cents) have been recovered in modern times bearing the inscription "D.H. Wood General Merchandise, Ring, NM," hinting that another general store competed against the CT&L commissary at

CT&L Sawmill #3, Bonito, New Mexico.

David O'Neill Collection.

Ring.[6]

The Continental Tie and Lumber Company would build its own mill at Bonito, known as "Mill No. 3" as referenced in historic photos and on the final company inventory in 1938. Located at the new terminus of the extended railway, Bonito would feature two rail sidings near the sawmill, a turning wye, and various shacks and housing for workers. In one of only two surviving photos of the mill site, C&N train #2 is pointed south toward the mill carrying stacked and loaded lumber on flatcars with a tank car in between the tender and caboose #2. While steam obscures a portion of the picture on the right-hand side, the loading sidings are visible on the left with flatcars and boxcars. A boxcar is seen at right on one leg of the wye, and various stacks of ties, props, and lumber are shown awaiting rail shipment across the line to Cimarron.

Like the other backcountry mills, Mill No. 3 was elevated off the ground and featured wood decking and a loading ramp. The 1938 inventory of Mill No. 3 denotes it was dismantled and the machines were stored in the Cimarron lumber yard hay shed, but it gives a clear pic-

6 All photos by Edward A. Troutman from Aztec Mill Museum's Historic Photographs Collection: "Pratt and Wood's Saw Mill, Ring N. Mex," #1; "Pratt and Wood's Saw Mill, Ring N. Mex," #3; "General View of Ring, N. Mex,"; "Ring, N. Mex, Old Baldy in Distance"; "Bird's Eye View of Ring, N. Mex;" James McGarvey: *The Chronicle-News,* (Trinidad, Colorado), 10 Nov. 1915; Ring post office, postal customers, and D.H Wood Gen. Merch. Coins: "Ring," Research binder by Nancy Robertson, Raton Museum.

CT&L Sawmill, Bonito #3, New Mexico.

New Mexico State University Library, Archives and Special Collections.

ture of the mill's construction and operation. The investment included a twenty-foot carriage with shotgun feed, saw husk with mandrel, a set of live rollers, a gang edger, chain slasher, lathe bolter, lathe machine, two sixteen-foot boilers, two stationary steam engines with one having a drive pulley, paving and fire brick, a log elevator chain with pulleys, a 200-foot chain conveyor, and 40,000 feet of used timbers and lumber. With this type of equipment and technology, the mill sites at Bonito and Ring were important in the process of milling raw logs into rough cut lumber for shipment to the CT&L planer mill at Cimarron and served as a collection point for mine props, poles, and crossties, with all products being shipped over the C&N to Cimarron.[7]

The harsh landscape and environment of northeastern New Mexico sometimes troubled the railroaders and loggers. July 30, 1910, witnessed a massive flood that struck the entire Poñil Park region, severely damaging milling and railroad operations. Described as a "cloudburst" by the *Albuquerque Morning Journal*, the waters "swept away Wolf's lumber mill, and injured one employee severely. The waters washed out the tracks of the Cimarron and Northwestern line for more than a mile, destroying eight small bridges. The heaviest loser was the Continental Tie and Lumber Company [...] and lost much lumber." The sole locomotive Sally, the C&N pile driver, and the railroad mainte-

7 Bonito mill site photo: "CT&L. Co. Sawmill #3 Bonito N. Mex," Edward A. Troutman, 1911-1916. David O'Neill Collection; Mill No. 3 inventory: Continental Tie and Lumber Company Inventory, March 8, 1938, Maxwell Land Grant Company Records. MSS 147, Box 8, File Folder 6,

C&N No. 1 leads a loaded log train past Pratt & Wood sawmill at Ring.

New Mexico State University Library, Archives and Special Collections.

nance crews, known as 'section gangs,' would be hard at work replacing track and bridges to restore service. In March 1911 a fire struck the Pratt & Wood mill at Ring. However, the *Cimarron News and Cimarron Citizen* reported that the newspaper just recently printed stationary for this mill and that "they [Pratt and Wood] are keeping at work as though nothing had happened."[8]

Setbacks aside, Theodore Schomburg, the CT&L, and the C&N would be featured, along with many other attributes of Colfax County, in a major broadsheet promoting the area in 1911. "COLFAX COUNTY RICHEST COUNTY IN UNITED STATES" would be the front-page headline with various sections on the climate, water resources, agricultural, ranching, mining, and lumbering opportunities. Alongside sale advertisements for 30,000 acres of the Rayado Ranch and land parcels near Miami, this edition of the *Cimarron News and Cimarron Citizen* would also detail the timber works:

> The Lumber company [CT&L] has established mills of a present annual capacity of 30,000,000 feet of lumber, and ship annually about 5,000 carloads of lumber, railroad ties and mine props. In the timber operations of the Continental Tie and Lumber Company about five hundred men find employment, and as the greater part of their operations are within a radius of twenty-five miles of Cimarron the

8 Flood washouts: *Albuquerque Morning Journal.* (Albuquerque, N.M.), 31 July 1910; Pratt & Wood news: *The Cimarron News and Cimarron Citizen.* (Cimarron, Colfax County, N.M.), 18 March 1911.

C&N log train stopped for a photograph with crew member on the boxcar.

New Mexico State University Library, Archives and Special Collections.

> different business enterprises of the city do a large amount of business with the company's employees. A planning mill and box factory [are] located here giving employment [to] a large number of men. Surfacers, finish and molding machinery are in constant operation, and turn out all classes of boxes and shipping cases, fruit crates, etc. A ready market is found for the product in Colorado, Oklahoma, Kansas and New Mexico.

Assuming three-hundred operating days a year, thirty million board feet would mean a daily output of 100,000 board feet of lumber. All this lumber was bound for the greater southwestern region, reaching as far as Oklahoma and Kansas through the C&N connection to the StLRM&P and its other railroad links. These same railroad connections assisted fruit growers such as the Chase Ranch who shipped "15,000 boxes of apples, approximately 22 rail boxcar loads" in a single year.[9] Cimarron and the surrounding area were growing and changing alongside the growth of the Cimarron and Northwestern and the Continental Tie and Lumber Company. The next decade would bring even more profound change.

9 CT&L output and fruit production: Cimarron Print. Co. "*Cimarron News Citizen*, 06-24-1911." (1911).

A Decade of Change
(1913 - 1923)

The ten years from 1913 and 1923 would be a decade of profound change for the Continental Tie and Lumber Company, the Cimarron and Northwestern Railway, and the entirety of Colfax County. The St. Louis, Rocky Mountain, and Pacific Company, unable to turn a profit on their subsidiary railway, sold the line in 1913 to avoid more losses. The CT&L would expand their Cimarron operations with a tie treating plant constructed in 1913 and a sawmill added in 1920. Freight and passenger declines on the Ute Park-Cimarron line would enable the CT&L to expand logging operations along this stretch of the Rocky Mountain Route, especially in Ute Park and the Cimarron Canyon. A major controversy would erupt regarding Eagle Nest Dam construction and Theodore Schomburg's goal to log the Moreno Valley by rail. Depleted timber would result in the railroad pulling back from Bonito and then abandonment of the line from Poñil Park to the South Poñil station. An oilman named Waite Phillips would purchase his first tract of land in the Cimarron area in 1922 and would quickly become one of the largest landowners in the region. Finally, Theodore Schomburg's son, Thomas W. Schomburg, would begin an active managerial role in the CT&L and the C&N beginning in 1920.

While some of these events happened before or after others, many of them were unfolding with considerable overlap during this decade. One prime example, which will be discussed in detail later in the chapter, was the tunnel above Eagle Nest Dam. Many players over an extended period were trying to find an economical way to expand rail access into the Moreno Valley. Business and economic development in

Colfax County were changing at a more rapid pace than ever before, and in many cases the Schomburg enterprises in Cimarron were leading the way.

The Rocky Mountain Route Changes Owners

The St. Louis, Rocky Mountain, and Pacific Railway began with grand plans to service the parent company coal mines and to haul other available commodities while building a rail route to Taos, Farmington, and beyond. However, the harsh reality was that once daily service started on the Cimarron-Ute Park portion of the line, it was not profitable for daily passenger and freight service. A more cost-effective gasoline powered motor car was put into service by 1907, and mixed trains ran to Ute Park only when needed for a major ore haul from the Baldy Mountain region or when a rancher was sending cattle to market. Daily mixed trains returned in 1909 to promote Ute Park business interests, but they were quickly reduced to a tri-weekly Monday-Wednesday-Friday schedule. The eastern portion of the StLRM&P Ry suffered similarly, and the daily train schedule was reduced in 1910 to every other day for the Raton-Des Moines portion and then only tri-weekly Monday-Wednesday-Friday by 1911 and 1912.

Agriculture and ranching shipments were largely seasonal, and the Continental Tie and Lumber Company was the only daily shipper with its ties, props, poles, and lumber from Cimarron. During the first six years of operation, the StLRM&P Ry had lost over $1,000,000 and in 1912 alone the losses totalled $168,000. The parent St. Louis, Rocky Mountain, and Pacific Company was ready to find a buyer for their unprofitable railroad.[1]

Avery Turner would be the key mediator between the St. Louis, Rocky Mountain, and Pacific Company and the Atchison, Topeka, and Santa Fe Railway that would eventually purchase the StLRM&P Ry in 1913. Turner, a civil engineer, had earlier worked as a surveyor and cartographer for the federal government, spending time on the Maxwell Land Grant in both Colorado and New Mexico. He would design the AT&SF tunnel through Raton Pass, which is still known as the Avery Turner Tunnel. He rose through the ranks to become a division superintendent and his experience and relationships in northeastern New Mexico put him in touch with Jan Van Houten, Charles Springer, Frank Springer, and other leaders working on the railroad

1 Bromley, 53-57.

StLRM&P station at Ute Park, New Mexico, showing water tank and loaded coal car. Sign points the way to a small hotel. Telephone/telegraph poles are visible for the line that served this station.

Aztec Mill Museum Collection, Cimarron, New Mexico.

sale. Negotiations were ongoing in 1911 and 1912, and the first contract of purchase was signed August 1, 1913. At that point, the AT&SF took possession of the railroad. After an ICC hearing in early 1914, the St. Louis, Rocky Mountain, and Pacific Railway was transferred to the AT&SF Corporation. On March 10, 1915, the original purchase contract was changed, and the StLRM&P Ry was renamed the Rocky Mountain and Santa Fe Railroad (RM&SF).[2]

At first the new owners made no changes as the AT&SF assessed the present state and possible future of the RM&SF. They explored the feasibility of extending the railroad beyond Ute Park, with the *Cimarron Citizen* reporting in March 1914 that the railroad would be extended to Taos and then to either Santa Fe or Gallup once funds could be secured. However, it became apparent that any extension would not be profitable and this decision would have a widespread impact in Colfax County.

The following changes were eventually made. First, daily mixed train operations resumed from Raton to Cimarron, an improvement from the prior tri-weekly service. Second, all maintenance operations were consolidated in Raton where the AT&SF already had a sizable roundhouse and maintenance hub. The former StLRM&P Ry roundhouse, turntable, blacksmith shop, machine shop, and powerhouse were all re-

2 Bromley, 69-75; Myrick, *New Mexico's Railroads*, 163.

moved from Cimarron by the end of 1914. This meant that any repairs and maintenance on C&N locomotive #1 and the rolling stock that could not be handled by the C&N shops would need to be taken to Raton. In some instances the C&N was able to secure rented locomotives from the AT&SF to continue daily service, but on other occasions service was suspended until maintenance and repairs were complete. The third change to the RM&SF was the abandonment of duplicate trackage. The Raton-Dillon line and the Clifton House-Preston line were formally abandoned and the rails taken up in September 1915.[3]

The final and most anticipated change involved staffing and personnel. Both the Cimarron and Northwestern Railway and modern-day researchers were the beneficiaries of one personnel change. Edward and Mary Troutman had come to Cimarron when the StLRM&P Co and its railway were started in 1905. Mary used a portion of their home for boarding, and Edward worked first in farming and then for the StLRM&P Ry as a foreman in charge of a section gang maintaining a particular portion of railroad track. But on March 15, 1914, Edward resigned his position with the StLRM&P Ry and joined the C&N.

Both Edward and Mary were professional photographers and took scores of photographs in Cimarron and the surrounding area with their Troutman Studios photography business. Many of their glass plate negatives and picture postcards, with distinctive white lettering, are preserved to this day for historians, researchers, and photography enthusiasts alike. When Edward joined the C&N as a section foreman he gained access and knowledge to photograph a wide range of C&N and CT&L equipment, people, operations, the outlying logging camps of Ring, Bonito, Poñil Park, and many subjects far too numerous to list. The Troutman photographs of the mills, the log trains, the teamsters, the wagon makers, the scenery, the landscape, and the loggers are a valuable resource which made possible this present-day picture of the C&N. The Troutmans, along with their descendants, would become prominent fixtures in Cimarron. Both Edward and Mary passed in the mid-1930s and are buried in Cimarron Cemetery, but their legacy lives on in their photographs which provide a portal to view their world.[4]

---

3 Bromley 74-75; Schomburg, Thomas W. Interviewed by Lawrence Murphy at Denver, Colorado, June 9, 1964; Cimarron Print. Co. "*Cimarron News Citizen*, 03-05-1914; 07-02-1914." (1914); *The Cimarron News and Cimarron Citizen.* (Cimarron, Colfax County, N.M.), 16 April 1914.

4 Cimarron Print. Co. "*Cimarron News Citizen*, 03-05-1914." (1914); Lamm, Gene, Email to Tucker Baker, May 6, 2020.

Edward A. Troutman wearing blanket (center) with two Native Americans at Troutman Photography Studios.

New Mexico State University Library, Archives and Special Collections.

Expanded Logging and Processing Plants

The changeover to the Rocky Mountain and Santa Fe Railroad led the CT&L Co to expanded its business with the AT&SF system. Shortly after the AT&SF purchase of the StLRM&P Ry in August 1913 the CT&L Co put out a call for 300 men to cut ties in the Ute Park area, either for Santa Fe expansion west of Ute Park or for trans-shipment to points elsewhere on the Santa Fe system. A few years later in the 1920s when Baldy Mountain mining interests revived, CT&L logging for both mine props and crossties expanded even further. Tie and mine prop yards were created in Ute Park as prop contractors were located up and down Ute Creek and along Tolby Creek. Additional mine prop yards were set up at the flag stops of Harlan and Nash on the RM&SF for logging Deer Lake Mesa and Devil's Wash Basin, both high points along the Cimarron Canyon. A large portion of these lands along the heights of Cimarron Canyon is now located on present-day Philmont Scout Ranch.

The area sustained such a significant number of contractors and employees that the CT&L Co opened another company store and commissary in Ute Park. Shipments to and from this commissary and the various tie and prop yards were facilitated over the RM&SF. It is not known whether the C&N had operating rights over the Ute Park-Ci-

CT&L mine props stacked along RM&SF flag stop of Nash west of Cimarron. A section crew's handcar loaded with tools rests on the siding.

Raton Museum Collection, Raton, New Mexico.

marron line. It is plausible, however, since the traffic on that line had declined significantly after 1913, with the Santa Fe discontinuing the StLRM&P's previous promotion of Ute Park as a tourist destination.[5]

The CT&L mill site in Cimarron experienced change as well in 1913, with the construction of a pressurized chemical tie treating plant that was expanded as business increased. Planning for the tie treatment plant began in 1912, including prospective costs of chemical treatment options and designing space for treated ties in the Cimarron yard. Correspondence related that approximately twenty acres would be needed to store 300 treated ties. Once the tie plant was in operation, the tie making process would start with hand-hewn ties, then later sawed crossties, shipped from the high country via the C&N Ry to Cimarron. The pressurized treatment process was described by Thomas Schomburg as "mechanically complicated." Ties would be placed into a heavy metal cylinder, doors were secured, the air pressure raised, and some heat applied and maintained. Then zinc chloride, an alternative preservative to creosote, was injected at high pressure, filling the cylinder with the preservative. The pressure and heat caused the zinc chloride to

5 "Flag stops" refer to railroad stops that are not normal station stops along the employee timetable, but trains stop only if a flagman or a flag has been raised at the stop. Call for 300 men to cut ties: *Santa Fe New Mexican.* (Santa Fe, N.M.), 26 Aug. 1913. Expanded logging in Ute Park and along Cimarron Canyon see Schomburg, Thomas W. Interviewed by Lawrence Murphy at Denver, Colorado, June 9, 1964; and MacDonald, Lamm, MacDonald, 53.

CT&L tie treating plant on right, lumber stacks on left, with boxcars on sidings.
Palace of the Governors Photo Archives (NMHM/DCA), Neg. No. 008967.

permeate the cells of the timber, not just the outside surfaces. After a specified period, usually a few hours, a vacuum was applied to remove the zinc chloride from the cylinder and to remove liquid from the ties. The result was a high-pressure, chemically treated crosstie which lasted longer in active use on railroad tracks.

The treated ties were commercially successful, and the Colorado and Southern Railway was a large customer with ties delivered to the C&S at either Trinidad, Colorado, or Des Moines, New Mexico. Business was so brisk that the end of 1913 saw the CT&L expanding the tie treating plant, with newspaper coverage reporting the local business success. A large elevated platform was built to stack treated ties at rail-car height for easier loading on outbound cars. Shortly thereafter in January 1914 more machinery, a hoisting derrick, and a tightly woven wire fence were installed in the tie treating area. The Santa Fe bought some treated ties, but mostly purchased untreated ties as they operated their own tie treating and seasoning plant in Albuquerque.

The newspapers reported that C&S Ry officials visited the plant in 1914 for a "very large order of ties." When the tie treating plant reopened for the 1915 summer season, it was reported that the CT&L held "a contract to treat one hundred thousand ties at this operation which will require a steady run of two months. […] About 1500 cross-ties a day with the present equipment can be treated." The "Tie Plant,"

CT&L planer mill, powerhouse, and locomotive engine shed.

Aztec Mill Museum Collection, Cimarron, New Mexico.

as it was known at that time, was located on the northwestern corner of the mill site, complete with large holding tanks for preservatives, the tie treating cylinders, and the railcar loading dock. The CT&L was a growing business and was maturing in technical operations with innovations that replaced hewing railroad ties by hand and seasoning in the New Mexico sun.[6]

As the treated tie business expanded and paid dividends, the backcountry sawmills were winding down and a new sawmill was constructed at the CT&L Cimarron mill site in 1920. This new mill was designed by Guy Palmes and Theodore Schomburg's son, Thomas, at the same time that trackage was being taken up and the Poñil Park rail line was slated to be partially abandoned. The Cimarron sawmill would replace the worn-out backcountry mills, and this caused a fundamental shift in how the C&N Ry operated. While CT&L Mill No. 2 at Poñil Park was being serviced by trucks and no longer by rail, the C&N was now primarily hauling raw logs on flatcars down to Cimarron. The Cimarron sawmill had a daily capacity of 30,000 board feet and included a log pond on site. The log pond allowed the logs to be stored, the outer fibers to be washed and softened before cutting, and to be sorted before being taken into the sawmill. The remaining backcountry mills

6 Planning correspondence on tie plant: Letter, B. Kuckuck to T.A. Schomburg, March 25, 1912, T.A. Schomburg Collection; Schomburg, Thomas W. Interviewed by Lawrence Murphy at Denver, Colorado, June 9, 1964; First expansion of tie plant: *Santa Fe New Mexican.* (Santa Fe, N.M.), 15 Dec. 1913; *The Cimarron News and Cimarron Citizen.* (Cimarron, Colfax County, N.M.), 15 Jan. 1914; second tie plant expansion: *Cimarron News and Cimarron Citizen* (Cimarron, Colfax County, N.M.), 24 Feb. 1915; Location of tie plant: Map, "Village of Cimarron, Colfax County, NM," G.E. Briggs, March 1922, T. A. Schomburg Collection, MSS.747.

used trucks for inbound logs as well as for outbound shipment to the planer mill in Cimarron.[7]

The Eagle Nest Dam Dispute

Theodore Schomburg was rarely idle and was constantly considering how to further expand his timbering enterprise on the Maxwell Land Grant. The CT&L contract with the Maxwell Land Grant Company was for all the timber on the New Mexico portion of the grant, and Schomburg firmly intended to log all economical timber by the most present means, the railroad. To this end, Schomburg took various actions through the years at the helm of the CT&L to bring about railroad construction into the Moreno Valley to log the valley by rail. At first, it appeared the StLRM&P Ry was going to complete their stated goal of building through Cimarron Canyon to the Moreno Valley during the initial construction of the railroad. According to Thomas Schomburg years later, "This route had been surveyed a number of times and the St. Louis, Rocky Mountain, and Pacific Railway had a very accurate survey." The poor financial returns of the StLRM&P, especially the failure of its Ute Park-Cimarron line, doomed any further expansion west from the terminus at Ute Park. However, the StLRM&P Ry held the right-of-way beyond Ute Park through its contract with the MLG Co., meaning that it was legally entitled to build a railroad into the Moreno Valley along the best route. Theodore Schomburg worked obsessively to convince the StLRM&P, and later the RM&SF, to extend their railroad to the valley.[8]

Everything moved from casual discussion to frantic action when on March 1, 1916, the MLG Co deeded 262 acres in Cimarron Canyon to the Cimarron Valley Land Company which was principally backed by Charles Springer. Springer and the Cimarron Valley Land Company planned to construct a private dam in the narrow opening at the end of the canyon. This dam would create a large reservoir of over 100,000 acres and would ensure a consistent water supply along the Cimarron River drainage, a long-held concern for farmers and ranchers in the area. The efforts by Charles Springer and other regional businessmen to build a dam on the Cimarron River had begun in 1907, but the financing for the project finally came through in 1916 when Springer himself

7 Murphy, *New Mexico Railroader*, Volume 7, No. 1. "The Cimarron and Northwestern: Historic Railroad of Northern New Mexico, Part III," pp. 1. January 1965. Arthur Johnson Memorial Library, Raton, New Mexico.

8 Schomburg, Thomas W. Interviewed by Lawrence Murphy at Denver, Colorado, June 9, 1964.

procured the needed land for the reservoir. A dam and the accompanying reservoir in Moreno Valley would make railroad construction impossible along the previously surveyed route. Instead it would require a double-track railroad tunnel through the southeast mountainside of Cimarron Canyon near Eagle Roost Rock. Heavy rock work, major blasting, and exponentially greater construction costs would be incurred to route around the dam. No provision in the dam agreement was made for a railroad right-of-way, so Schomburg stood to lose the chance to log Moreno Valley by rail when construction on the dam started in late 1916. Schomburg began exploring every alternative in early 1917.[9]

The Continental Tie and Lumber Company, by virtue of its contract with the MLG Co, also had the right to construct wagon roads, traction roads, and railroads on the grant lands to harvest the timber. With the Poñil Park condition well satisfied, this allowed Schomburg to devise and execute a plan to reach the Moreno Valley by rail. He directed Frankenburger to monitor the progress of dam construction in February 1917, while Schomburg negotiated with MLG Co officials for a railroad right-of-way around the dam site. With Frankenburger reporting that dam construction was moving along, but with no conclusion to his MLG Co negotiations, Schomburg called a special meeting of the CT&L board of directors on March 10, 1917, where the decision was made to begin a railroad right-of-way survey and brush clearing straight through the middle of the dam site.

Since the Rocky Mountain and Santa Fe Railroad, as successor to the StLRM&P Ry, held the right-of-way and had already surveyed the best route, Schomburg generated ideas for lowering the construction costs to entice the Santa Fe to build into the Moreno Valley.

The logic behind this decision was that the prior CT&L and MLG Co agreement allowed railroad construction for timber harvesting, and if the CT&L could lower RM&SF's costs by preparing the way, then the Santa Fe might be persuaded to extend their line to Taos and beyond as originally planned. Other options included the Santa Fe selling their survey and right-of-way to Schomburg, or Schomburg might persuade Springer and the Cimarron Valley Land Company to contribute toward the additional expenses for routing the railroad around the dam

9 Maxwell Land Grant Company Records, Minute Book 124, Special Meeting of Board of Trustees, March 3, 1916; Pearson, 238; Murphy, *Out in God's Country: A History of Colfax County, New Mexico*, 83-87.

Eagle Nest Dam construction site showing the originally surveyed railway route.

Aztec Mill Museum Collection, Cimarron, New Mexico.

site.[10]

The evaluation of these options would involve an interesting series of discussions, and fortunately scores of letters between Frankenburger, Schomburg, Van Houten, MLG Co. superintendent James K. Hunt, and Charles Springer would leave a detailed paper trail. After the March CT&L special board meeting, Schomburg had Frankenburger direct men to set up camp, have Palmes begin surveying a right-of-way, and then begin clearing brush on the RM&SF right-of-way. As specifically directed by Schomburg, Palmes set out surveying stakes and Frankenburger had "Jesse and six Mexicans at the site maintaining our engineering presence" by clearing brush directly through the dam construction site itself. By the end of March fifteen-hundred feet of right-of-way had been located and three-hundred feet cleared of trees, rocks, debris, brush, and other items. Frankenburger even reported that all this activity was in full view of the dam construction workers who continued to toil on their own project with this spectacle going on in front of them daily.

In April, the affair escalated even further when Frankenburger reporting to Schomburg that Colfax County commissioner Mason Chase, allegedly deputized by the Colfax County sheriff, had ordered Jesse and the Mexicans to leave the dam site or face immediate arrest. Schomburg fired back in a telegram to Frankenburger that he wants a list of who the sheriff actually deputized, wants answers as to why these deputies are only at the dam construction site, and says Mason Chase cannot be both county commissioner and a deputy sheriff. From this

10 Letter, H.G. Frankenburger to T.A. Schomburg, February 12, 1917, File Folder 12, T.A. Schomburg Collection; Minutes of the Special Meeting of the Board of Directors of the Continental Tie and Lumber Company, March 10, 1917, File Folder 12, T.A. Schomburg Collection.

point onward, the letters between Schomburg and Charles Springer increased in length and in frequency. Both gentlemen were fully convinced of the rightness of their own actions and their legal standing. Springer held the title and deed of land from MLG for the dam, but Schomburg held the surveys, a right-of-way, and was fully within his rights to build a railroad for the purpose of timber harvesting. Both sent letters to each other detailing how they were in the right and trying to resolve this in a "friendly manner."[11]

For Schomburg, the result was indeed friendly. In 1918, the Maxwell Land Grant Company joined with the Cimarron Valley Land Company to help finance a railroad tunnel on an alternate route around the dam site. Schomburg contributed $4,000 of his own money, the Cimarron Valley Land Company pitched in $8,000 and the MLG Co contributed the remaining $9,098.97 for a total cost of $21,098.97. The resulting tunnel ran through hard rock above the southeast corner of Eagle Nest Dam, and it was wide enough for two railroad tracks side by side. The tunnel was built as double track since it would be the local high point for the route coming up Cimarron Canyon and then descending into Moreno Valley. Double track allowed for trains to pass each other, whereas a passing siding on a heavy grade was not ideal as stopping trains on a steep grade is never easy or safe.

On March 8, 1919, Schomburg went a step further and incorporated the New Mexico and Western Railway (NM&W) to receive ownership of the tunnel and the right-of-way. The incorporators were Theodore A. Schomburg, Thomas W. Schomburg, Harry K. Holloway, Charles G. Waters, and Henry G. Frankenburger, an almost exact match of CT&L management and leadership. The official incorporation listed the eastern terminus at Ute Park, the western terminus at Taos Pass, a branch line to Elizabethtown of eight miles, a twenty mile main line between Ute Park and South Moreno Valley, and a ten mile branch line to Taos Pass, for a total of thirty-eight miles. Ostensibly, this corporation was intended to preserve single ownership over the right-of-way and the tunnel, as well as to pave the way for the RM&SF expansion into the Moreno Valley perhaps by simply selling or leasing the NM&W Ry to the Santa Fe.

The Santa Fe was noticeably absent from the Eagle Nest Dam dis-

11 T.A. Schomburg Collection, File Folder 14: Letter, Frankenburger to Schomburg, April 1917; Telegram, Schomburg to Frankenburger, April 1917; Letter, Schomburg to Charles Springer, April 1917; Letter, Charles Springer to Schomburg, April 1917.

The completed railroad tunnel above and south of Eagle Nest Dam.
New Mexico State University Library, Archives and Special Collections.

pute during the voluminous correspondence, and despite periodic conversations with Theodore Schomburg, the Santa Fe never extended its rails beyond Ute Park. By the time the tunnel and the Eagle Nest Dam were completed in 1920, advancements in motor trucks and the thin timber reserves remaining on the northern end of the Moreno Valley rendered logging by rail uneconomical. In the late 1930s, the CT&L would begin to log the southern Moreno Valley by truck. Yet the historical record is clear: Theodore A. Schomburg and the Continental Tie and Lumber Company built a railroad tunnel above Eagle Nest Lake. The tunnel would be listed on the 1925 CT&L *Memorandum of Property* showing a line item of $8,000.[12]

The evidence of this drawn-out drama are still present today. The Eagle Nest Dam is the largest privately constructed dam in the country, and it continues to serve the residents of Cimarron and Eagle Nest by providing consistent water resources and recreation on the expansive Eagle Nest Lake. Portions of the area, including the railroad tunnel, came under New Mexico Department of Game and Fish control as the Cimarron River is an active fishery. The CS Ranch, a direct descendant

12 Letter, Hunt to Cimarron Valley Land Company, June 19, 1918, Maxwell Land Grant Company Collection; Articles of Incorporation, New Mexico and Western Railway, March 8, 1918, File Folder 14, T.A. Schomburg Collection; Schomburg, Thomas W. Interviewed by Lawrence Murphy at Denver, Colorado, June 9, 1964; Continental Tie and Lumber Memorandum of Property, November 30, 1925, Maxwell Land Grant Company Collection.

of Charles Springer's ranch, continues to own the dam and the immediate area around it privately. Eagle Nest Lake was transferred to the State of New Mexico who operates it as a state park.

As for the tunnel, all construction materials were removed from it long ago, leaving large openings on both mountainsides. Extensive trestle works were needed on the Eagle Nest side of the tunnel and the virgin redwood timbers used for these trestles were repurposed into a barn and machine shop of sorts on the CS Ranch near the dam control structure. In 1995, the barn was dismantled and repurposed yet again as a private cabin in Eagle Nest. Its builder remarked that not a single knot was seen in the large 6"x14" timbers and was the finest wood around, fit for a cozy cabin.[13]

The First Pull-Back

The rate at which the Continental Tie and Lumber Company was harvesting timber on the Maxwell Land Grant would lead to the eventual rerouting of the railroad to reach other timber reserves. The first step had been the expansion of the Cimarron and Northwestern beyond Poñil Park to Bonito where new mills were set up to work stands of timber. The next decision was whether to continue with railroad expansion or reroute the available resources to other areas, meaning that certain sections of the line would be abandoned, the rails lifted, and then reused for track in a new stand of timber. Expanded operations would lead to increased operation costs. New tracks and relatively new rolling stock would mean lower maintenance and operation costs, but as equipment and tracks aged, expenses would increase.

Total C&N Ry expenses grew from $20,730.94 in 1909 to $24,331.58 in 1910, then increasing further to $33,049.66 in 1911 after the expansion to Bonito. With timber thinning out in the Bonito area and 1915 expenses totalling $41,387.88 (a net loss of $8,635.87 for the C&N), the decision was made to relocate sawmills and to abandon some existing sections incrementally over time. As early as 1914, the *Cimarron News-Citizen* newspaper heard "authentic word" that logging would be finished in the Bonito area and the sawmills there relocated, further stating that a good stand of timber provides only three to four years' worth of logging. "It was believed," the front-page article continues, "that the present setting at Bonito could be cleared by the

13 Email, David Werhane to Tucker Baker, August 10, 2020; "Eagle Nest Dam," Sidetracked Charley, June 14, 2014.

CT&L mill, lumber yard, and tracks at Cimarron.

Raton Museum Collection, Raton, New Mexico.

middle of August [1914] but owing to the heavy rains in the summer mills were forced to close down for several months causing somewhat of a delay."

Rain and floods would create constant problems as that same year another front-page headline displayed, "Rain Plays Havoc with Lumber Works," bemoaning the constant rains' potential for delaying seasoning and production of lumber for fruit crates and boxes desperately needed by the CT&L to fulfill orders. Just as the timber was thinning out on the northern end of the C&N, demand was spiking for timber products.

DEMAND FOR LUMBER GREAT

> For the first time in its history the Continental Tie and Lumber Company of Cimarron is unable to meet the demand of lumber, ties, and props occasioned by the unprecedented demand for building material [...] Superintendent Frankenburger has stated that all orders are being accepted on condition that they can be filled within two or three months. The lumber camps are working at their utmost capacity at present.

The manpower redirected into the American effort in World War I in Europe could have certainly led to both the greater demand for timber products and a shortage in manpower in the high-country camps. It appears that the C&N Ry tried to cash in on the heightened demand

Poñil Park sawmill and yard during motor truck logging.

Raton Museum Collection, Raton, New Mexico.

for timber at this time in terms of railroad shipping rates. However, the New Mexico State Corporation Commission forced refunds in September 1917 when the C&N made the rates effective on July 1 of that year without seeking consent from the commission. Weather, transportation costs, maintenance costs, rate increase refunds, and major lumber demand, all contributed to abandoning sections of the CT&L logging railroad system.[14]

Indeed, partial abandonment would start in 1916 as track was pulled up between Bonito and Ring. No formal abandonment procedures or regulations were needed as that track was privately held by the CT&L. In that year, the CT&L held eight miles in addition to the C&N's twenty-two miles, with only five miles in use the preceding year. Five miles was essentially the distance from Poñil Park to Ring and the yard limits of the Pratt-Wood sawmill siding there. By 1920 only the main twenty-two miles of C&N and two miles of CT&L track remained, evidently for continued logging along the remaining CT&L trackage. Additional trackage had been removed between 1919 and 1920,

14 C&N financials: *Decisions of the Interstate Commerce Commission of the United States of America*, Vol. 106, Valuation Reports. October 1925 – February 1926, pp 570-571; Bonito area exhausted of timber: Cimarron Print. Co. "*Cimarron News Citizen*, 09-17-1914." (1914); "Rain Plays Havoc with Lumber Works": *The Cimarron News and Cimarron Citizen*. (Cimarron, Colfax County, N.M.), 30 July 1914; CT&L cannot keep up with demand: *New Mexico State Record*. (Santa Fe, N.M.), 08 June 1917; *Albuquerque Morning Journal*. (Albuquerque, N.M.), 12 July 1917.

as the New Mexico state tax commission assessed a value of $12,500 on the five miles of CT&L-owned track and $66,000 for the twenty-two miles of C&N track. The timber around the twenty-two miles of C&N track had obviously been cut, so this section was used only for transport back to Cimarron. By the end of 1921 only the twenty-two miles of C&N track remained from Poñil Park to Cimarron as all the CT&L rail had been abandoned, recovered, and stored in Cimarron for later use. Frankenburger gives some insight as to the developments of this period when, in a letter concerning the Eagle Nest Dam, he asks Schomburg about the plans for the 30 lb. rails lifted from the Bonito mill site in 1916.[15]

By 1923 the time had come for the partial abandonment of Cimarron and Northwestern Railway trackage. C&N General Manager Henry G. Frankenburger petitioned the Interstate Commerce Commission on August 3, 1923, to allow for abandonment of its line from South Poñil to Poñil Park, a distance of fourteen miles. The case was handled without a formal hearing and Frankenburger testified in writing to the ICC as to why the line should be allowed to be abandoned.

> The applicant represents that there is no further need of the line from South Poñil and Poñil Park, as the available supply of timber in that territory is exhausted and no other tonnage can be obtained. It is estimated that 90 percent of the traffic has been furnished by the timber industry. Passenger traffic has been unimportant. [...] There are no cities, towns, or villages on that portion of the road proposed to be abandoned. It is represented that only about 20 inhabitants will remain in that vicinity after the timber camps are moved.

On August 29, 1923, ICC Finance Docket No. 2980 was decided, and the formal certificate of Public Convenience and Necessity was issued, thereby allowing the immediate abandonment and lifting of rails and track. As was common in the timber industry during that period, and as mentioned by the ICC commissioners, the main body of people living along the C&N line planned to follow the company wherever the line was re-laid for further CT&L timbering. However, photographic evidence shows log trucks all around Mill No. 2 in Poñil Park and the entire mill yard was reconfigured for motor vehicles, suggesting that some logging and milling continued in the area for a few

---

15 Active track miles: *Annual Report on the Statistics of Railways in the United States, Interstate Commerce Commission*; 1916, pp 687; 1920, pp 434; 1921 pp 388-389; New Mexico state tax valuations: *Albuquerque Morning Journal.* (Albuquerque, N.M.), 7 March 1920; Letter, H.G. Frankenburger to T.A. Schomburg, February 12, 1917, File Folder 12, T.A. Schomburg Collection.

View today of tie and spike left after the Poñil Park trackage was pulled up.

Steve Lewis Collection.

years after railroad abandonment. The rail pickup, however, was hasty, as the ties and much other-track-material, known as "OTM" or "jewelry," was left behind during abandonment. Hikers on Philmont Scout Ranch and in the Valle Vidal continue to find joint bars, spikes, bolts, nuts, and trestle timber rebar along the remains of the right-of-way today.[16]

In the same volume of Decisions of the Interstate Commerce Commission allowing the first partial C&N abandonment in 1923, a deficit settlement was reached regarding a period of federal control of the C&N. Finance Docket No. 1918 of October 13, 1923, determined that the C&N Ry was due $25,228.35 during the period for which it operated under federal control from January 1, 1918 to June 3, 1918. Section 204 of the Transportation Act of 1920 allowed for the payment of deficits incurred by common carrier railroads while under federal control during World War I. The US federal government had nationalized common carrier railroads during the war and placed Army and federal employees in charge over them to directly facilitate full railroad support for the war effort.[17]

16 Decisions of the Interstate Commerce Commission of the United States of America, Vol. 82, Finance Reports, July – December 1923, pp 217-218; Photo Collection: "Poñil Park Mill No. 2, May 1, 1921," Raton Museum, Raton, NM.

17 Ibid, pp 441-442; Nationalization of railroads during WWI: Bromley, 78-79.

Waite Phillips

Oilman Waite Phillips would be one of the later characters to impact the Cimarron and Northwestern and the Continental Tie and Lumber story. It would be Phillip's consolidation of lands logged by the CT&L into ranch/agricultural land under single ownership that would eventually lead to the creation of Philmont Scout Ranch and would place a large portion of the CT&L and C&N operational areas within its boundaries. Born in 1883 near Conway, Iowa, Phillips would first encounter the West on a long western trip with his twin brother Wiate. After the death of his brother, Phillips returned to Iowa and took a position as bookkeeper for a Knoxville, Iowa, coal company. Similar to Theodore Schomburg, his humble start as a bookkeeper would pale in comparison to his later success. By 1925 Phillips would receive around $25 million when he sold his highly successful Waite Phillips Petroleum Company that had plied the oil fields of Oklahoma. Phillips would additionally expand his investments and commercial success in Tulsa, Oklahoma, his then hometown, by investing in banks and commercial real estate with the construction of the twenty-three-story Philtower office building.[18]

Phillips would eventually have over 300,000 acres of contiguous land around Cimarron by 1926. It would begin in 1922 when Phillips purchased 44,000 acres of George Webster's Urraca Ranch south of Cimarron near modern day Philmont's camping headquarters and administration area. He continued buying parcels of land in the succeeding years from the Sauble, Heck, and Chandler families, as well as small farming plots near Rayado. In 1923, Phillips acquired the remaining 30,000 acres of the Urraca Ranch from Webster. Phillips would also purchase land from the Maxwell Land Grant Company, and this included the lands the Continental Tie and Lumber Company was logging along the South Poñil and Wilson Mesa. 1926 saw the purchase of 121,000 acres on the Poñil drainages by Phillips and additional acquisitions in the Cimarron, Turkey, Dean, and South Poñil Canyons.

By virtue of the timber contract with the MLG Co, the CT&L held the timber rights on a portion of the lands Phillips was purchasing. Thomas Schomburg explained how the CT&L handled timbering with Phillips: "Part of the country [Phillips bought], the Continental

18 Murphy, *Philmont: A History,* 188-189.

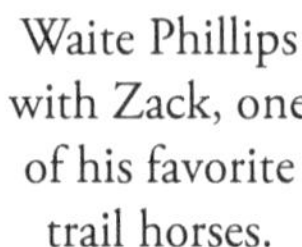

Waite Phillips with Zack, one of his favorite trail horses.

National Scouting Museum Collection, Cimarron, New Mexico.

Tie and Lumber Company had relinquished timber rights. On other parts, the company still held it and did cuttings over there. Over around Urraca and Rayado, the company had relinquished their timber rights several years before. Phillips never sold any timber rights he owned to the Continental Tie and Lumber Company. He sold some to some other interests, but not to us." Phillips subsequently purchased land with remaining timber stands as well as cut-over timber lands still suitable for cattle grazing. Phillips continued acquiring and consolidating his holdings, and he would have a major impact in the region during the years after the end of the C&N Ry.[19]

Thomas W. Schomburg

As 1920 approached and the Continental Tie and Lumber Company and the Cimarron and Northwestern Railway continued to evolve through ten years of heavy change, Theodore Schomburg's son, Thomas, would begin to take a more active role in the management of the companies. Since the names were similar, earlier historical accounts often erroneously considered Thomas the only "Schomburg" involved in the operation. While the two were not one and the same, Thomas did continue his father's legacy by having an active part in the timber industry. It was Thomas who would see the close of C&N and CT&L operations.

Born Thomas Whigham Schomburg in Raton, New Mexico, Thomas would move with his family to Trinidad in 1901 when the elder Schomburg became Vice President and General Manager of the

19 Zimmer and Lewis, 157; Pearson, 239-240; Schomburg, Thomas W. Interviewed by Lawrence Murphy at Denver, Colorado, June 9, 1964.

Thomas W. Schomburg (right) caught red handed in a college prank.

T.A. Schomburg Collection, PH.605. History Colorado Center.

Rocky Mountain Timber Company. Thomas would move with the family again in high school when the Schomburgs relocated to Denver in 1908 as the CT&L and C&N were getting underway in Cimarron.

Young Thomas would study at the University of Colorado in Boulder, where in December 1913 he and another cohort, Harold W. McCraffey, were involved in a prank. Looking to make a mark in the friendly college rivalry between their school and the Colorado School of Mines in Golden, the two were caught attempting to paint "U of C" on one of the Mines buildings. The Mines students relished the occasion by shaving Schomburg's and McCraffey's heads, painting "MINES" on their foreheads, and delivering them to the train station to head back to Boulder wearing painters' overalls with "MINES" painted across them. Newspapers documented the whole affair because the rivalry had intensified after the attempt to steal the Mines' mascot, a goat, had taken place some weeks prior. Thomas' studies were interrupted by service in World War I, and after the war Thomas finished his studies at Columbia University in New York City.[20]

Maturing and entering the timber business like his father, Thomas

20 Schomburg, Thomas W. Interviewed by Lawrence Murphy at Denver, Colorado, June 9, 1964; Caught in a college prank: *The Colorado School of Mines Magazine*, Alumni Association of the Colorado School of Mines, Vol. 3, No. 12, December 1913, pp 285-286.

was working at the Pagosa Lumber Company on the Jicarilla Apache reservation near Dulce, New Mexico, in 1920. When the time came for his transfer to Cimarron, his first assignment teamed him with Guy Palmes to design and construct a sawmill at the Cimarron CT&L mill site. The CT&L was moving away from maintaining smaller back-country sawmills in the high country and was using the C&N to haul logs back to Cimarron. A sawmill would allow for the complete milling process to take place in one location: cutting logs, sending the lumber through the planer mill, pressurized treating of ties, seasoning, storage, and outbound delivery. After the sawmill was operational, Thomas returned to Colorado and expanded his forestry background working in various Colorado timber companies during 1922 and 1923. His next Cimarron assignment would come in 1923 as new railroad construction commenced for the C&N route from South Poñil.[21] He would return to Cimarron periodically through the 1920s and would take a more active managerial role in the Cimarron companies after his father's death in 1929.

21 Schomburg, Thomas W. Interviewed by Lawrence Murphy at Denver, Colorado, June 9, 1964

Wilson Mesa and the South Poñil Branch

Even before the South Poñil to Poñil Park portion was granted formal abandonment in 1923, the Continental Tie and Lumber Company began constructing what would be the last section of the Cimarron and Northwestern Railway. Beginning in 1922, Guy Palmes went to work again as railroad locating engineer, with Thomas Schomburg supervising the construction of the new route. The goal was to log the Wilson Mesa area, including the virgin timber on top of the expansive mesa. The timber contract with the Maxwell Land Grant Company was still in effect and logging by rail was still considered the most economical option. Palmes and the Schomburgs knew that this track would not be a permanent line and that the timetable for construction, logging, and abandonment was only a handful of years.

At this point a geographical note might be helpful. Period historical maps refer to the mesa in question as both "Wilson Mesa" and "Stern Mesa." The surname of Nat Stern, a ranch owner in the area, appeared in several places on some older maps. By comparing historic maps and photos it is clear that "Stern" was located at the South Poñil-Middle Poñil confluence, the site of Philmont's Poñil camp, while "Wilson" was further west at the confluence of Pueblano Creek and South Poñil, the site of Philmont's Pueblano camp. "Wilson Mesa," being both the historical and modern-day name, will be used in this account.[1]

Track construction started at South Poñil station on the C&N at the

1 Schomburg, Thomas W. Interviewed by Lawrence Murphy at Denver, Colorado, June 9, 1964; Murphy, *New Mexico Railroader*, Volume 7, No. 1. "The Cimarron and Northwestern: Historic Railroad of Northern New Mexico, Part III," pp 3, January 1965; Map, "New Mexico North Central Part," Continental Tie and Lumber Company, March 1922, T.A. Schomburg Collection.

Nat Stern's ranch at the junction of the Middle Poñil and South Poñil Canyons.
New Mexico State University Library, Archives and Special Collections.

confluence of the North Poñil and Middle Poñil Canyons. The track would proceed northwest up Middle Poñil Canyon through the Stern Ranch at what is now modern-day Poñil Camp. At Stern, the railroad would then take a large sharp westward curve to enter the mouth of South Poñil Canyon. To make this curve, the railroad approached from the eastern side of Middle Poñil Canyon, maintained a constant grade over the canyon bottom and creek with a large 96-foot trestle, and continued curving to successfully enter the narrower South Poñil Canyon. A photograph of this trestle in 1924 noted that it was the "same length as bridge #10 on the old line," which was located approximately at mile marker 4 near the mouth of Dean Canyon.

Reaching the top of Wilson Mesa posed a formidable challenge for Palmes and the younger Schomburg. At first, they considered extending the railroad itself to the mesa top. The only feasible route would have been to continue further west in the South Poñil Canyon for several more miles, then circle back, heading east to reach the mesa top. A route such as this, while being costly for the engineering, earth works, and extra miles needed, also would have incurred steep railroad grades. Thomas would recall that they considered going this route and using a geared locomotive such as a Shay, Heisler, or Climax, but the costly plan was nixed altogether. Another idea was to build a timber skid, using gravity on a designated slope site to ground skid the logs down to

Stern, New Mexico, 96 ft long bridge approaching the curve to enter South Poñil Canyon.

T.A. Schomburg Collection, MSS 747, F.32.783. History Colorado Center.

the rail line. A third idea was to build a massive log flume from the top of the mesa down to the rail line. Even an overhead tramway of cables and tongs was considered. However, the final plan was for a motor vehicle road which was surveyed, designed, and constructed by Palmes from the top of the mesa to the rail line in the canyon below using existing trails. The first motor logging trucks in the area were used on this road and they provided the most efficient and cost-effective solution for logging the top of Wilson Mesa, with the rail line hauling the logs to Cimarron.[2]

After this decision was made, the track from South Poñil to the terminus at Wilson was built by the CT&L and owned in the name of the CT&L as a private logging railroad. It connected at South Poñil with the C&N's common carrier track into Cimarron. Years later Palmes and Thomas Schomburg would describe the nature of this line's construction to Lawrence Murphy:

> Like its companion canyon to the north, the South Poñil was a historic area. Many arrowheads and graves left from the period of prehistoric Indian occupation were found during construction. At the junction of the South Poñil and Pueblano Creek, which ran off Wil-

2 Schomburg, Thomas W. Interviewed by Lawrence Murphy at Denver, Colorado, June 9, 1964; Murphy, *New Mexico Railroader*, Volume 7, No. 1. "The Cimarron and Northwestern: Historic Railroad of Northern New Mexico, Part III," pp 3, January 1965; Photo, Neg. No. F32.783, "Railroad bridge at Stern, N.M", T.A. Schomburg Collection, PH.605.

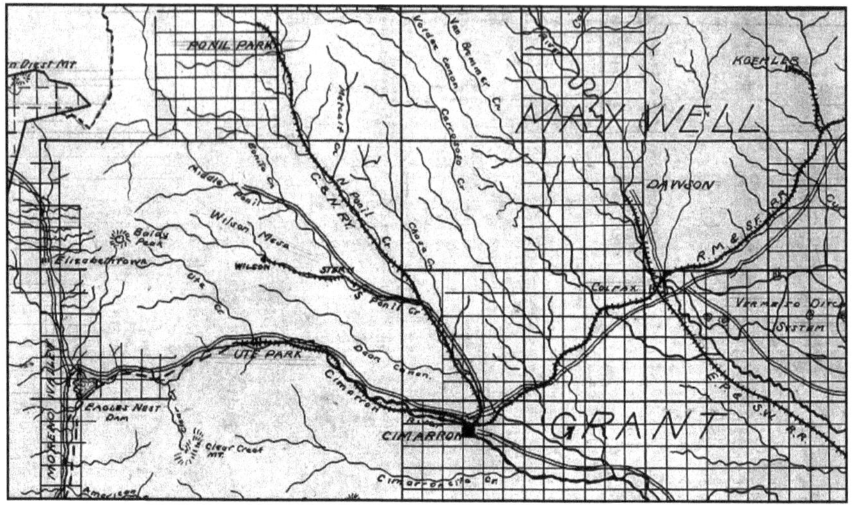

C&N trackage to Poñil Park and on the South Poñil in 1922.

T.A. Schomburg Collection, MSS 747, Oversize Maps. History Colorado Center.

> son Mesa very near the terminus, was an old stone fort where outlaws and anti-granters had guarded the canyon against officers employed by the Maxwell Land Grant company.[3]

Thomas Schomburg would mention that the line was built "more like a standard logging railroad," although it was still sturdily constructed. The track was ten miles long, built from rail used previously on the North Poñil Canyon portion, with ties from the CT&L mill in Cimarron. Since the line was not a common carrier, no public timetables were published. Wilson would be the terminus that included a wye to turn trains. Thomas Schomburg recounted that "on the South Poñil, there was a minor ranch, later owned by Nat Stern, where we later had our operations. Not many small squatter types." Indeed, the South Poñil Branch operated in a different time, place, and circumstance than the earlier Poñil Park line.

Modern LIDAR imagery shows that the grades were mild going from South Poñil to Stern, generally 2% or less, but the last five miles approaching Wilson were 4%, a steep climb for any train whether loaded or empty. The ten miles of CT&L South Poñil trackage, along with the eight remaining miles of C&N trackage, gave the C&N a total of eighteen operating rail miles. For these eighteen miles, a 1925 *Memorandum of Property* for the CT&L listed the South Poñil Railroad

3 Schomburg, Thomas W. Interviewed by Lawrence Murphy at Denver, Colorado, June 9, 1964.

Logging by motor truck in the Poñil Canyons.
Raton Museum Collection, Raton, New Mexico.

Line at $100,000.[4]

Unlike the original twenty-two miles and the extension to Bonito, no backcountry sawmills were located along the tracks. Timber was cut, skidded, or trucked to the rail line at various points, and then the C&N would haul the logs stacked on flatcars down to the sawmill at Cimarron. No other industries existed on the line. Lumbermen Bert Pratt, C.S. Wood, and others either moved to other ventures or had completed their timbering operation by the time the C&N pulled up the track from Ring and Poñil Park. The prior practice of spotting empty flatcars at various sidings and spurs, picking them up loaded by C&N #1, and dropping off more empty flatcars, likely continued on the South Poñil branch.[5]

A logging camp did develop near the terminus at Wilson. Located slightly west of the wye along South Poñil Creek, the camp was known as Pueblano, using an old Spanish term for a small community or village. At Pueblano, loggers built cabins and shacks with culled lumber as they continued the practice of living near their logging sites. Today Philmont's Pueblano camp occupies the location of Wilson and the

4 Murphy, *New Mexico Railroader*, Volume 7, No. 1. "The Cimarron and Northwestern: Historic Railroad of Northern New Mexico, Part III," pp 3, January 1965; Letter, Everett Lueck to Tucker Baker, April 25, 2020; *Continental Tie and Lumber Memorandum of Property*, November 30, 1925, Maxwell Land Grant Company Collection.

5 Schomburg, Thomas W. Interviewed by Lawrence Murphy at Denver, Colorado, June 9, 1964; Murphy, *Philmont: A History*, pp 174-175.

wye and "Pueblano Ruins" now mark the location of the old logging camp. Supplies, equipment, and machinery could still be brought in by train if needed. As South Poñil Canyon and Wilson Mesa were being logged using the combination of trucks and the C&N Railway, the CT&L also expanded its cutting operations along Deer Lake Mesa, Harlan, and Ute Park for the same timber products as in all other locations: crossties, mine props, and commercial saw timber.

The actions taken by the CT&L and the C&N at this time do raise questions for researchers, but fortunately the historical record affords many answers to these questions. First, with the terminus at Wilson being tantalizingly close to the mines on the north slope of Baldy Mountain, did the C&N ever consider expanding to the mines in attempt to gain more business? According to Thomas Schomburg, none of the mines on the north slope were in operation at the time the C&N operated on the South Poñil. Second, if the grade was steeper in South Poñil Canyon, why were the tracks not simply constructed further along the mild grade in Middle Poñil Canyon? The CT&L *Estimate of Timber* dated November 28, 1919, answers that question. With a greater concentration and higher quality timbers estimated in South Poñil Canyon and on Wilson Mesa, more saw timber, ties, and props could be had on the South Poñil, so the railroad was built to that point. An existing wagon road led from Stern up the Middle Poñil Canyon and into Greenwood Canyon, so these areas could be logged by livestock, wagons, or motor trucks and brought down to the track with greater ease than coming off Wilson Mesa. Third, was any consideration given to extending the South Poñil branch further west? Again according to Thomas Schomburg, this was not considered since the last cutting on the South Poñil was done between 1928 and 1930, and by that time the end was in sight for logging by rail.[6]

6 Schomburg, Thomas W. Interviewed by Lawrence Murphy at Denver, Colorado, June 9, 1964; *Continental Tie and Lumber Company, Estimate of Timber*, Nov. 28, 1919, Maxwell Land Grant Company Collection.

The End of the Line

By the late 1920s the end was in sight for the Cimarron and Northwestern Railway. The timber sought in the South Poñil and nearby drainages had been sufficiently cut and the Continental Tie and Lumber Company had turned its sights to the Moreno Valley for further logging on Maxwell Land Grant Company lands. A combination of factors contributed to the final decision to end the rail line. The contributing factors included declining concentrations of timber that could be reached by railroads, improved technology of motor trucks, decreased timber demand, and a lack of available capital brought on by the Great Depression. Finally, the company founder, Theodore A. Schomburg, would pass shortly before the C&N Ry was fully abandoned.

While the CT&L performed well financially, the C&N Ry incurred steep financial losses during the years of operation on the South Poñil branch. The annual net losses fluctuated between $12,000 to just over $20,000. In 1923, the first full year of the South Poñil branch, the net loss was $23,546. The following year saw a net loss of only $12,313 but the loss increased in 1925 to $22,651. This pattern continued until the end with a $21,231 net loss in 1929 and a $9,093 deficit in 1930, the final year of operations. From 1923 to 1930, just seven years of railroad operations on the South Poñil incurred a total net loss on the C&N Ry books of $134,134. As the timber revenues dwindled, there was no economic motivation to extend the railroad any further. The Bonito expansion had proved that railroad extensions brought additional costs which could not be easily recovered, even with a stand of virgin timber to harvest and sell.

The areas immediately adjoining the South Poñil railroad line had already been cut over. The slopes around Baldy Mountain had been heavily cleared by the various mine claims in the area. Nearby Dean Canyon had already provided an estimated 9,577,000 feet of saw timber and had been a target of early CT&L logging efforts. Further south of Dean Canyon was the Cimarron Canyon where the CT&L was finishing up as well. To the north were the cut-over lands of Poñil Park, Ring, and Bonito. A large portion of the countryside to the north and west of Cimarron had been cut over. There were simply not many timber stands left which could support a logging railroad.[1]

Time and technology had also caught up with the C&N. The stock market crashed in October 1929 and the resulting start of what would become the Great Depression was taking hold across the nation. The depressed economy led to significantly decreased lumber demand. Furthermore, with the financial markets in disarray, the amount of available capital for railroad expansion disappeared. Few financiers were interested in spending large sums on a short-term logging railroad that had to navigate mountainsides to reach the last stands of remaining timber in a remote portion of the country. Finally, the advancement of motor trucks made it feasible and more profitable to log smaller, less-dense stands of timber in remote areas. Logging trucks needed only minimal roads to access timber, were more versatile and easier to maintain, and were significantly less expensive to purchase. Bulldozers and log trucks were positioned to fully replace livestock, wooden wagons, and the mighty iron horse.

Theodore Schomburg would not live to see the final abandonment of the Cimarron and Northwestern Railway. After two weeks of illness, Schomburg died on January 20, 1929, at a hospital in Berkeley, California. He was visiting one of his daughters during Christmas and passed with Thomas and his daughter, Mrs. J.K. Balantine, at his side. In each obituary, newspapers noted his upbringing in England, his rise from a bookkeeper for the Maxwell Land Grant Company, his successful business enterprises, and his various philanthropic efforts in Colorado and New Mexico. The 64-year-old was a noted member of the Denver Club, a former director of the First National Bank of

1 *Annual Report on the Statistics of Railways in the United States*, Interstate Commerce Commission; 1923, p 274; 1924, p 237; 1925; 1926, p 238; 1927, p 238; 1928, p 184; 1929, p 184; 1930, p 248.

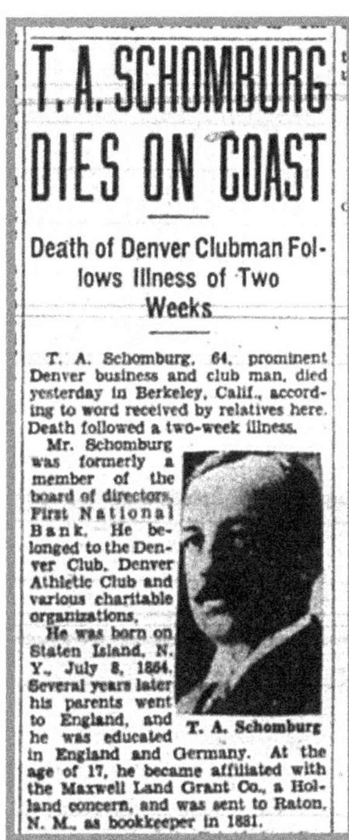

T. A. SCHOMBURG DIES ON COAST

Death of Denver Clubman Follows Illness of Two Weeks

T. A. Schomburg, 64, prominent Denver business and club man, died yesterday in Berkeley, Calif., according to word received by relatives here. Death followed a two-week illness.

Mr. Schomburg was formerly a member of the board of directors, First National Bank. He belonged to the Denver Club, Denver Athletic Club and various charitable organizations.

He was born on Staten Island, N. Y., July 8, 1864. Several years later his parents went to England, and he was educated in England and Germany. At the age of 17, he became affiliated with the Maxwell Land Grant Co., a Holland concern, and was sent to Raton, N. M., as bookkeeper in 1881.

T. A. Schomburg

Rocky Mountain News, 20 Jan. 1929, Denver Public Library.

Denver, President of the Trinchera Timber Company and the Continental Tie and Lumber, and Vice President of the Feather River Lumber Company in California. His wife, Lulu, had passed a year earlier. He was survived by his children and a sister who resided in England. Theodore and Lulu were buried at Fairmont Cemetery in Raton, the town where they met, and the town Theodore came to as a young seventeen-year-old from England. He had risen from those early years to be known by the time he met Guy Palmes as "the great builder of the West." From this point onward, his son Thomas W. Schomburg would take the reigns as president of the CT&L Co, doing everything from "bookkeeping to logging road engineering." Thomas would preside over the end of the C&N Ry and the final years of the CT&L Co.[2]

The end of the Cimarron and Northwestern began in 1929 and it was abandoned formally in 1930. When Henry Frankenburger applied for abandonment on June 3, 1930, trains were not regularly operating. Rather, only clean-up runs were being made to empty out the on-line lumber yards. In 1929 only 6,307 tons of freight were moved, of which 6,145 tons were timber products. That left only 162 tons of other merchandise and a paltry $32.40 in passenger revenue. The ICC commissioners noted that since 1923 the lumber industry had furnished 95% of the freight traffic. The final statement presented to the ICC in Finance Docket No. 8317 succinctly encapsulates the abandonment and its role in the region:

> No cities, towns, or village are located on the line except Cimarron, which has an estimated population of 600. The only residents within 10 miles of the line are the employees of one cattle ranch and grazing lands, which are not served by the railroad. The railroad is located in a mountain canyon and can not be reached by inhabitants

2 *Denver Post*, 20 Jan. 1929, Denver Public Library; *Rocky Mountain News*, 20 Jan. 1929, Denver Public Library; Schomburg, Thomas W. Interviewed by Lawrence Murphy at Denver, Colorado, June 9, 1964.

> of outside districts. With the exhaustion of the timber supply there are no industries remaining in the adjacent territory, except the one cattle range above referred to. It appears that the railroad has served the purpose for which it was built, and that no public convenience or necessity require its continued operation.

The Certificate of Public Convenience and Necessity allowing for abandonment was issued on August 12, 1930, and removal of the track began shortly thereafter. During the fall and winter of 1930, all remaining rails would be lifted and removed to Cimarron.[3]

The removal of the railroad was undertaken as the final operation of the Cimarron and Northwestern and was a process directly managed by Thomas Schomburg himself. The rails and other significant track material were likely collected by a crew working in tandem with C&N #1 and several flatcars. The salvage crew was mainly interested in the rails and ties, with a significant number of joint bars, spikes, bolts, nuts, and lock washers being left where they laid. Many of the ties and track hardware are still present on the former right-of-way today. If the trestle timbers could be repurposed for another use, they were taken up, yet most of the trestle works were simply left in place or used as part of a roadway that was built over the right-of-way grade.

Most of the rails were "sold to a firm in San Francisco [California] where it was shipped to Japan" in the period immediately following removal, according to Thomas Schomburg. More than likely, the metal was melted down and perhaps even used during World War II which would break out within a decade. The Cimarron and Northwestern Railway corporation was officially suspended on December 1, 1931. At that point, the C&N ceased to exist as an entity and any remaining assets of the C&N were transferred to the Continental Tie and Lumber Company. Thomas recalled, "the rolling stock didn't amount to anything" and was sold for scrap value. The locomotive, a small pile of rail, handcars, and other railroad equipment did remain in Cimarron until the end of the CT&L company.[4]

Almost all the lands logged by the C&N were now under the fence of Waite Phillips and his large Philmont Ranch. Many of the remaining employees referenced by the ICC commissioners would become ranch employees, such as Shorty Murray who tended cattle on the vast

---

3 *Decisions of the Interstate Commerce Commission of the United States of America*, Vol. 166, Finance Reports, June – December 1930, pp. 391-392.

4 Schomburg, Thomas W. Interviewed by Lawrence Murphy at Denver, Colorado, June 9, 1964.

ranch. Many of the old logging roads designed by Palmes continued to be used as ranch roads to access various portions of the region. Scouts hiking at Philmont continue to use the Wilson Mesa logging road as the main trail between Pueblano camp and Rich Cabins on the neighboring Vermejo Park Ranch. Some portions of the original C&N rails found their way into other uses and remain today as cattle gaps on an old logging road near Rich Cabins in Middle Poñil Canyon. This was the end of the line for the Cimarron and Northwestern Railway, a company that lasted just twenty-four adventurous years.

The Final Years of Timber Operations

The Continental Tie and Lumber Company continued logging for roughly eight more years after the abandonment and removal of the Cimarron and Northwestern Railway. The original timber contract between the CT&L and Maxwell Land Grant Company was still in effect, and closing the C&N Ry was just one step in keeping the CT&L in profitable operation. Logging, milling, and production would continue, but the final years of CT&L operations were markedly different from the first twenty-five years.

The Final Years of Logging

The contractual timber rights between the CT&L Co and MLG Co would undergo numerous extensions and updates. First, the original requirements of April 1, 1904, were formally acknowledged in 1910, recognizing that the CT&L had fulfilled its obligation to build a common carrier railroad to Poñil Park. Second, the contract would be updated in an agreement dated August 1, 1913, largely pertaining to an extension of the timber rights. When the contract ended in 1926, Theodore Schomburg requested and received a ten-year extension on the timber rights. By this point the Poñil Park line had been abandoned and the South Poñil branch was also nearing timber exhaustion, motivating Schomburg to prepare for the final iteration of timbering by the CT&L Co. A final contract extension was agreed upon ten years

Interior, Poñil Park sawmill during motor truck logging.
Raton Museum Collection, Raton, New Mexico.

later, on January 6, 1936, to cover the closing of the CT&L Co.[1]

The primary focus of the CT&L shifted to the southern portion of the Moreno Valley for the final years of logging. Three sawmills would be built and operated by the CT&L in the Moreno Valley as Thomas Schomburg continued to lead the company. The Cieneguilla Mill would be located near the base of Cieneguilla Mountain on the east side of the valley. Another CT&L company store, including a butcher shop, would be located at Cieneguilla as well. Two more mills would be established on the western side of the valley, the Apache Mill near the base of Apache Mountain, as well as Mill No. 3 which had probably been relocated from Bonito to be the third sawmill on the western Moreno Valley slopes. Its exact location is undetermined at the time of this writing. The primary logging activity was along American Creek on the east side and in the vicinity of Palo Flechado Pass on the west side, which led to Taos. Thomas would note how the pattern of land

1 1926 and 1936 extension: Pearson, pp 243-244, 267-268; Contractual fulfillment by CT&L: Agreement between the Maxwell Land Grant Company and the Continental Tie and Lumber Company dated May 20, 1910, File Folder 22, T.A. Schomburg Collection; Maxwell Land Grant Company records: Contract between Maxwell Land Grant Company and T.A. Schomburg dated April 1, 1904; Agreement between Maxwell Land Grant Company and the Continental Tie and Lumber Company dated August 1, 1913; Contract between Maxwell Land Grant Company and the Continental Tie and Lumber Company dated January 6, 1936.

Logging by motor truck in the final years of operation.

Raton Museum Collection, Raton, New Mexico.

purchases dictated the location of the remaining timber in the Moreno Valley:

> To the west and north of Eagle Nest the timber was sold along with the land. The biggest stands of timber were on the south end, as earlier purchases of land in the area by settlers and ranchers did not include the timber rights. On the west side of the Moreno Valley, there was a lot of good timber, a good part of it spruce, but it was too high up and the cost of getting it out was too great, so the CT&L never operated there. On the south end, there was good amounts of ponderosa pine and red spruce. We could get it out at that time without having to build so many roads.

Building roads was the new logging method, as bulldozers and trucks were exclusively used to haul timber in the final CT&L years. The CT&L used two Caterpillar Diesel tractors, a Diesel 40 with a Le Tourneau angledozer, and a RD4 tractor with power winch and cable. The tractor with the angledozer, commonly known as a bulldozer, would be used to carve out logging roads and the tractor with the winch and cable could be used for a variety of purposes, from hauling logs across terrain that motor trucks could not reach, to bringing in road building materials and removing stubborn boulders and debris

New way of cutting timber using a tractor with large circular saw and push bar.

New Mexico State University Library, Archives and Special Collections.

from roadways.

The Moreno Valley operations were similar to the early years of the CT&L and the C&N, albeit with trucks instead of livestock-powered wagons. The three Moreno Valley mills would produce rough cut lumber and trucks would haul it back to Cimarron for final processing in the planer mill and seasoning in the yard. Ute Park continued to operate as a tie yard and company store location for the CT&L as all ties from the Moreno Valley were gathered at this location. The ties would then be trans-shipped over the Rocky Mountain and Santa Fe to either Cimarron or other points on the AT&SF Ry system.[2]

The CT&L continued to operate the mill in Cimarron with some modifications in the final years. Thomas observed that, "two or three smaller sawmills in Cimarron were picking up odd tracts of timber we couldn't reach while the company was growing, by using trucks, which were getting better as they could haul more." Indeed, improved technology aided the continuance of the local timber industry. The Rocky Mountain and Santa Fe Railroad continued to provide common carrier service to the CT&L Cimarron mill and other local industries.[3]

In 1932, the CT&L Cimarron tie-treating plant was sold to the Na-

2 Schomburg, Thomas W. Interviewed by Lawrence Murphy at Denver, Colorado, June 9, 1964; Continental Tie and Lumber Company Inventory, March 8, 1938; Box 8, File Folder 6, CT&L Co Files, Maxwell Land Grant Company Collection.

3 Schomburg, Thomas W. Interviewed by Lawrence Murphy at Denver, Colorado, June 9, 1964,

tional Lumber and Creosoting Company of Denver which relocated the plant to Denver. The National Lumber and Creosoting Company would eventually be merged into Koppers, the chemical and treated wood company. Koppers continued to operate the tie treatment plant in Denver even after the CT&L closed their own sawmill in 1938. At the time of the Murphy interview with Thomas Schomburg, this tie treating plant was still in operation.

Closure and Liquidation

The Continental Tie and Lumber Company came to an end in 1938, a full thirty years after the opening of the Cimarron and Northwestern Railway. Factors that contributed to the closure of the C&N Ry likewise contributed to the end of the CT&L Co. "Being in the timber business," Thomas would relate in 1964, "the costs were getting higher, the regulations were getting stiffer and stiffer, and timber getting further and further back." The depressed market for timber during the Great Depression reduced financial returns on what were already thinning margins for the CT&L.

A new contributing factor, a result of the growing "conservation movement" in that period, was the desire to leave remaining forests intact. Pearson writes that "although the Continental Tie and Lumber Company paid the Maxwell company an average of over $4,000 a year from 1930 to the end of 1935, the Amsterdam directors seriously considered keeping the remaining timber intact rather than allow further lumbering." In fact, when the existing timber contract between the CT&L and MLG Co was to expire April 1, 1936, the MLG Co considered terminating the contract. However, negotiations between Thomas W. Schomburg and Jan Van Houten resulted in an extension on January 6, 1936. Van Houten remarked in a letter in April 1936 to Thomas, "I did the best I could, but probably under existing circumstances, considering markets, finances and other matters, this conclusion is better for all parties concerned." The positive news of the extension was short lived and as hinted by Van Houten, the following year saw the CT&L standing at almost $30,000 in debt. Regarding the final days of the CT&L, Pearson remarked:

> After liquidating $7,7000 in debts that September [1937], it still owed about $20,000. Satisfying the creditors within a reasonable time seemed remote and no bank would lend the money. Two months later, the Maxwell company sold $2,500 in United States

C&N locomotive #1 in Cimarron yard on September 17, 1937.

Dennis Hogan Collection.

> Liberty Bonds deposited with the First National Bank as escrow, for the unpaid royalties since July [1937]. December 27, Schomburg was notified that because the November 25 royalty payment was in default for thirty days, the lease was being declared null and void.

The end had come for the Continental Tie and Lumber Company, and the Maxwell Land Grant Company closed the final chapter on large-scale lumbering on grant lands.[4]

The final liquidation of Continental Tie and Lumber Company assets took place in the spring of 1938, including the remaining railroad equipment of the Cimarron and Northwestern Railway. The March 8, 1938, inventory presents the clearest picture of CT&L operations during the 1930s. Insights gained from the inventory show that company housing was maintained in this period with "4 log shacks" at Ute Park, "10 houses – employees" at the Cieneguilla mill site, and "4 houses – employees" at the Apache mill site. The company stores at Cimarron and Cieneguilla had complete butcher shops with the Cimarron store even having a "Winter air display case," a chilled case used to display and store cuts of meat. Mill No. 3 had already been dismantled and the machinery was stored in the hay shed. Despite the heavy uses of diesel tractors and motor logging trucks, seven horses, wagons, saddles, and associated livestock equipment were maintained until the last day of the company. Unfortunately, the inventory also shows that one 1936 Ford pickup was to be repossessed by the Raton Motor Company. Finally, the railroad inventory still on hand was noted. This included

4 Pearson, pp 267-268; Letter, Jan Van Houten to Thomas W. Schomburg, 9 April 1935. Letters, January 1, 1933 to December 30, 1935, Maxwell Land Grant Company Collection.

239 sticks of 52-pound rail in thirty foot sticks, 38,000 angle bars (also known as joint bars or fishplates, used to join together two sticks of rail), 24,000 spikes and rail braces, fifteen low target switch posts, fifteen ground throws for switches, one derail (a large block used to prevent railcars from exceeding beyond a certain point), two push cars, one pile driver hammer, numerous track tools of jacks, wrenches, and finally, "1 60 ton Baldwin locomotive."[5]

Sally, C&N locomotive #1, did not immediately leave Cimarron after the C&N Ry was closed. Perhaps she was used as a yard switcher for the CT&L mill. The CT&L might have held onto the locomotive and the other rail equipment to either sell as a "starter kit" for another railroad operation or in case logging by rail was needed again. Unfortunately, the final fate of Sally is unknown. "The locomotive was sold," Thomas would later recall, "and I forget now where it did go. It was shipped some place I don't remember." In 1938 Sally was a forty-year-old outdated steam locomotive. She may have been used on another small yard or line, but she was likely sold for parts or scrap.

Before Sally was to depart Cimarron, Gretchen Sammis, the great-granddaughter of Manly and Theresa Chase, tried to save one item from the locomotive. She "did not have a wrench big enough to break the bolts loose that held the bell on the wonderful old locomotive." Born in 1925, Sammis was raised on the Chase Ranch and would be the last head of the ranch when she passed in 2012. She heard the bell and whistle of Sally each time the train rumbled near the Chase Ranch headquarters in Poñil Canyon. If the train kept a fixed schedule as its public timetables proclaimed, Sammis could know the exact time of day by the whistle of C&N No. 1. Unfortunately, thirteen-year-old Sammis was unable to save Sally's bell.

All Continental Tie and Lumber Company assets were liquidated in the spring and summer of 1938 to pay outstanding debts. The liquidation did allow the CT&L to pay the remaining balance of $5,142.25 owed to the Maxwell Land Grant Company. The entire Cimarron mill site still owned by the CT&L was sold, but various small sawmill enterprises continued to operate on the site. The tie treating plant was already sold and removed from the site in 1932. The Cimarron Lumber Company, on the western side of Cimarron, with R.E. Adams as the main stockholder and a prosperous timberman himself, continued log-

5 Continental Tie and Lumber Company Inventory, March 8, 1938, Box 8, File Folder 6, Maxwell Land Grant Company Collection.

ging in the Cimarron area.[6]

After the liquidation, the key characters of the various Cimarron Schomburg enterprises moved on. Thomas Schomburg returned to Denver in 1938. He worked in a retail lumber yard, then during World War II, worked for the Lumber Production Division of the War Production Board for Colorado, Wyoming, and New Mexico, to keep up lumber production. He noted that there was not much lumber production in Cimarron during WWII. After the war, Thomas was then involved with a pulp and paper mill that was cutting timber near Glenwood Springs, Colorado. Finally, he began doing "some sales work," then got into the real estate game. Thomas said that after a lengthy career as a timberman in Colorado and New Mexico, this was "about as far away from timber operations as you can get." His son graduated from Yale in chemical engineering, served in the Army during World War II, and lived in Tulsa, Oklahoma, with his two children at the time of Schomburg's interview with Lawrence Murphy in 1964. The other railroad employees likely began working for other railroads after the closure of the C&N in 1930. The final chapter of Henry Frankenburger, Ike Torrance, Alex McElroy, and other key business players in the CT&L are unfortunately unknown at the time of this writing.[7]

The end of the Continental Tie and Lumber Company in 1938 rang down the curtain for large-scale logging on the Maxwell Land Grant. Certainly, as predicted by early timber estimates and confirmed by Thomas Schomburg, the CT&L was very profitable through the years. "Over the years, the cost of getting lumber out just got too high," Thomas recounted years later. The CT&L "was a very close corporation," he continued, "with only 5 to 6 stockholders through the years."

By the late 1920s and 1930s, the Maxwell Land Grant Company began to focus on selling large tracts of its land and keeping the remaining timbered areas intact for eventual sale for recreation purposes. Earlier land sales to William Bartlett and Waite Phillips for recreational and ranching purposes paved the way for a 1949 sale of the 33,324-acre Cimarron Canyon tract to the New Mexico Game and Fish Department. W.J. Gourley also purchased large tracts of MLG Co lands in the late 1940s. Pasture lands were desired for large cattle operations, and high-country timber was prized for its natural beauty. These fac-

6 Bromley, pp 46; "Chase Ranch: History," Philmont Museums, Philmont Scout Ranch, Web; Pearson, pp 268.

7 Schomburg, Thomas W. Interviewed by Lawrence Murphy at Denver, Colorado, June 9, 1964.

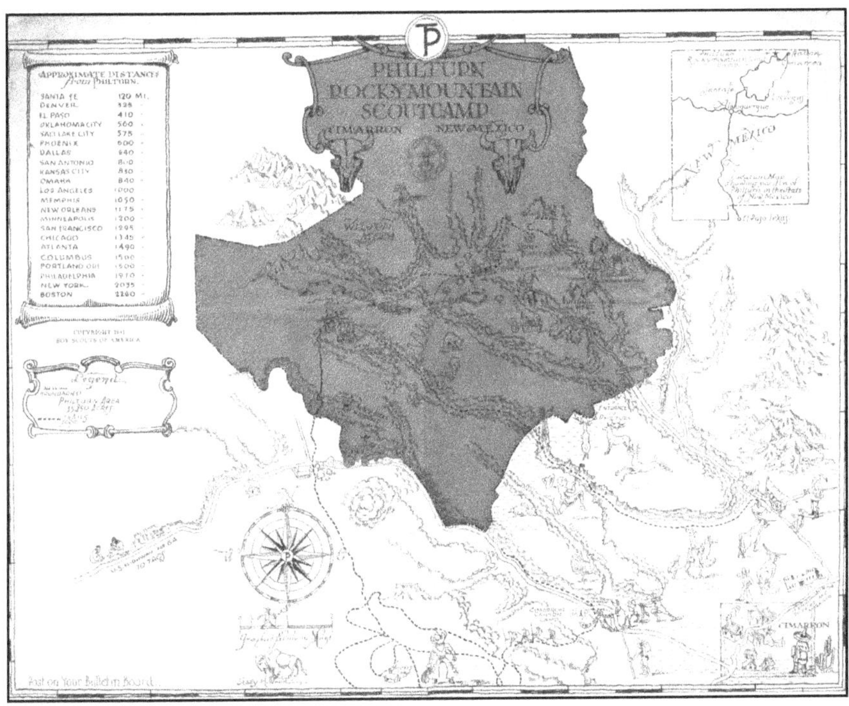

Map showing extent of Philturn Rocky Mountain Scout Camp.

National Scouting Museum Collection, Cimarron, New Mexico.

tors formally closed the door to large scale timbering by the mid-20th century. No longer would huge swaths of timber country be cleared by a small army of loggers working alongside a railroad.

Finally, as 1938 witnessed the close of the CT&L, the land encountered one more transition. Waite Phillips donated 36,000 acres in the Poñil area to the Boy Scouts of America which became Philturn Rocky Mountain Scout Camp, the predecessor of modern day Philmont Scout Ranch. "Philturn" came from Phillip's name and the Boy Scout slogan of doing a good turn daily. Most of Philturn would consist of the very first timberlands traversed by the C&N Ry, including the North Poñil Canyon with the former station stops of South Poñil and Metcalf, and the South Poñil Canyon with the later South Poñil railroad branch. Another donation of 138,000 acres from Phillips in 1941 would lead to the creation of Philmont Scout Ranch. Boy Scouts would be hiking and riding along the very canyons and mountainsides that had witnessed Schomburg's logging efforts only a few decades before.[8]

8 Pearson, 273, 276; Murphy, *Philmont: A History*, 207-208.

Daily Life Along the Line

A look at daily life along the Cimarron and Northwestern Railway during the twenty-two years of its operation yields insights into not only the toils and triumphs of the loggers and railroaders, but also into the culture of northern New Mexico in the early 20th century. People and their families lived, died, struggled, and succeeded during the course of C&N Ry history, and many of their stories provide a rich context for how lives were impacted by the CT&L and the C&N.

Many people enjoyed economic success as a result of the Schomburg enterprises in Cimarron. Communities throughout the region were built or changed with the coming of the iron horse to haul timber. Just as quickly as new communities grew along the railroad, many would dissolve as the timber was depleted. The Continental Tie and Lumber Company, by virtue of its company stores and issuance of company scrip, was intimately involved in the daily life of its employees and contractors.

The C&N Ry section crews encountered more than their fair share of surprises and incidents in their daily lives, from discovering a fatality while moving along the line in a handcar, to saving a man's life from drowning. Surprisingly, the period also witnessed growing concerns over the environmental impacts wrought by large scale timbering and its associated sawmills and railroads. Daily life alongside the Cimarron and Northwestern was rich, varied, difficult, dangerous, and adventurous.

The Commercial & Social Impact

The Continental Tie and Lumber Company and the Cimarron and Northwestern Railway represented the major economic engine to those who benefited from this success. With the major mill site and rail terminus in Cimarron, CT&L and C&N employees complemented the population in Cimarron which was already growing after the StLRM&P Ry shops were located there. Carpenters, sawmillers, millwrights, painters, mechanics, railroad crew members, office clerks, yard laborers, teamsters, wagon drivers, and many more trades and livelihoods would be needed by the timber and railroad companies. The town of Cimarron grew when a new section was platted by the Cimarron Townsite Company.

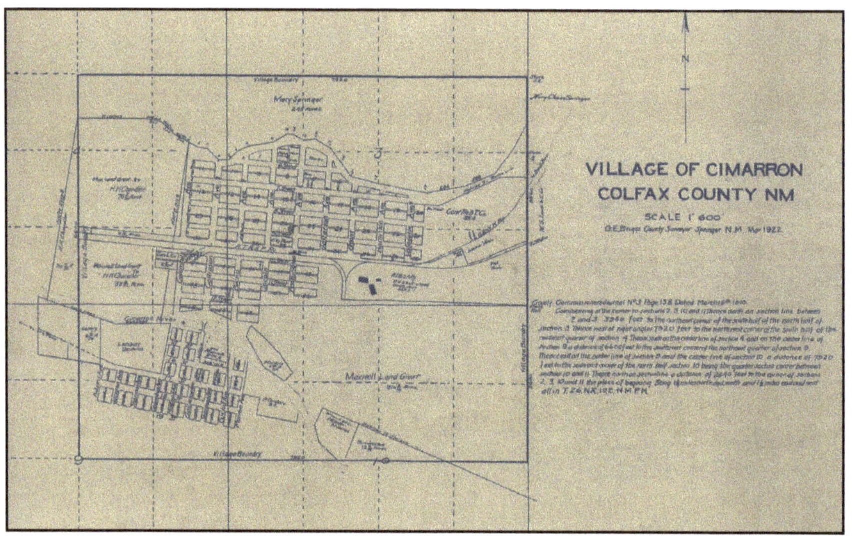

March 1922 plat map of Cimarron "New Town."

T. A. Schomburg Collection, MSS.747, History Colorado Center.

Outside of Cimarron, communities sprang up along the C&N Ry and existing communities grew as well. Dean Canyon was home to a backcountry sawmill with its associated loggers and sawmillers. Metcalf grew around the telephone office, Pratt's sawmill, and the logging of the nearby canyons. Poñil Park grew to include lumber yards, a US Post Office, a school, a small depot, and a grocery store. A similar community sprouted at Ring in 1910 when the railroad expanded. Ring, New Mexico, grew around the new Pratt-Wood sawmill, a CT&L company store, wagon makers and repairers, and corrals for livestock. Bonito, Wilson, and Pueblano all started as logging camps associated with the railroad and evidence of sawmill foundations and living quarters from these sites can still be found today.

The C&N Ry aided the development of these communities by providing an efficient means of transportation. Supplies, machinery, equipment, livestock, and people could be brought deep into the timbered backcountry. Residents of these communities could easily make regular business trips to Cimarron or Raton in a single day. Day trips over the C&N for fishing or hunting were quite common and Thomas Schomburg himself described such trips. Many oral histories recount that even the crew of the daily C&N train would partake in a quick hunt for turkey or deer, or a quick fishing break over their mid-day mealtime. Many people enjoyed the economic benefits and simple daily pleasures wrought by the C&N Ry.[1]

Stopping to hunt along the rail line.

Aztec Mill Museum Collection, Cimarron, New Mexico.

The Continental Tie and Lumber Company's influence in the communities through company stores and through technology was quite pervasive. In many industrial fields in the late 19th and early 20th centuries, issuing company scrip and providing company stores was quite common. Sawmills, logging companies, mining companies, railroads, and even canal and turnpike companies issued company scrip and operated company stores. As was true throughout the lumber and mining industries in the United States, the lands worked by the CT&L and the C&N were in remote areas without any major infrastructure,

1 Murphy, *Philmont: A History*, 173.

Continental Tie and Lumber Company scrip No. 3077 valued at one dollar.

National Scouting Museum Collection, Cimarron, New Mexico.

including roads, bridges, churches, schools, stores, streets, towns, utilities, banks, or other institutions important to daily living. The CT&L had to deploy and manage its people in proximity to the resources they sought, so they needed to provide sufficient infrastructure to facilitate these remote operations.

Company stores in Cimarron, Ute Park, Cieneguilla, and Ring, along with the issuance of Continental Tie and Lumber Company scrip, provided a source of needed supplies for workers in remote areas, and it facilitated monetary exchange where there was a dearth of both physical money and nearby banks. Examples of CT&L company scrip survive today, decorated with ornate depictions of logging operations. Unique serial numbers were printed on each scrip, along with disclaimers saying "not to be used as money" and a note that it could be redeemed at any company store of the CT&L.

The 1938 CT&L liquidation inventory shows that the company stores, also referred to as "commissaries," functioned as general stores, with the inventory listing livestock feed, butcher counters with refrigerated display cases, and produce weighing instruments at each store. It was common practice to stock everything from foodstuffs to chairs, tables, home furnishings, sewing supplies, cloth, fabric, tools, hardware, shoes, soap and so on. The company stores even had their own masking tape that read "The Continental Tie and Lumber Co. – General Merchandise – Cimarron N.M." The CT&L sought to stock all the daily necessities of life in a convenient mercantile located near their workers.

The CT&L valued their company scrip to be competitive with other

On payday horses and wagons line the street in Cimarron.

Aztec Mill Museum Collection, Cimarron, New Mexico.

companies competing for labor in the area. The scrip could also function as a sort of interest-free loan, as scrip could be redeemed for goods before payday. But come payday, all workers could redeem their scrip for cash or get paid in cash directly. When that day came, it was time for a family trip to Cimarron. Zenas and Margaret Ward of Cimarron provided a glimpse into this time: "The company had commissaries for the workmen but many began driving to Cimarron to trade. Payday would see the wagons coming to town. The women and children sat on the floor of the wagon beds while the men occupied the seat."

The single wire company telephone at Metcalf used by Theodore Schomburg, A.G. Allen, and Frankenburger to communicate with construction and grading crews in 1907 played a key role in social life. Cowboys, loggers, and other laborers in North Poñil Canyon could pay to use the telephone to arrange weekend dates with Cimarron ladies. Zenas Ward, a cowboy at the XA Ranch north of Metcalf, used the telephone to court his future wife, Margaret. Apparently true love is only a timber company single wire telephone call away! In these remote areas the CT&L became more than just an employer, but was also a mercantile operation and a connection to the outside world for the loggers, cowboys, and laborers of the New Mexico high country.[2]

2 General history of scrip: Fugera, William, "A History of Scrip," June 2005, Aztec Mill Museum; For a detailed breakdown on timber company stores, see Barnett and Lueck, "Sawmill Towns: Work, Community Life, and Industrial Development in the Pineywoods of Louisiana and the New South." Gen. Tech. Rep. SRS-257; CT&L Co scrip No. 3077 issued Feb. 1, 1909, National Scouting Museum; CT&L Co masking tape, National Scouting Museum; Ward, Margaret, *Cimarron Saga*, 71.

This social event in Ute Park was typical of frequent community gatherings at many points along the area's railroad lines.

Aztec Mill Museum Collection, Cimarron, New Mexico.

While hunting and fishing were enjoyed by local residents in the high country, the railroad also served to facilitate recreation and gatherings throughout the region. Cimarron Methodist preacher Rev. J. Alfred Morgan announced in the local paper in 1908 that religious meetings would be held at Pratt's sawmill in Metcalf Canyon near Metcalf twice a month to minister to the surrounding logging camps and communities. The same paper announcing these religious services also saw Metcalf residents and mill workers preparing for grand Independence Day festivities:

> WILL HOLD CELEBRATION – June 28 Big Day at Pratt's Mill – Ball Game, Horse Races – Log Loading Contest
>
> Sunday, June 28, promises to be a big day at the Pratt mill in Metcalf canon. The mill has been the scene of a great many large days, but if the plans now under way are carried forward to completion, the 28th will eclipse them all in magnitude and in real live fun. The boys at the mill are planning for a sort of Fourth of July celebration – ball games, horse races, foot races, wrestling, shooting, jumping, and last but not least, they will have a big log loading contest that will be an eye opener to some one. The boys at the mill never do things by half, and they are in this celebration to make it go clear up to the hilt. Big purses have been offered and if any of the local athletes think they know anything about athletics, they will have a chance to show what they are made [of. The] events will be pulled off without fear or favor. His excellency, Le Marshal von Harris, will be master of ceremonies and speaker pro tem and all the tem.

Typical Sunday picnic along the rail line with men and women dressed in Sunday finery.

Raton Museum Collection, Raton, New Mexico.

> In the afternoon a big ball game will be played between the Mill Crew Sluggers and the Woods Crew Knockers, and judging from the amount of money that has already been bet on the result of the game, the spectators will see a red hot contest at every stage. Taking it all in all, Sunday, the 28th, will be a red letter and red eye day.
>
> Next Thursday there'll be preaching at the mill.

Metcalf and the nearby mill were certainly a scene of activity in the opening days of the C&N Ry. A few years later in 1911, the C&N was involved in another holiday event, this time with a special train excursion:

> Picnic at Poñil Park - The C. & N. will run an excursion train to Poñil Park, Tuesday, Decoration Day. The train will leave here at 7:30 am, returning at 6:00 pm. Fare for round trip will be $1.00, children under ten years of age, half fare. The ladies of the Methodist church will furnish lunch and refreshments on the train and picnic grounds. This will be a good opportunity to spend the day in a pleasant manner.

Decoration Day was the original name for Memorial Day, as the graves of military veterans would be decorated in recognition of their service. At a small Poñil Park cemetery, Decoration Day was both a patriotic and recreational holiday with the C&N Ry facilitating round-trip transportation from Cimarron. It is possible, but unconfirmed as of this writing, that the C&N rented passenger coaches or cabooses from the St. Louis, Rocky Mountain, and Pacific Railway to provide

Women walking on the tracks between stacks of CT&L mine props and crossties.

New Mexico State University Library, Archives and Special Collections.

a full passenger train consist for this trip instead of trying to make do with their only passenger conveyance, C&N caboose #2. These are just a few examples of the railroad's impact on the daily life along the line.[3]

The People Along the Line

The C&N Ry was fully operational during only one US census, but the census of 1910 captures the extent of the population working on the railway, the timber company, and related enterprises. The 1920 census would see the C&N scaling back, with declining train movements, and by 1930 the line had run its course and was ending operations altogether. Fortunately, the 1910 census affords numerous inferences regarding the people and their daily lives. On May 11, 1910, Isaac P. Littrell enumerated the Thirteenth Census of the United States for Poñil Precinct 26, Colfax County, New Mexico, which included the northern region of the CT&L and C&N operating area.

Casines Hernandez ran his own barbershop. Parfirio Algin, Cardinas Romero, Rudolph Trajea, and Jose Archuleta were laborers in a nearby sawmill. Frank Siaz, Margarito Romero, Pedro Maiz, Antonio Gonzales, and Francisco Giagas were tie choppers. Manual C. Chavez from Texas was listed as a "tie contractor." The Rich brothers, Joe, Lou-

3 Preaching at Pratt's Mill and upcoming Fourth of July competition: *The Cimarron Citizen.* (Cimarron, N.M.), 17 June 1908; Decoration Day train excursion: *The Cimarron News and Cimarron Citizen.* (Cimarron, Colfax County, N.M.), 27 May 1911.

Christmas Day at Ring, New Mexico, 1911.

Aztec Mill Museum Collection, Cimarron, New Mexico.

is, John, and Dave of Austria, were listed as ranchers on their own ranch in Middle Poñil Canyon. A fellow Austrian and his family, Joe Wirrtz, was also working on the Rich Ranch. Clara Brook from Missouri was a schoolteacher in a nearby public school. John Troy, age 51, from Pennsylvania was a section foreman for the Cimarron and Northwestern Railway. The section crew included eight other crew members: Rafael Labatto, 41, Jose Agular, 18, Pedro Leyba, 45, Juan Lara, 19, Jose Ledesma, 20, Stike Santacruz, 18, Manual Trada, 25, and Catrino Santacruz, 15. Abran and Fred Arreno were listed as teamsters, wagon drivers of livestock.

While these are only a handful of the people enumerated on this census sheet, they provide a wealth of information. Most of the names listed were Spanish speakers born in New Mexico. Only a handful were from other states and listed English as their language, while the Rich and Wirrtz families spoke German. About half of the names listed were heads of households, so their families were included since many families were living in the area. The other half were boarders and young male laborers working for the railroad or in logging. Several persons had recently come to the United States. Five members of the C&N section crew immigrated to the US in 1910, the same year as the combined C&N and CT&L railroad expansion to Bonito. The Rich family immigrated in 1892 while the Wirrtz family showed 1900 as their year

Loggers with a horse team and a loaded log wagon stuck in the mud.

Aztec Mill Museum Collection, Cimarron, New Mexico.

of arrival.[4]

This single census sheet shows a milieu of people, cultures, and languages in the C&N Ry area and this was no accident. The CT&L was active in recruiting laborers, regardless of background, for its timber operations. In fact, multiple advertisements in Spanish were run in newspapers at Taos and Santa Fe in 1919 and 1921. The Spanish-language newspapers *La Voz del Pueblo* and *La Revista de Taos* carried advertisements with more details on logging life. The advertisement in *La Voz del Pueblo* of Santa Fe in 1919 read: "SE NECESITAN TIROS – para jalar madera – se paga $5.00 el mil de pies – se jalará a diez millas de distancia. Diríjase a la máquina de acerrar, 25 millas al Noroeste de Cimarrón, N.M." The CT&L was willing to pay $5.00 per thousand board feet of timber cut and pulled about ten miles to the backcountry sawmill.

The need for laborers must have been great because the CT&L operation was a considerable distance northeast of Santa Fe. The advertisement in *La Revista de Taos* in 1921 read: "QUEREMOS – Cortadores de propes y tallas. Pagamos por cortar propes ásperos un peso por cien pies lineal. Diríjanse a Continental Tie & Lumber Co, Cimarrón, N.M., M. Baurecesley, Gerente." This ad demonstrates the need for

4 Department of Commerce and Labor, Bureau of the Census. Thirteenth Census of the United States: 1910 – Population. Poñil Precinct 26, Colfax County, New Mexico. The entries were handwritten into the census ledger by Littrell and the authors have attempted to accurately reproduce the name spellings. However, the possibility that Littrell misspelled names cannot be ruled out. The authors welcome any potential corrections on the names.

Family cabins in Poñil Canyon.

New Mexico State University Library, Archives and Special Collections.

mine prop cutters who would be paid a dollar per 100 board feet.[5]

The 1910 census record and local newspaper accounts paint a vivid picture of daily life for the section crews of the Cimarron and Northwestern Railway. Each crew inspected and maintained their assigned section of track. Normally consisting of a section foreman and five to seven crew members, each crew would have a handcar to ride daily over the track to inspect ties, joint bars connecting two rails, tightness of nuts and bolts on the joint bars, rail flange wear, loose spikes, washouts, rocks, or any other railroad maintenance item. In the early 20th century, section crews were assigned twenty to thirty miles of track, depending on the terrain, carrying their hand tools of spike mauls, lining bars, claw bars, shovels, track wrenches, spikes, nuts, bolts, lock washers, joint bars, and other items on their handcar.

In mountainous country, such as on the Cimarron and Northwestern, section crews generally maintained a smaller portion of track, such as ten to fifteen miles, as washouts, steep terrain, lack of accessibility or visibility, rock slides, and the like made maintenance by hand tools much more difficult. The C&N probably employed two full section crews to maintain all the railroad trackage under C&N and CT&L control, given the length of the C&N Ry at twenty-two miles in mountainous country, later extended to thirty-five miles, the 1938 CT&L inventory listing two handcars, and two confirmed names of

5 *La Voz del Pueblo*. (Santa Fe, Nuevo México), 26 April 1919; *La Revista de Taos*. (Taos, Nuevo México), 14 Jan. 1921.

A maintenance of way crew loading rocks onto two C&N flatcars at the Poñil Park wye. Stacks of mine props and crossties can be seen in the background along with a boxcar spotted on the tail of wye. A handcar push trailer loaded with the workers' lunch pails is also on flatcar No. 101.

New Mexico State University Library, Archives and Special Collections.

section crew foremen working at the same time. John Troy oversaw one crew in the Poñil Park vicinity and Edward Troutman was the section foreman for the other.

Both crews maintained their tools and handcar at a small section crew shed and these were likely located at Poñil Park, Metcalf, or Cimarron. Poñil Park and Metcalf have some evidence for section crew dwellings, since Poñil Park served as the northern terminus and provided easy access to the Bonito extension in later years. Edward Troutman is noted in the local press as coming down from Metcalf to join his family for Christmas, suggesting that Troutman's section crew was based at Metcalf, site of the company telephone and the approximate halfway point on the original twenty-two miles of track.

Newspaper accounts describe how a C&N crew discovered the dead body of Samuel Metcalf, age 50, and a sawmill worker at Pratt's Metcalf mill in 1909. Reports in the *Albuquerque Morning Journal* mentioned murder as a possible reason for Metcalf's death, but subsequent articles told how he suffered from epilepsy, likely suffering an epileptic fit while riding his horse to Cimarron, and then freezing in the wintery conditions. Just two years later in 1911 the C&N section crews prevented another man from suffering a similar fate:

Rains dislodged a large boulder in Poñil Canyon at Stern Ranch near the confluence of the Poñil and South Poñil Canyons.

Palace of the Governors Photo Archives (NMHM/DCA), Neg. No. 001657.

> G.W. Manning who went to the saw mill last Friday, was reported drowned in the Poñil Monday afternoon. He drove into the creek about four miles above the Chase ranch, his horse went into quicksand and upset the buggy. With the aid of the section men on the C. & N. he managed to save his horse and buggy. When he returned to town Thursday afternoon some of the boys having heard that he was drowned wanted to know when he was resurrected.

Maintaining track and experiencing the environment's hostile conditions were all part of the daily life of C&N Ry section crews.[6]

The activities around Metcalf provide a typical microcosm of life during the heyday of the C&N. During the construction phase, camps of graders, contractors, track workers, team drivers, engineers, and surveyors would have moved through or camped at Metcalf. Chief engineer A.G. Allen was a frequent visitor, and many members of the engineering party used the company phone to communicate with Allen and Frankenburger in Cimarron. Once the railroad was in operation, Bert Pratt arrived in Metcalf to build his sawmill site and arrange for railcar

6 Section crew information: Bromley, 54; E.A. Troutman in Cimarron for Christmas: *The Cimarron News and Cimarron Citizen.* (Cimarron, Colfax County, N.M.), 31 Dec. 1914; Samuel Metcalf frozen to death: *Santa Fe New Mexican,* (Santa Fe, N.M.). 20 Dec. 1909; Journal Publishing Company. "*Albuquerque Morning Journal,* 12-19-1909." (1909).

shipments of construction materials and machinery over the C&N. Theodore Schomburg himself passed through while looking after timber and railroad business. Thomas Schomburg and Big Ike rode the daily C&N train through Metcalf to Poñil Park on their storied fishing trip.

Log cabin interior, "Mr. Chapman's bachelor quarters" at Poñil Park.

Raton Museum Collection, Raton, New Mexico.

Daily denizens of Metcalf could have included a telephone operator, as the telephone was likely housed in a small company office at Metcalf. Loggers, sawmill laborers, teamsters, tie cutters, mine prop crews, and their families all would have lived in and around Metcalf in cabins or shacks of culled lumber. As related by Zenas Ward, cowboys from nearby ranches frequented Metcalf to use the telephone or perhaps to ride the train into Cimarron. A corral for livestock was likely part of the Metcalf infrastructure. Edward Troutman and the section crew he oversaw could have had their handcar storage shed and tools at Metcalf. The people of Metcalf were working around a new railroad and their world, however big or small, was typical of the Cimarron and Northwestern Railway story.

Environmental Impacts

The environmental impacts of local industry were noticed early in the history of the Cimarron and Northwestern Railway and the Continental Tie and Lumber Company. Alongside a front-page article about a new sawmill for the CT&L Co, *The Cimarron Citizen* ran a story about potential harm to the fine fishing in area streams.

> TO PROTECT GAME FISH – Authorities Endeavor to Stop Throwing Trash in Water
>
> The Cimarron river and the Poñil river were at one time as clear and pure as any stream in the country, but owing to the fact that placer mining has been carried on the upper Cimarron, [...] the Cimarron

river is now a muddy and unsuitable stream for trout and other game fish.

Sawmills along the Poñil were also singled out: "On the Poñil those running saw mills have allowed their saw dust, etc. to either fall in the river itself, or to be placed where it pollutes the stream, and no fish are to be found in the Poñil either." These strong words advocating for local game wardens to enforce the law protecting game fish were written, surprisingly, in June 1908.

Indeed, as both mining and timbering continued in Colfax County and the lands surrounding Cimarron, the depletion of natural resources was part and parcel of this progress. When the C&N Ry ceased operations in 1930, the thick timber stands that afforded a home for deer, turkey, and bear were gone. Gone also were the days of C&N train crews stopping to hunt or fish on their lunch breaks. Many photos of C&N trains show large virgin timber logs stacked high on flatcars, leaving only deformed, diseased, or undesirable trees to repopulate the forest. The clear-cutting method did not leave a healthy stock of trees for proper regeneration of timber once the CT&L had finished all its cutting in 1938.[7]

At the same time these negative environmental impacts were becoming apparent early in the history of large-scale logging by railroad, there was a growing effort by timbermen to implement better forestry practices and a desire to leave the land in a timbered state for recreation. The ICC correctly noted that Theodore Schomburg's goals did not include any interest in the cut-over lands logged by the CT&L and the C&N Ry. However, his son Thomas became very much interested and engaged in using good timber practices during his lengthy forestry career. Thomas spoke at length on the forestry practices of the CT&L in his interview with Lawrence Murphy, and his corpus of forestry documents comprise a significant portion of the T.A. Schomburg Collection at the History Colorado Center.

First, Thomas related that there was no burning or clearing of brush left from logging by the CT&L. Brush, which included treetops, tree limbs, bark, and woody biomass remaining after logging, was left where it was and "that was better for the country for preventing erosion." He mentioned that in several Colorado projects, landowners and existing regulations required the collection and burning of brush, and Thomas

7 *The Cimarron Citizen.* (Cimarron, N.M.), 03 June 1908.

says this left the soil denuded in the areas where it was burned which contributed to erosion problems. Thomas further remarked that natural regeneration of the forests the CT&L cut was aided by the fact that the land was primarily cattle country, "as sheep eat everything down, including small trees. Cattle don't do that." At the time of the interview in 1964, Thomas remarked he still had many contacts with the US Forest Service, likely related to cutting on Forest Service lands and current timber and logging regulations of the day.

Second, Thomas' contributions to the T.A. Schomburg Collection includes dozens of documents related to his forestry career and forestry practices of the period. This includes lumber grading booklets with one containing a small table on railroad shipping rates from Cimarron, aerial photographs of timber on the Maxwell Land Grant Company land and Vermejo Park Ranch, and a timber cruise completed by T.W. Schomburg Forest Products in 1955. Within the lifetime of the C&N, the negative environmental impacts of large-scale logging and the development of good forestry practices occurred simultaneously while the railroad continued chugging along.[8]

8 Schomburg, Thomas W. Interviewed by Lawrence Murphy at Denver, Colorado, June 9, 1964; T.A. Schomburg Collection, File Folders 114, 117, 185; Maxwell Land Grant Company Records, MSS 147, Box 13, Folder 18, Tom Schomburg timber cruise, 1955.

Comparison to Peer Operations

Cut-over timberlands grew quietly across the nation once large-scale logging came to an end with the conclusion of World War II. The days of operations such as the Cimarron and Northwestern Railway and the Continental Tie and Lumber Company were no more. Fortunately, the passage of time and the collection of primary historical documents afford a unique opportunity for comparisons among peer operations in the southwestern United States. This brief survey will show how the Cimarron enterprises were both typical of their period and unique in their operations. This chapter provides a high-level examination of the C&N Ry and the CT&L compared to logging in and around Catskill, New Mexico, the Feather River Lumber Company of Plumas, California, and the Pagosa Lumber Company of Dulce, New Mexico.

Catskill Comparison

The logging and railroading conducted and operated by the C&N and the CT&L was vastly different from the operation in and around Catskill, New Mexico, primarily because many lessons were learned from the twelve-year logging period in Catskill. First, the Maxwell Land Grant Company would not directly finance the construction of a railroad into a timbered area and then let timber contracts to independent sawmillers. Second, no longer would the MLG Co select a townsite and work to develop it. Both factors directly resulted in the initial timber rights contract of 1904 between the MLG Co and Theodore Schomburg. Schomburg gained control over the timber rights for the entire New Mexico portion of the grant and could directly control the sequence and location of logging. In exchange for this right, the burden was on Schomburg to build his own common carrier railroad to an existing community. All the risk of sawmilling, logging logistics, and operating a common carrier railroad would fall to Schomburg and his enterprises, not to the MLG Co.

Third, the C&N operated in concert with the CT&L due to the managerial overlap and close connection of the enterprises. The MLG Co would not act as the intermediary between railroads, sawmillers, and townspeople as they had done in Catskill with the Union Pacific, Denver, and Gulf Railway and then later with the Colorado and Southern Railway. The CT&L decided where timber was going to be cut and that is where the C&N Ry went. When the timber in one section was cut over, the C&N and CT&L trackage was extended and then later pulled up and re-laid in a new timber section. All of this was spearheaded by the timber company, not the MLG Co.

Fourth, the CT&L matured and evolved over the three decades of its operation. The Cimarron mill site was rebuilt after a fire, expanded with a high-tech tie treating plant, and finally continued logging without rails using bulldozers and trucks. The passage of time allowed for technological innovation and adaptation to keep logging moving, unlike the brief period of livestock and wagon-focused lumbering around Catskill.

Fifth, no related industry, such charcoal or coke ovens, developed alongside the C&N Ry. A.C. Drake's brick beehive-shaped charcoal ovens near Catskill, which relied on leftover treetops, can still be seen to this day, but the remains of the CT&L backcountry sawmills are almost invisible in the present-day landscape. Schomburg's efforts to attract an outside coal mining outfit never materialized and timber products consistently dominated C&N Ry railcar traffic. The lessons and experience from Catskill are discernible in the differences in how logging was conducted by the CT&L Co.

Despite the lessons learned from Catskill, some similarities did exist in Schomburg's Cimarron enterprises. First, the initial logging period lasted approximately twelve years in both cases. Major logging around Catskill ran from 1890 to 1902 and the initial phase of CT&L logging along the C&N Ry ran from 1908 to 1920. Second, when the lands were cut over, only a handful of persons continued to live in the area. All the timber camps and communities would die out as people followed the timber or moved on to other opportunities. Catskill, Poñil Park, Ring, Bonito, Wilson, and Pueblano would all end together as former communities known only as names on a map with the fallen remains of old cabins and shacks. Third, the land gave way to large cattle ranches after timbering came to an end. Most CT&L cut-over lands reverted to the MLG Co or were purchased by Waite Phillips. The transition from logging to cattle grazing would be seamless in both Catskill and the region logged by the Continental Tie and Lumber Company.

Schomburg's Other Timber Interests

Perhaps the closest comparison to the Continental Tie and Lumber Company and the Cimarron and Northwestern Railway were in other timber companies in which Theodore Schomburg had a controlling interest. This included the Feather River Lumber Company and the Pagosa Lumber Company. The Pagosa Lumber Company itself bears a compelling and fascinating history much like the CT&L and the C&N Ry. Alexander T. Sullenburger owned and operated the original Pagosa Lumber Company with three sawmills and a network of narrow-gauge logging railroads in and around Pagosa Springs, Colorado, from 1900 to 1916. On August 6, 1916, the final whistle of the Pagosa Lumber

Pagosa Lumber Company log train south of Dulce, New Mexico, c.1920.

T.A. Schomburg Collection, MSS 747, F.35.507. History Colorado Center.

Company's mill signaled the first phase had come to an end.

The company was then purchased by Theodore Schomburg and another veteran lumberman, Edgar H. Biggs. Biggs had owned and operated the New Mexico Lumber Company with a major mill at Edith, Colorado, just over thirty miles south of Pagosa Springs. The new phase of the Pagosa Lumber Company started with Schomburg as President and Biggs as Vice President and General Manager. Their first action was to move the old mill from Pagosa Springs to Dulce, New Mexico, roughly fifty miles to the south, directly in the heart of the Jicarilla Apache Reservation. Incorporation documents estimated that ninety million board feet of timber was available on company owned land with a potential for access to another seventeen million board feet. Pagosa Lumber Company letterhead would proclaim "Lumber, lathe, and moldings" as the principal finished products. The main mill at Dulce was fed by a logging railroad that reached an area known as Mills Lake at its terminus. Outbound common carrier service was provided by the Denver and Rio Grande Railroad. Pagosa Lumber Company operations ended in 1930 with the timber at hand exhausted and the Great Depression sweeping the nation.[1]

The Pagosa Lumber Company presents numerous comparisons to Schomburg's Cimarron lumbering efforts. The main differences are that the logging railroad extending from the mill at Dulce was operated as a narrow-gauge private industry track under the name of the Pagosa Lumber Company, not as a common carrier like the standard-gauge Cimarron and Northwestern Railway. However, both railroads served a large, centrally located mill and brought raw logs in for processing. Both companies operated tie treating plants, utilized steam-driven mills powered by burning scrap wood and sawdust, elevated the mills for loading out finished products, utilized log ponds from 1920 onward, and built housing for workers and managers.

In both railroad operations, locomotives were purchased second-hand. Pagosa Lumber Company No. 70, a 4-6-0 locomotive purchased from the Denver and Rio Grande Railroad, was much like Cimarron and Northwestern No. 1 as it retained an oil headlight and simple furnishings. Again like C&N No. 1, Pagosa Lumber Company No. 70 pulled primarily flatcars loaded with raw logs. Based upon the oil

---

1 *The Pagosa Springs Sun*, (Pagosa Springs, Colo.), 9 Feb. 2017, "Pagosa Lumbers into the 20th Century," by John Motter; Myrick, *New Mexico's Railroads*, 207-209; Incorporation of the Pagosa Lumber Company, 1920, File Folder 115, T.A. Schomburg Collection; Letter, Walter R. Sheldon to T.A. Schomburg, April 15, 1920, File Folder 107, T.A. Schomburg Collection.

Pagosa Lumber Company mill south of Dulce, New Mexico, c.1920.

T.A. Schomburg Collection, MSS 747, F.26.934. History Colorado Center.

headlights never being converted to electric headlights in either rail operation, Schomburg did not appear to heavily invest in the finer trappings of locomotive technology available during the period. Pleasure outings were supported by both companies with the C&N Ry hosting an excursion to Poñil Park on Decoration Day and the Pagosa Lumber Company hosting a company picnic in an idyllic stand of towering virgin timber. Finally, both logging railroad enterprises terminated by 1930.[2]

The Feather River Lumber Company of Plumas County, California, would have a longer life span than its contemporary timber enterprises, and it too has a dynamic and interesting history. Numerous companies operated under the name of the "Feather River Lumber Company" in northern California, but the one under examination here was incorporated in Colorado on December 23, 1904, and principally backed by Theodore Schomburg, William H. Deleker, and George Laws. Deleker had also partnered with Schomburg as a backer of the Continental Tie and Lumber Company and was involved in logging around Catskill. Laws would be the point man in California, and the company got underway by purchasing established sawmills near Portola, California, in 1905. Mill No. 1, the former Totten Mill near Clairville, was pur-

2 Photo, Neg. No. F26.934, Pagosa Lumber Company sawmill, T.A. Schomburg Collection, PH.605; Photo, Neg. No. F35.507, Pagosa Lumber Company log train, T.A. Schomburg Collection, PH.605; Pagosa Lumber Company picnic photos, File Folder 178, T.A. Schomburg Collection.

chased along with 2,400 acres of timberland. Mill No. 2 was located at what would become the town of Deleker, named for the principal backer, and was J.W. Webster's former Humbug Valley Mill. A third mill was located south of Clio and all three mills were serviced by the Sierra Valleys Railway.

A 1905 prospectus sought additional backers and funding, but the major support came from the Western Pacific Railroad building through the Middle Fork Feather River Canyon. A 1907 contract with the Western Pacific Railroad for seven thousand crossties spurred the company to the success it had anticipated. Logging railroad operations began in 1914 to serve Mill No. 2 at Deleker with two narrow-gauge Shay locomotives from Argentine Central Railway in Colorado. The Feather River Company would operate until the end of 1946 when a letter to all shareholders announced that cutting was complete, final dividend payments were forthcoming, and the company would close.[3]

Schomburg's other timber operations had much in common with the Continental Tie and Lumber Company. The operational goals and practices were similar, due to the common vision and experience of the incorporators.

3 Myrick, David F. *Railroads of Nevada and Eastern California: Volume 3*: More on the Northern Roads, 241-250; Letter, Feather River Lumber Company to all shareholders, received by Thomas W. Schomburg, November 29, 1946, File Folder 109, T.A. Schomburg Collection

The Quiet Years

While the Cimarron and Northwestern did not operate after 1930, the history of the railroad continued to be uncovered, interpreted, and kept alive through many decades of serendipitous discoveries, purposeful actions, and historical connections to the abandoned railroad. People from all backgrounds and walks of life interacted with the history and the remains of the C&N. The land had grown quieter in some respects, as the sounds of axes and steam locomotives had given way to smaller logging operations, cattle ranching, and recreational land supporting hikers, campers, sportsmen, and naturalists throughout the area.

After the closure and liquidation of the Continental Tie and Lumber Company in 1938, the Rocky Mountain and Santa Fe Railroad continued operations from Raton to Cimarron and Ute Park. However, the former interchange partner and outbound carrier for the C&N was experiencing its own tough times. In 1936 the RM&SF lost the US Postal Service contract as the postal service began delivering mail to rural stations via truck. The 1938 closure of the CT&L mill was a significant loss of carload traffic for the RM&SF, and the train schedule for the Raton-Ute Park route was modified from a daily mixed train to a three-days-per-week schedule of Tuesday-Thursday-Saturday. The remaining shippers in Ute Park and Cimarron would not see RM&SF service last much longer as that section of the line continued to perform poorly financially.

The low traffic volumes resulted in decreased maintenance and the RM&SF trackage significantly deteriorated. The track was originally rated for forty-five miles per hour, but the deterioration led to significantly reduced speeds whenever trains were operated. Declining volumes and the onset of World War II hastened the end. Steel was needed for the war effort and not even active rails would be spared in the recycling effort. Abandonment of the RM&SF came at great protest from several sources in New Mexico. C.A. King, a manager at Philmont, wrote to New Mexico Governor John E. Miles in July 1942 to file a letter protesting the potential abandonment, since rail transportation was seen as critical for getting Scouts and supplies to and from the remote Philmont Scout Ranch. Governor Miles agreed with King's assessment and agreed that the RM&SF should not be abandoned. However, the protests went unheeded as abandonment from Koehler Junction to Ute Park was granted by the ICC on December 8, 1942, and the rails were taken up by the end of the same year. Rail service in Cimarron lasted only 36 years from 1906 to 1942.[1]

Interestingly, one of the last customers that shipped over the RM&SF would get up close and personal with the terrain along the old C&N line. They would be carrying shovels, picks, trowels, and sifters, outfitted with a chuckwagon and cowboy cook, and exploring and digging all over North Poñil Canyon. They were not railroaders, nor modern ferroequineologists. They were, in fact, archaeologists. As recounted in *Let the Coyotes Howl: A Story of Philmont Scout Ranch*, Samuel Bogan and what would be called the "Philmont Archaeological Expedition," were one of the final shippers on the RM&SF and one of the early Boy Scout groups to gain firsthand experience with the remains of the C&N.

Bogan was an archaeologist at Yale University, and his goal was to explore Philmont in the summer of 1941 and conduct archaeological studies in North Poñil Canyon, focused on the indigenous peoples who had lived there. Their supplies were shipped from New Haven, Connecticut, all the way to the RM&SF depot in Cimarron. The Saturday train did not have their shipment as initially planned, so they anxiously received the delivery the following Tuesday. By the end of the next year, 1942, rail service was gone from Cimarron. Archaeological tools were some of the last goods unloaded from boxcars at the depot in Cimarron. After receiving their supplies and beginning their trek, Bogan noted in his account the obvious features of the C&N, in-

---

1 Bromley, 91-95, 100; "St. Louis, Rocky Mountain, and Pacific Train," Charlie McCandless; Letter, New Mexico Governor John E. Miles to C.A. King, July 7, 1942, National Scouting Museum

Scouts in the area explored by the Philmont Archaeological Expedition.
National Scouting Museum Collection, Cimarron, New Mexico.

cluding the raised rail bed and numerous crossties remaining in North Poñil Canyon, especially in the area surrounding what would become modern-day Indian Writings camp. This occurred only two decades after the C&N abandoned its trackage to Poñil Park, so it is possible that the remaining trestle timbers and other right-of-way features were still clearly discernible. Succeeding years would see generations of Boy Scouts plying the same canyons as Bogan and his archaeological team as they too enjoyed the land all across Philmont Scout Ranch.[2]

Two decades later and a few miles further north, a certain Robert E. Mahn, Jr. revived the history of the C&N through his program at Old Camp. A true lover of railroads and railroad history, "Big Bob Mahn" as he was known, would be the Philmont camp director at Old Camp in 1962, just one of his many positions in a storied seasonal staff career at Philmont. Old Camp was located at the site of Metcalf. How the name transitioned from "Metcalf" to "Old Camp" is unclear, but perhaps it was a reference to "the old logging camp" that once resided there.

Old Camp was one of the many backcountry camps staffed by Philmont during the summer as participants hiked from camp to camp

2 Bogan, 18, 62.

on extended backpacking treks. While the official program for Philmont participants at Old Camp centered on geology in North Poñil Canyon, Mahn and his staff shared the history of the C&N through artifacts and stories that summer. In fact, an unused cookshack was converted into a small railroad museum featuring recovered railroad artifacts, and Mahn provided entertaining discourses on railroading in the area. While an unofficial program, Mahn's efforts earned him recognition among his peers for starting Philmont's first railroad program.

Mahn would go on to a career in the National Park Service, but his time on the Philmont staff kept the memory of the C&N alive and planted the seed for interpreting the history of local railroading to future generations of visitors. Like one of the many railroad trestles that spanned North Poñil Creek, Mahn bridged the gap between the period of actual railroading and the time of reincarnating the railroad for historical interpretation and learning.[3]

Two decades later and a few miles to the north of Old Camp, the land that was once traversed by the C&N would again change hands. Land belonging to Waite Phillips to the north of what became Philmont would transition to other private ranch owners and even further north, W.J. Gourley's WS and Vermejo ranches, including the sites of Poñil Park, Ring, and Bonito, would come under new ownership.

The Phillips land not included in Philmont would become the Kimberlin Poñil Ranch after the purchase by the Kimberlin family. The Kimberlin Poñil Ranch continues as an operating cattle ranch with cattle herds grazing along the old C&N rail bed that winds its way through North Poñil Canyon. Gourley, on the other hand, would sell his land to Pennzoil Co. in 1973. Pennzoil managed the 500,000-acre tract as a hunting park, similar to William Bartlett's land several decades earlier. In 1982, 100,000 acres of this hunting park were donated by Pennzoil to the federal government which formed the Valle Vidal Unit of the Carson National Forest. The remaining acreage of Pennzoil's land was sold to media mogul Ted Turner in 1996 to become part of his growing Vermejo Park Ranch. Although that portion did not contain any of the C&N right-of-way, the northern extent of the C&N would now be preserved as public forest land.[4]

3 "Big Bob Mahn and Philmont's Railroading Program," *High Country*, Vol. 42, No. 6, Philmont Staff Association, December 2019.

4 Dunn, Scott. "Bountiful Valley," *Albuquerque Journal.* 2 Nov. 2000.

By the time Ted Turner was building up his Vermejo Park Ranch, lumbering in Colfax County had come to the end of its second phase. The first phase was the large-scale logging wrought by the likes of the Continental Tie and Lumber Company and the Cimarron and Northwestern Railway clear-cutting large timber stands. The second phase consisted of smaller lumber enterprises working on smaller parcels of timber using bulldozers to carve logging roads, livestock to skid the timber to the roads, and logging trucks to bring the raw logs to a mill site or a sawmill in Cimarron or Springer. The CT&L sawmill and yard were sold to the Capital Land and Timber Company who operated a smaller sawmill footprint. They renovated the old two-story CT&L-C&N office building, removing the second story and constructing a conventional wood-framed roof.

The CT&L tie treating plant had already been sold and relocated in 1932 to the National Creosoting and Lumber Company in Denver, so only the mill and lumber yard remained at the east Cimarron site. As recounted by Thomas Schomburg, lumber production in Cimarron was not great during World War II and would never again reach that of the days of Schomburg's timber enterprise. The Cimarron Lumber Company mill in west Cimarron, located at Highway 64 and Columbus Avenue, the present-day site of baseball fields, would end operations sometime after World War II. However, remote lumber camps continued during the postwar era. Heck Canyon, near White Peak southwest of Rayado, witnessed significant logging from the 1920s to 1941 with Robert E. Adams operating a sawmill there. Heck even featured a post office from 1927 to 1941, a school, and a company commissary run by Adams. Families moved away to other logging endeavors when the timber was "cut out" in 1941.

Cimarron Lumber Company on the west side of Cimarron.

New Mexico State University Library, Archives and Special Collections.

CT&L lumber yard in Cimarron, late 1930s; Slate Hill in background.

Raton Museum Collection, Raton, New Mexico.

Roy Cartwright operated a mill in Cimarron where the present-day Cimarron High School now stands. Cartwright also operated numerous logging camps near La Grulla Ridge and Moras Creek south of Rayado Peak in the 1940s. Willie Vernon Carter and his family conducted logging near Harlan, Black Lake, and Heck Canyon in the 1940s as well. The Gray Lumber Company of Ute Park, while only operating for a few years from 1946 to 1948, logged MLG Co lands north of US Highway 64 around Touch-Me-Not Mountain and on the Atmore Ranch along Ute Creek. Roy Gray, a former CT&L worker, when he purchased the existing sawmill at Ute Park, contracted with the Douglas-Guardian Warehouse Corporation of New Orleans, Louisiana, to build and run a lumber warehouse in conjunction with the Gray Lumber Company sawmill.

Clyde Martin would come to Cimarron from Oklahoma and after first logging in Tolby Canyon south of Eagle Nest Dam, would purchase the former Cartwright mill site in Cimarron. Martin's Interstate Lumber Company would operate in Cimarron from 1956 until 1978. Doyle Holbird was the force behind the Capital Land and Timber Company which operated at the former CT&L site. After the local school district used eminent domain to demolish the Interstate Lumber Company site at Collison Ave and 9th Street to build a new school, and a fire took the Capital mill in 1970, Martin moved his mill site to the Capital mill site at the former Continental Tie and Lumber Company location. In 1978, Martin sold the mill site and his lumber

Operator near a trim saw, with scrap being fed by conveyor into the sawdust burning teepee, which still stands today in Cimarron.
Raton Museum Collection, Raton, New Mexico.

company to Bud Davis and the Pacific Stud Lumber Company who continued to operate a lumber mill there into the late 20th century.[5]

At the time of Turner's purchase of Vermejo Park Ranch, Pacific Stud Lumber Company was doing business as Tricon Timber at the CT&L site and was the only remaining mill operating in Cimarron in the 1990s. However, in 2001 the sawdust pile at Tricon Timber caught fire and the resulting fire destroyed the mill operations. The fire claimed several bulldozers and the smoke even forced families to evacuate the area nearby. Only sawdust, an old burn teepee, and few tattered buildings were left at the mill site to sit forlornly as the second phase of Colfax County lumbering ended abruptly. For almost two decades the former CT&L mill site sat idle. With the end of the second phase of logging around Cimarron, the timberlands in the region continued to flourish and accumulate fuel for potential wildfires. Many timberland owners watched helplessly as the Poñil Complex Fire in 2002 and the Ute Park Fire in 2018 burned thousands of acres of timberland primarily on Philmont and public recreational land.

However, it is possible that a third phase of Colfax County lumbering may be underway. In December 2019, with a $350,000 invest-

5 Schomburg, Thomas W. Interviewed by Lawrence Murphy at Denver, Colorado, June 9, 1964; Contract of Lease between Gray Lumber Company and Douglas-Guardian Warehouse Corporation, July 20, 1946, Maxwell Land Grant Company Records, MSS 147; Capital Land and Timber Company mill site and renovation of former CT&L-C&N office building: New Mexico State University Library, Archives and Special Collections, Alpers Collection; Second phase of Colfax County lumbering: Serna, Louis F., *A History of Cimarron, The Sawmills Camps Nearby, and the People Who Worked Them*, April 2020.

ment from the New Mexico State Economic Development Department, northern California timber company Lance Forest Products announced plans to relocate their sawmill in Redding, California, to the former CT&L sawmill site in Cimarron. An expressly stated goal of this effort to relocate a sawmill to Cimarron was to reduce the risk of major wildfires on recreational land and to improve forest health by providing a market outlet for the region's timber. Owners John and Art Lance noted that the Cimarron location would provide studs for the housing markets in Colorado, Oklahoma, New Mexico, and Texas. The global COVID-19 pandemic interrupted the planned 2020 relocation of the sawmill. As of this writing, the sawmill site in Cimarron awaits its fate in the next chapter of lumbering, but perhaps soon the site that witnessed the Continental Tie and Lumber Company providing lumber products throughout the Southwest will bear a sawmill serving the same region once again.[6]

6 "Fire Burns Sawmill in Cimarron, Smoke Forces Dozens of Families to Evacuate," KAOT Action News, April 15, 2001; Kirkland, Jacqlyn, "New Mexico Gains New Sawmill Venture," *Timber Harvester and Forest Operations*, December 13, 2019; Krasnow, Bruce, "NMEDD Awards $350,000 LEDA Grant to Resurrect Cimarron Sawmill," KRTN Radio, Raton, NM, December 11, 2019.

Canyon Walls Ring Again

A new chapter of the Cimarron and Northwestern Railway started in much the same way as the original founding of the railway over a hundred years prior. Indeed, it would take a collection of individuals, teams, and a series of starts and stops, much like the original endeavor to reach Poñil Park by rail, to bring the C&N back to life in a vibrant and dynamic way previously unseen at Philmont or in the world of heritage railroading. Some background will help in understanding what was needed to make a railroad for Boy Scouts. This is the story of modern-day Metcalf Station.

The idea of building a railroad at Philmont involved a long journey that began at the high adventure base's inception. Waite Phillip's stated goal for his donations to the Boy Scouts of America was to benefit youth through an outdoor experience in northeastern New Mexico. His intention was to provide Scouts an experience with the land, with its heritage, history, lore, and environment, that would prove tremendously beneficial to those who spent time there. Teaching and sharing the history of the American Southwest has been a component of the Philmont program from the beginning. In the first summer of operation in 1938, Scouts participated in gold panning, wildlife study, and viewing indigenous petroglyphs in North Poñil Canyon near the remaining C&N railbed, all while pulling burros on a twelve-day adventure, complete with a chuck wagon and cook.

In the late 1940s, the program expanded to include a 21-day Wagon Train Trek, eight- to fifteen-day backpacking trips, a seven-day horseback ride known as Cavalcade, a Ranch Pioneering Trek focused on

Scouts on an early Philmont trek with chuckwagon and cook.
National Scouting Museum Collection, Cimarron, New Mexico.

ranching and related vocations, a winter-focused "Operation 10" mountain adventure, and even a mountain lion hunt around Thanksgiving each year. In the early 1950s, the program was shifted to focus on shorter backpacking expeditions, with burros still available for packtrain use in the northern portion of the ranch. In Philmont's backcountry, camps are categorized as "trail camps" where only the visiting expeditions stay overnight, and "staff camps" where a team of seasonal staff members are stationed for the summer to provide a unique program to participants. Early programs varied from gold panning to Dutch Oven cooking, natural plant dyes, burro packing and care, rifle and shotgun shooting, and archaeology at Indian Writings Camp in North Poñil Canyon.[1]

In the early 1970s, a new approach for teaching history was implemented at some of Philmont's staffed camps. Historical interpretation was done through a method known as "living history." The backcountry staff interpreted a period of Southwest history, ranging from fur trapping in the 1830s, homesteading in the 1860s, life along the Santa Fe Trail in the mid-19th century, gold mining in the early 20th century, and of course logging. The staff would dress in interpretive clothing, referred to as "in kit" in the living history industry, and provide historical programs including fur trapping demonstrations, tomahawk throwing, black powder muzzleloading riflery, candle making, garden-

1 Murphy, *Philmont: A History*, 210, 215, 220-221, 224.

ing, animal care, spar pole climbing, gold mining in formerly active gold mines, panning for gold, crosstie making, fur trade rendezvous trading and bartering, fly fishing, wool spinning and weaving, axe and saw sharpening, historic cabin tours, adobe brick making, fence-mending, and a litany of chores or routine daily activities from periods in the nation's past.

The staff would fully immerse themselves in the specified time period, as if they were actually living during the camp's selected year in history. They would adopt a manner of speech and language appropriate to the context of their historical period. As nearly as possible they went about living in a remote work setting as people would have lived during that time. This included using woodburning stoves, kerosene lanterns, and in may places hauling food and supplies by burro. Metcalf Station would become the latest in this series of living history camps.

Getting this idea in motion would require an understanding of the fund-raising opportunities, the development of a team with a unified vision, and most importantly a burning desire to succeed. This description fit Theodore Schomburg in the early 20th century, but the same could be said for the Philmont professional staff and civilian volunteers that made Metcalf Station come to life in the early 21st century.

Seasonal staff in interpretive garb on the new track at Metcalf Station.

Philmont Scout Ranch, Cassidy Johnson.

The Metcalf Station story starts with John Van Dreese, an Associate Director of Program at Philmont and an individual with a long family history in railroading. It was a personal passion for Van Dreese, who had spent time with a railroad maintenance crew and whose father, grandfather, and great-grandfather worked for railroads. He was familiar with the C&N railbed in North Poñil Canyon as part of as introductory driving tour during his 2004 orientation on the Philmont professional staff. During this tour Van Dreese often caused Director of Program Mark Anderson to pump the brakes or turn around because he had spotted some artifact or recognized a historical railroad site. Van Dreese began researching the history of the Cimarron and Northwestern Railway, and he explored the potential for a railroading program at Philmont.

The next few years saw Van Dreese giving talks and slide presentations on local railroad history, prominently featuring the C&N Ry, to local civic clubs and historical groups in Colfax County. The original concept of the railroading program was to be a reconstruction of a portion of the C&N by a living history staff teaching Philmont participants how to lay railroad track with hand tools. They would interpret western railroad history using handcars, an historically accurate railroad depot, a blacksmith shop, and an evening campfire program featuring railroad history, songs, and lore. A partnership was formed with BNSF Railway in 2006, successor to the AT&SF Ry which operated the RM&SF in Cimarron, to provide initial supplies, funding, and most importantly, an accurate survey for track construction. Building a fresh railroad track on an abandoned railbed in a canyon beset with geographical challenges necessitated a professional engineering approach. Despite several attempts from 2006 to 2008, the survey was unable to be completed and for various reasons the spark died out and the project went dormant.[2]

In 2011 the Metcalf Station story received new life and continued down the road toward having spike hammers swinging again in the arid canyons of northern New Mexico. Philmont Associate Director of Program David O'Neill began program development and Sid Covington, a volunteer and seasonal Philmont staff member, began building a team of railroaders to assist with the physical design and implementation of a track construction program. In 2012 and 2013, through

2 Van Dreese, John. Phone Conversation with Tucker Baker, May 20, 2020; Van Dreese, John. "Railroading in the Poñil," Philmont Scout Ranch, slide presentation.

much discussion, planning, fundraising, and site visits to North Poñil Canyon, Metcalf Station's physical components were assembled.

Much like the incorporators of the C&N, each member of the Metcalf Station project team helped make the vision a reality. Bill Glavin secured the donation of rails from the Texas Pacifico Railroad, operator of the South Orient Railroad that runs between Brownwood and Presidio, Texas. Some of the donated rail even had a connection to the C&N with several 75-pound sticks rolled in 1914 in Pueblo, Colorado, at the Colorado Fuel & Iron Works, the same CF&I whose founder J.C. Osgood attempted and failed to reach Poñil Park by rail, thereby opening the way for Theodore Schomburg to build the C&N.

The rail was ordered by and delivered to the Kansas City, Mexico & Orient Railroad, later becoming the South Orient Railroad. Most of the donated rail was a 70-pound variety rolled in 1907 at the Carnegie steel mills in Pittsburgh, Pennsylvania. A few sticks of 85-pound rail from the Maryland Steel Company were also included in this initial donation. The Texas Department of Transportation purchased the South Orient Railroad in 2001 and later upgrades of the line replaced the 70-pound rail with modern, heavier 120-pound rail. To put the donated rail to use, Glavin, Mike Marler, and Darwin Desen compiled a Track Construction Assessment and a staff instruction guide

Herzog delivering railroad ties at the site of Metcalf Station.

Sid Covington Collection.

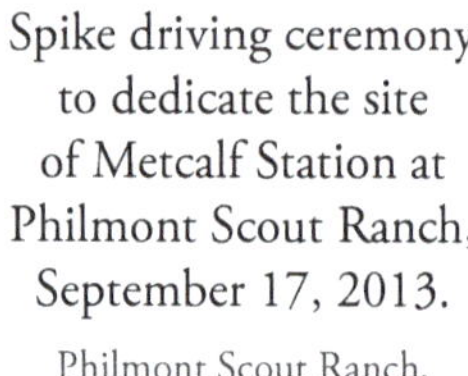

Spike driving ceremony to dedicate the site of Metcalf Station at Philmont Scout Ranch, September 17, 2013.

Philmont Scout Ranch, Cimarron, New Mexico.

to direct the efforts for the soon-to-be-built track. Lonnie Blaydes secured the donation of used crossties from the New Mexico Rail Runner and Herzog Transit Services, Inc. Herzog transported the crossties and McClatchy Brothers Trucking of Midland, Texas, brought the rail to Philmont from the South Orient Railroad siding at Miles, Texas.

The other track material, known as "OTM" or "jewelry," was delivered to Philmont from San Angelo, Texas, with a work crew led by Sid Covington. To announce the opening of Metcalf Station, a spike driving ceremony was held at the site of Metcalf on September 17, 2013. Only a short panel of track was spiked together, using two short sticks of rail, a few crossties, sledgehammers, and a handful of spikes. The enthusiasm and excitement on that day was palpable. Pictures were taken, invitation cards printed up as train tickets, and every spike was driven fully down into its respective crosstie for a track within the proper standard gauge. A seasonal backcountry staff was hired the following winter, and Metcalf Station was on track to commence a new chapter for the C&N.[3]

In the summer of 2014, the North Poñil Canyon walls started ringing again with the sound of spike mauls driving spikes into wooden

3 Covington, Sid. "The Making of Metcalf Station: 2008 – 2014." Philmont Scout Ranch, Boy Scouts of America, September 2014; Covington, Sid. "Metcalf Station," *TXDOT Internal Newsletter,* Feb. 2015; "New Backcountry Staff Camp on Track," *PhilNews* June 7, 2013, Issue 1

Philmont Scouts ballasting track near Metcalf Station.
Philmont Scout Ranch, Skyler Ballard.

crossties. The seasonal staff for that summer hailed from North Carolina, Iowa, Indiana, Arizona, Mississippi, and Louisiana. Hands-on track construction training was conducted with the seasonal staff under the tutelage of Bill Glavin and Mike Marler. To get an understanding of operating steam railroads, the staff spent an entire day at the Cumbres & Toltec Scenic Railroad in Chama, New Mexico, riding the daily train, discussing operations with the staff, and immersing themselves in the world of 19th and early 20th century railroading through first-hand experience. From there, the staff would teach and supervise Scouts on track construction as the new rail line grew each day.

The 2014 summer would see 1,592 participants at Metcalf Station, and many had their first experience with railroad engineering at the camp. The participants received a safety briefing, worked in proper personal protective equipment including hard hats, safety eyeglasses, gloves, and steel toe covers for their hiking boots, and spent hours in the hot New Mexico sun hearing the ringing of steel-on-steel. The original C&N track had been constructed by hand, using hand tools and manual labor. By following 1907 track construction standards, using the same type of hand tools and methods, the sounds echoing from the canyon walls and heard by the Boy Scouts were indeed the same as those heard by track laborers in 1907.

Crater Lake and Pueblano, Philmont's two living history logging camps that interpret the history of the Continental Tie and Lumber

Scouts learn basic blacksmithing in the shop at Metcalf Station.

Alex Moushey Collection.

Company, "tied" into the Metcalf program by producing hand-hewn crossties. As part of the program at those camps the Scouts learn how to cut crossties, and the finished ties were hauled to Metcalf Station for use in track construction.

The Metcalf blacksmith shop was constructed in the summer of 2014 and received one of the finest collections of blacksmithing tools in the area. A blacksmith from nearby Questa, New Mexico, Les Micheles, passed away shortly before the 2014 summer began. His sister, unsure of what to do with his extensive blacksmith shop, was in contact with a fellow blacksmith and Cimarron resident, Steve Rick. He arranged for the donation of much of Micheles' shop to Metcalf Station, and in July 2014 Micheles' anvil was again in active use, teaching thousands of Scouts the art of blacksmithing.

Rounding out the physical camp were two false-front structures with canvas walls, reminiscent of early railroad "boom town" tents. The Rail Office building included a station sign of "METCALF" and it was stocked as an office typical of early 20th century stations, including typewriters and telegraphs. The combined Post Office and general store building was not yet stocked, so it functioned as the staff cookshack that summer. Signs and banners for Old Dutch Maid Soap, Heinz

Two new false-front buildings at Metcalf Station camp.

Tucker Baker Collection.

Pickles, Carhartt Overalls, and bottled Coca-Cola adorned the door frame of the cookshack, a harbinger of the building's future use.

The seasonal staff on that inaugural summer compiled an evening campfire program for crews staying the night, complete with traditional railroad songs and stories of "John Henry" and "Casey Jones," but it also included adaptations of "Been All Around This World" to share the history of the C&N and Theodore Schomburg. Staff member Kyle Soyer wrote a new song, "Manly's Folly," to commemorate the relationship with Manly M. Chase, his famed Chase Ranch apple orchard, and the building of the C&N through the orchard on its way to Metcalf and Poñil Park.[4]

The following summers from 2015 to 2019 would see continuous improvement and expansion of the Metcalf Station program. Many of the seasonal staff would return to Metcalf summer-after-summer, which was unusual for Philmont staff rotations. However, Metcalf Station is a most unusual camp based on the unique nature of its program. The seasonal staff and professional Philmont staff would work together to develop safe operating procedures for the growing collection of roll-

4 Covington, "Making of Metcalf Station," 7; "Metcalf Station Camp Profile," Philmont Scout Ranch, 2019.

A work crew of Scouts lining track under the supervision of trained seasonal staff members.

Alex Moushey Collection.

ing stock at the camp, and these procedures were reviewed with each group before riding the rails. The rolling equipment roster included one gear-and-crankshaft driven traditional handcar, one chain-and-sprocket driven handcar, a railroad velocipede, a maintenance-of-way flatcar trailer, and a hand-cranked Fairmont bridge crane. Perhaps the track at Metcalf Station is the only track in existence completely constructed, maintained, and operated by Scouts, running on the same railbed over which the C&N originally operated.

As the program developed, the Philmont professional staff and the Metcalf seasonal staff continued to conduct historical research. Their efforts illuminated the world of the past for the staff to then share with participants visiting Metcalf. The 2015 staff began referring to the track under construction as the 'Pride and Glory' of the canyon, from the perspective of past laborers and workers who had lived along the C&N in North Poñil Canyon. Those rails represent the livelihood of hundreds of people, both in the past and in the present, and today's Scouts are now able to directly experience aspects of the lives of those who had gone before them during the last century.

In 2019, through the support of the BNSF Railway, a replica of a 1910 AT&SF railway depot was constructed at Metcalf Station facing

Left: Scouts constructing track under the direction of trained seasonal staff.

Philmont Scout Ranch, Dominic Baima.

Right: Track with flatcar, velocipede, and handcar. Baggage wagon at right.

Tucker Baker Collection.

the two existing false-front buildings. The depot was based on donated blueprints for a standard depot from the Santa Fe Railway Modeling & Historical Society. An architect at the BSA national office modified the plans to fit Philmont's needs, including an extension of the roof to create a large covered porch for crews, a replica ticket office and telegraphy office with a bay window, a room for the camp director, and modern kitchen facilities in what would have been the freight room. The depot was stocked with historic furnishings and fixtures, even down to the replica lanterns in the interior, which are powered by hidden solar panels on the back of roof. While no building of this kind ever existed at Metcalf, the new depot is an historically accurate rail office, and it was needed for proper camp operations and to enhance the interpretation of the region's rich railroad history.[5]

Just as the Cimarron and Northwestern Railway expanded over the course of its lifetime, so too will today's Metcalf Station. Plans call for an expanded blacksmith area to more accurately recreate a railroad repair shop, construction of large wooden trestles over North Poñil Creek to expand the new track

New depot at Metcalf Station.

David O'Neill Collection.

5 "Philmont Metcalf Station Project," the Santa Fe Railway Historical and Modeling Society, Web; "Living History: BNSF Helps Philmont Scout Ranch take Campers on an Unforgettable Adventure," *Rail Talk*, BNSF Railway, Web, August 12, 2020.

construction, relocation of a donated Colorado & Southern Railway standard gauge boxcar to the camp, and the acquisition of more boxcars and a caboose. A water tank is planned that will resemble a typical wooden tank, but it will have a modern plastic lining which will provide sanitary water storage for camp use.

The ultimate vision is to construct several miles of track over the original railbed and to build a telegraph and telephone system along the line. At each end, line shacks or converted boxcars or cabooses will house telegraph desks and a direct line telephone. Crews would help install poles and wire up and down the line, and as hikers arrive at each end, a staff member would teach them telegraphy and single-wire telephone operation. After using that technology to contact Metcalf Station, more staff members could arrive by handcar with a trailer. The hikers could then load their gear and "pump" their way to Metcalf. These experiences would directly connect participants to the history of railroad section crews, the power of communication by wire at Metcalf, and the great changes in transportation brought about by the coming of the railroad through North Poñil Canyon. As a result of this interpretive experience at Phlmont Scout Ranch, the Cimarron and Northwestern Railway will never completely die.

Conclusion

Railroads as remote and obscure as the Cimarron and Northwestern Railway largely fade from history once the line is abandoned and all those connected to the railroad pass on. Normally, ordinary logging railroads do not get a new lease on life, nor are the timbermen and railroaders memorialized through in-depth research and published works. However, the Cimarron and Northwestern Railway, and its parent company, the Continental Tie and Lumber Company, were no ordinary enterprises. They ushered in important changes with a deep impact on the rich history of northeastern New Mexico. In a place already having a vibrant history, full of colorful characters and events, the C&N Ry and the CT&L Co were among the most important in shaping and developing the area.

The railroad began as a method for meeting the contractual obligations of a new logging company using remote steam-powered mills. Yet these enterprises developed and matured into vertically integrated firms controlling timber rights, railroad transportation, manufacture of lumber, treatment of crossties, and purveyors of benefits and mercantile establishments for people throughout the region. Characters such as Theodore Schomburg, Henry Frankenburger, Alex McElroy, A.G. Allen, Edward & Mary Troutman, Frank & Charles Springer, and Gretchen Sammis have come and gone, but their legacy lives on. Their accomplishments are memorialized in local historical markers, museums, photographs, railbed remains, Philmont Scout Ranch programs, the Chase Ranch Foundation, as well as the living history site of

Metcalf Station. The land and the people, past, present, and future, will be remembered and celebrated by the 'Pride and Glory' of the Cimarron and Northwestern Railway through North Poñil Canyon.

Cimarron & Northwestern Railway resurrected at today's Metcalf Station. These Scouts are experiencing the thrill of powering themselves over railroad tracks that they helped to build with their own hands.

W. Garth Dowling, BSA File Photo.

Historical Timeline

1864 – Theodore A. Schomburg born at Staten Island, New York.

1875 – September: Parson Tolby murdered in Cimarron Canyon. Colfax County War commences in earnest.

– Deputy Sheriff William Metcalf is ambushed at confluence of North Poñil Canyon and what would be named Metcalf Canyon in his honor [unattested account].

1879 – AT&SF reaches New Mexico through Raton Pass after beating out the Denver & Rio Grande.

1881 – T.A. Schomburg works as office boy for Maxwell Land Grant Co in Cimarron after growing up in Germany and England (Father worked in London office of MLG Co).

1887 – April: US Supreme Court confirms Maxwell Land Grant title to over 2 million acres in New Mexico and Colorado in *United States v. Maxwell Land Grant Company*. Frank Springer was the lead attorney for the MLG Co and Schomburg helped him prepare the case.

1890 – Six orders for class 10-32-E locomotives (2-8-0s) are built for the Western New York and Pennsylvania Railway by Baldwin Locomotive Works in Philadelphia. Locomotive #10568 would become #165 on the WNY&P Ry roster.

– Catskill, New Mexico, founded when the Union Pacific, Denver, and Gulf Railroad builds 16 miles to headwaters of Canadian River and Maxwell Land Grant Co erects multiple sawmills there.

– J.C. Osgood and his Maxwell Timber Company operated out of Catskill.

1893 – Manly Chase awarded gold ribbon for his apples at the Chicago World's Fair.

1901 – March: J.C. Osgood gets timber contract on the Colorado portion of the Maxwell Land Grant.

– Osgood forms Rocky Mountain Timber Company with Theodore A. Schomburg and W.H. Deleker.

– Colorado and Southern [now parent company of the Fort Worth and Denver ("Denver Road") which took over the Union Pacific, Denver, and Gulf] unwilling to invest in maintaining the line to Catskill for limited timber remaining, so abandons line to Catskill.

1902 – January: Colorado and Southern removes rails from Catskill branch line. Trackage on the branch remains only on the Colorado side. Mills close and Catskill is abandoned.

– Osgood faces cash flow problem due to modernization of Colorado Fuel & Iron mill in Pueblo, brings in George Jay Gould who in turn brings in John D. Rockefeller. The latter would engineer a corporate takeover of Colorado Fuel & Iron and their related railroad interests (Colorado and Wyoming Railroad).

1904 – Osgood forced out of Colorado Fuel and Iron; Gould and Rockefeller interests now run CF&I.

– April: Schomburg secures timber rights on New Mexico portion of Maxwell Land Grant.

1905 – St. Louis, Rocky Mountain, and Pacific Company formed.

– October: Theodore Schomburg organizes Continental Tie and Lumber Company.

1906 – St. Louis, Rocky Mountain, and Pacific Railway reaches Cimarron.

1907 – January 21: T.A. Schomburg organizes Cimarron and Northwestern Railway.

– February: A.G. Allen is chief engineer and surveys route up Poñil and North Poñil Canyons.

– March 23: G.W. Whitescarver of Trinidad wins the initial grading contract.

– June 13: Company contractors begin laying track from Cimarron heading northwest.

– August: C&N Ry purchases what will become locomotive #1 "Sally" from the Southern Iron and Equipment Works in Atlanta.

– St. Louis Rocky Mountain &Pacific Ry reaches Ute Park.

1908 – January 6, 1908: C&N Ry now operational. Rough cut lumber, props, and tie are hauled to Cimarron and feed, hay, and other supplies brought in boxcars on the trip north.

– Chicago, Burlington, and Quincy Railroad buys Colorado and Southern Railroad.

1909 – Late March: Major fire breaks out at CT&L yard; burns planner mill, storage house, and lumber stacks; planer mill was built of metal beams, so it did not completely collapse.

1910 – Expansion to Bonito Canyon is planned and surveyed by Guy H. Palmes.

1911 – Continental Tie and Lumber Co extends railroad through Lowery Canyon (now Seally Canyon) and establishes another sawmill at Bonito in the Bonito Canyon (Mill #3). Ownership of track in name of CT&L Co and leased to C&N Ry.

– Sawmill established by Pratt and Wood at Ring (would later show on maps as "Ring Town").

1912 – January 6: New Mexico becomes 47th state in the Union.

1913 – CT&L Co begins work on tie treating plant in Cimarron.

– AT&SF purchases StLRM&P Ry; renames it Rocky Mountain and Santa Fe.

1914 – AT&SF relocates Cimarron shops to Raton (roundhouse, machine shop, car shop).

1915 – CT&L Co tie treating plant in Cimarron opens with 100,000 orders of treated ties already on the books.

– Manly Mortimer Chase dies.

1916 – October: Timber exhausted in Bonito area; five miles of track from Bonito to Ring pulled up. This was private industry track, so no formal abandonment application to ICC needed.

– March: MLG Co deeds land to Cimarron Valley Land Company for construction of the Eagle Nest Dam.

– October: Schomburg begins legal battle regarding dam construction.

– November: Schomburg and business partners form the New Mexico and Western Railway to obtain right of way through the dam site.

1917 – March: Schomburg has Frankenburger and the "NM&W Ry" begin clearing right of way at the dam site.

– May: Map of right of way and track by C&N engineer Guy Palmes is completed and counter-signed by General Manager H.G. Frankenburger. Map now resides in National Archives and Record Administration in Washington, DC.

1918 – Schomburg, MLG Co, and Cimarron Valley Land Company pay to have a double track railroad tunnel blasted above the Eagle Nest Dam site. By the time of completion, the feasibility of logging the Moreno Valley by rail is gone. The tunnel remains to this day on NM Dept of Game and Fish land.

1920 – Six miles of track from Ring to Poñil Park abandoned. Private CT&L Co trackage requires no ICC approval.

– CT&L Co builds sawmill on their site in Cimarron with 30,000 board feet/day capacity and a mill pond. CT&L now has a planer mill, tie treating plant, box factory, and sawmill in Cimarron.

1921 – Edward Troutman photographs Ring and Poñil Park sawmills; these sawmills are logged primarily by truck when the photos are taken.

1922 – Waite Phillips purchases 42,000 acres of George Webster's Urraca Ranch. According to the Murphy interview of Thomas W. Schomburg, Phillips owned the timber rights on some properties, but CT&L Co retained the timber rights on others.

1923 – H.G. Frankenburger petitions ICC to abandon 14 miles of track from Poñil Park to South Poñil (modern day 6-Mile Gate).

– Construction under direction of Guy Palmes builds railroad track under CT&L Co ownership up South Poñil to Stern, at base of Stern Mesa (now Wilson Mesa) where a wye and logging camp are built at nearby Pueblano (modern day Pueblano Ruins). Logging is now a combination of trucking to railhead at Stern and various rail sidings. Raw timber is hauled out to the mill at Cimarron.

– Phillips purchases another 30,000 acres of the Urraca Ranch.

1926 – Waite Phillips has over 300,000 acres in his Philmont Ranch with most acquisitions between 1923-1926 contiguous to the original Urraca Ranch.

1929 – January 20: Theodore A. Schomburg dies.

– June 3: Frankenburger requests ICC permission to abandon C &N trackage from South Poñil (6-Mile Gate) to Cimarron. Tracks under ownership of CT&L were already removed.

– October 31: ICC grants permission to abandon all remaining trackage of C&N Ry.

– Logging by CT&L Co is primarily by truck for all mills and operations. Primarily logging southern Moreno Valley.

1931 – December 1: C&N Ry corporation suspended.

1932 – CT&L Co tie treating plant in Cimarron sold to the National Lumber and Creosoting Company of Denver. (NLCC became part of the Koppers Company in later years.)

1937 – Thirty year contract between CT&L Co and MLG Co for timber rights expires.
– CT&L Co and all remaining assets, including C&N Ry, are liquidated to pay creditors.

1938 – Waite Phillips donates first gift to Boy Scouts of America. Philturn Rocky Mountain Scout Camp established.

1941 – Philmont Archaeological Expedition in North Poñil Canyon.
– Phillips gives second gift to BSA, Philmont Scout Ranch formed.

1942 – Rocky Mountain and Santa Fe Railway is abandoned and trackage taken up.

1962 – "Big Bob Mahn" was Camp Director at Old Camp, with railroading program featured during that summer. Staff collected C&N artifacts into a small museum.

1964 – June 9th: Lawrence Murphy interviews Thomas W. Schomburg at Schomburg's home in Denver. This interview would form the foundation for Murphy's writings on the C&N and the CT&L Co in the *New Mexico Railroader* newsletter and *Philmont: A History of New Mexico's Cimarron Country.*

2002 – Poñil Complex Fire devastates the second growth forest lands north of Highway 64 in Cimarron. The burn scar is almost exactly where the C&N and CT&L Co had operated.
– Tricon Timber mill in Cimarron, on the same site as the CT&L mill and yard, burns down in a sawdust fire. Koppers had ended the tie treating plant in prior years and only the stud mill of Tricon remained. For the first time since 1907, a timber mill was no longer operating at this site.

2006-2008 – Railroading program concept origination, design, promotion, and development by Philmont Associate Director of Program John Van Dreese.

2012 – August: Consultant team led by Sid Covington visits Philmont to assess creation and development of Metcalf Station.

2013 – January: Metcalf Station Project Report delivered to PSR. Funds are transferred from a prior-given Union Pacific Foundation grant to start Metcalf Station.
– September: Philmont announces opening of Metcalf Station with a spike driving ceremony.

2014 – First Metcalf Station staff hired and trained by Bill Glavin and Mike Marler for track construction and maintenance, blacksmithing by Steve Rick, and steam railroad operations at the Cumbres and Toltec Scenic Railroad in Chama, NM.

– Cookshack and rail office are built with false front style and canvas walls on three sides. Blacksmith shop is built and the donated Les Micheles blacksmith shop becomes the foundation of the Metcalf Station blacksmithing program. New well is completed for untreated water.

– August: Dodge handcar arrives at Metcalf Station. 934 ft of track laid.

2015 – Second year of Metcalf Station operations. Safe operating procedures, track construction & maintenance manual, and troubleshooting guide are written by Tucker Baker and Matthew Hauser covering handcar, flat car, derrick (crane) car, velocipede, and track construction operations. Derrick car arrives at Metcalf Station. 634 feet of track are added.

– June 27 – Poñil Complex Flood wreaks havoc at Metcalf.

– Trevor Lombardi sketches what will become the modern-day Cimarron and Northwestern Railway logo featuring a Zia and an arrow to the northwest. No prior logos or heralds are known as of this writing.

2016 – Velocipede and a second handcar (chain driven) arrive at Metcalf Station.

2017 – Treated water system begins operation at Metcalf Station. Walls are added to cookshack and rail office. Sliding doors are added to blacksmith shop. Boxcar is acquired and stationed at 6-Mile Gate.

2018 – Ute Park Fire devastates Philmont and surrounding lands; summer program is cancelled. Under direction of Camp Director Trevor Lombardi, track panels on steepest grade of hill at Metcalf Station are removed and grading commences to lessen ruling grade on the track.

2019 – August: Track at Metcalf Station reconnected now at a lower ruling grade.

– December: Lance Forest Products plans to relocate a sawmill to Cimarron from Redding, California, on the former site of the CT&L Co mill with NM state economic development funds.

2020 – Metcalf Station depot constructed in style of a 1910 AT&SF depot.

Selected Bibliography

Articles

Alpers, Audrey. "The Continental Tie and Lumber Company and the Cimarron and Northwestern Railway." Cimarron Historical Society, June 5, 1994. Arthur Johnson Memorial Library, Raton, New Mexico.

Covington, Sid. "Metcalf Station." Texas Department of Transportation Internal Newsletter. February 2015. Copy provided to the authors, May 2020.

Gunnerson, James A. "Chase Orchard: A Poñil Phase Pueblo in the Cimarron District, Northeastern New Mexico with a Suggested Reconstruction of Tanoan Origins and Migrations." Memoir 11 of the Oklahoma Anthropological Society. Robert E. Bell Monographs in Anthropology 4 of the Sam Noble Oklahoma Museum of Natural History. 2007.

Lamm, Gene, and the Cimarron Historical Society. "A Brief History of the Village of Cimarron." Cimarron Chamber of Commerce. 2008.

Laurie, Karen P. "History of Vermejo Park, New Mexico." New Mexico Geological Society 27th Annual Fall Field Conference Guidebook, pp 87-92, 1976. New Mexico Geological Society.

Murphy, Lawrence. *New Mexico Railroader*. Arthur Johnson Memorial Library, Raton, NM.
—— Volume 6, No. 11. "The Cimarron and Northwestern: Historic Railroad of Northern New Mexico, Part I." November 1964.
—— Volume 6, No. 12. "The Cimarron and Northwestern: Historic Railroad of Northern New Mexico, Part II." December 1964.
—— Volume 7, No. 1. "The Cimarron and Northwestern: Historic Railroad of Northern New Mexico, Part III." January 1965.

Philmont Staff Association. "Big Bob Mahn and Philmont's Railroading Program," *High Country*, Vol. 42, No. 6. Cimarron, New Mexico. December 2019.

Books

Albi, Charles, and Willian C. Jones. *Otto Perry: Master Railroad Photographer.* Chicago: Johnson Publishing Company, 1982.

Alumni Association of the Colorado School of Mines. *The Colorado School of Mines Magazine.* Vol. 3, No. 12, December 1913. Accessed via Google Books.

Bogan, Samuel D. *Let the Coyotes Howl: A Story of Philmont Scout Ranch.* New York: G.P. Putnam's Sons, 1946.

Bromley, Ronald E. *The Last Train to Leave Cimarron, New Mexico: Why the Trains Left Cimarron.* Bloomington: Author House, 2013.

Caffey, David L. *Frank Springer and New Mexico: From the Colfax County War to the Emergency of Modern Santa Fe.* College Station: Texas A&M University Press, 2007.

Graybeal, Johnny. *Along the ET&WNC Volume II: The Ten Wheelers.* Hickory, North Carolina: Tarheel Press LLC, 2001.

Keleher, William A. *Maxwell Land Grant.* Santa Fe: Sunstone Press, 2008.

MacDonald, Randall M., Gene Lamm, and Sara E. MacDonald. *Cimarron and Philmont.* Mount Pleasant: Arcadia Publishing, Images of America series, 2012.

Moody's Manual of Railroads and Corporation Securities. United States: Moody Manual Company, 1915. Accessed via Google Books.

Murphy, Lawrence. *Out in God's Country: A History of Colfax County, New Mexico.* Springer, New Mexico: Springer Publishing Company, Inc, 1969.

—— *Philmont: A History of New Mexico's Cimarron Country.* Albuquerque: University of New Mexico Press, 1972.

Myrick, David F. *New Mexico's Railroads: A Historical Survey.* Albuquerque: University of New Mexico Press; Revised edition, 1990.

—— *Railroads of Nevada and Eastern California: Volume 3: More on the Northern Roads.* c ed., Reno: University of Nevada Press, 2007.

New Mexico State Corporation Commission. *Fourth Annual Report of the State Corporation Commission of the State of New Mexico, 1915.* Accessed via Google Books.

Official Guide of the Railways. United States: National Railway Publication Company. June 1916. Cimarron and Northwestern Railway January 1915 public timetable.

—— June 1921. Cimarron and Northwestern Railway January 1921 public timetable.

Pearson, Jim Berry. *The Maxwell Land Grant.* Norman: University of Oklahoma Press, 1961.

Pietrak, Paul V., Joseph G. Streamer, and James A. Van Brocklin. *The History of the Western New York & Pennsylvania Railway Company and its Predecessor and Successors.* Hamburg, New York, 2000.

The Railway Age. Vol. 43, January 1 to June 30, 1907. Chicago: The Wilson Company, 1907. Accessed via Google Books.

Rohrbacher, Charles "Rock." *Philmanac: A Trekker's Guide to the Philmont Backcountry.* Eighth Edition, 2020.

Serna, Louis F. *A History of Cimarron, The Sawmills Camps Nearby, and the People Who Worked Them.* April 2020.

Taylor, Morris F. *Basil (Bill Metcalf) and His Toll Gate, Now in Union County, New Mexico Formerly in Colfax County, New Mexico 1872-1885.* Trinidad: Trinidad State Junior College, n.d.

Ward, Margaret. *Cimarron Saga.* Pampa, Texas: Pampa Print Shop, 1959.

Zimmer, Stephen, and Steve Lewis. *It Happened in the Cimarron Country.* Eagle Trail Press, 2013.

Private Collections

Sid Covington Photograph Collection.

Dawson Association Photograph Collection.

Friends of the Cumbres & Toltec Scenic Railroad.

Dennis Hogan Photograph Collection.

Steve Lewis Photograph Collection.

Alex Moushey Photograph Collection.

David O'Neill Photograph Collection.

Philmont Scout Ranch, Cimarron, New Mexico.
—— Photograph Collection.
—— Internal documents.
— Covington, Sid. "The Making of Metcalf Station: 2008 through 2014." Philmont Scout Ranch, Boy Scouts of America, September 2014.
— "Metcalf Station Camp Profile." 2019.
— "New Backcountry Staff Camp on Track," *PhilNews*, June 7, 2013, Issue 1.
— Van Dreese, John. "Railroading in the Ponil."

Stephen A. Zimmer Photograph Collection.

Public Collections

Aztec Mill Museum. Cimarron, New Mexico.
—— Fugera, William. "A History of Scrip." June 2005.
—— Historic Photographs Collection.
—— Koehler, Jr., Henry. *Prospectus: St. Louis Rocky Mountain and Pacific Company.* May 10, 1905.
—— McCandless, Charlie. "St. Louis, Rocky Mountain, and Pacific Train." Originally written for the *Raton Range*.
—— Williams, F.M. "St Louis, Rocky Mountain, and Pacific Railway: The Scenic Route of New Mexico." Reprinted brochure, Railroad Club of New Mexico, 1962.

Boston Public Library, Photographs of the American West: "The Raton Mountains, Line of Southern Colorado and New Mexico," Lead Photographer: Alexander Gardner.

Collection of Baldwin Locomotive Works Records. DeGolyer Library, Southern Methodist University, Dallas, Texas.
—— Baldwin Locomotive Works engine specifications, 1869-1938, Series 2, Volume 17, Page 143.
—— Baldwin Locomotive Works, Index of Companies, Construction Numbers from May 1889 to July 1896, Nos. 10000 – 14999, p 65.

Chase Ranch Foundation, Cimarron, New Mexico.
—— Historic Photographs Collection.
—— Memorandum of Agreement between Charles Springer and T.A. Schomburg, signed January 24, 1907.

Arthur Johnson Memorial Library, Raton, New Mexico.

—— Historic Photographs Collection.

Maxwell Land Grant Company Records. MSS 147. Center for Southwest Research, University of New Mexico Libraries, Albuquerque, New Mexico.

—— Continental Tie and Lumber Company, Estimate of Timber, Nov. 28, 1919.

—— Letter, Hunt to Cimarron Valley Land Company, June 19, 1918.

—— Letter, Jan Van Houten to Thomas W. Schomburg, 9 April 1935.

—— Minute Book 124, Special Meeting of Board of Trustees, March 3, 1916.

—— Agreement between Maxwell Land Grant Company and the Continental Tie and Lumber Company dated August 1, 1913.

—— Contract between Maxwell Land Grant Company and the Continental Tie and Lumber Company dated January 6, 1936.

—— Box 8, File Folder 6, Continental Tie and Lumber Company.

— Contract between Maxwell Land Grant Company and T.A. Schomburg dated April 1, 1904.

— Maxwell Land Grant Company Timber Royalties Due. October 1907, November 1907, December 1907, January 1908.

— Agreement between Maxwell Land Grant Company and the Continental Tie and Lumber Company dated January 31, 1908.

— Contract of Lease between Gray Lumber Company and Douglas-Guardian Warehouse Corporation, July 20, 1946.

— Letter, CT&L Co to J. Van Houten, December 10, 1924.

— Continental Tie and Lumber Company Inventory, March 8, 1938.

— Continental Tie and Lumber Memorandum of Property, November 30, 1925

—— Box 13, Folder 18, Tom Schomburg timber cruise, 1955.

Library of Congress Prints and Photographs Division, Public Domain Images.

National Scouting Museum. Philmont Scout Ranch, Cimarron, New Mexico.
—— Historic Photograph Collection.
—— Box 7A – Railroads – Rayado
— Roehm, Peter, "Taos and the Ghost Railroads of Philmont." 1955.
—— "Chase Ranch: History."
—— Continental Tie and Lumber Company, scrip No. 3077, issued Feb. 1, 1909.
—— Continental Tie and Lumber Company, masking tape.
—— Letter, New Mexico Governor John E. Miles to C.A. King, July 7, 1942.
—— Letter, H.G. Frankenburger to M.M. Chase, July 29, 1908.
—— Memorandum of Agreement between Charles Springer and T.A. Schomburg, signed January 24, 1907.
—— Schomburg, Thomas W. Interviewed by Lawrence Murphy at Denver, Colorado, June 9, 1964. Reel to reel tape transferred to MP3 file.

Raton Museum. Raton, New Mexico.
—— Historic Photographs Collection, Folder 43.
—— Copy of "Cimarron and Northwestern Railway, Located Line," Deed Book #31, 1907, Colfax County, New Mexico.
—— Right of Way Deed. Manly M. Chase to the Cimarron and Northwestern Railway Co. April 30, 1907.
—— "Ring." Research Binder by Nancy Robertson.

T. A. Schomburg Collection, MSS.747. History Colorado Center. Denver, Colorado.
—— File Folder 3, Correspondence 4/19/1898 – 6/13/1907.
—— File Folder 4, Correspondence 11/25/1903 – 3/13/1909.
— Letter, T.A. Schomburg to J. Hearne, August 30, 1904.
— Letter, T.A. Schomburg to Albert A. Miller, September 13, 1904.
— Letter, T.A. Schomburg to Albert A. Miller, February 9, 1905.
— Letter, T.A. Schomburg to Senator W.A. Clark, June 16, 1908.
—— File Folder 5, "History of the Administration of the Maxwell Land Grant 1887-1907."

—— File Folder 10, Raton and Elizabethtown Railway Prospectus, 1903.
—— File Folder 12
— Letter, H.G. Frankenburger to T.A. Schomburg, February 12, 1917.
— Minutes of the Special Meeting of the Board of Directors of the Continental Tie and Lumber Company.
— Undated and unaddressed document by T.A. Schomburg with elevation figures.
—— File Folder 14
— Letter, H.G. Frankenburger to T.A. Schomburg, April 1917.
— Telegram, T.A. Schomburg to H.G. Frankenburger, April 1917.
— Letter, T.A. Schomburg to Charles Springer, April 1917.
— Letter, Charles Springer to T.A. Schomburg, April 1917.
— Articles of Incorporation, New Mexico and Western Railway, March 8, 1918.
—— File Folder 16
— Hand-drawn timber estimate map, "Tp 29 N – R 17 E."
— Hand-drawn timber estimate map, "Tp 30 N – R 17 E."
—— File Folder 17, Letter, H.G. Frankenburger to T.A. Schomburg, February 1, 1909, "Estimate of Timber Controlled by CT&L Company," with attachment, "Estimate of Timber – February 1, 1909."
—— File Folder 22, Agreement between the Maxwell Land Grant Company and the Continental Tie and Lumber Company dated May 20, 1910.
—— File Folder 48.
— Theodore Schomburg's personal folded 1889 Maxwell Land Grant map in a leather pocketbook.
— Map of the Beaubien and Miranda Grant or Maxwell Grant in Colorado and New Mexico, 1889, as annotated by Theodore A. Schomburg
— Map Showing General Character of Lands Adjacent to the St. Louis, Rocky Mountain & Pacific Railway. Undated.
—— File Folder 50, Map of Rocky Mountain Timber Company timber estimates.
—— File Folder 105
— Letter, Rocky Mountain Timber Company to Maxwell Land

Grant Company, April 15, 1902.
— Letter, B. Kuckuck to T.A. Schomburg, March 25, 1912.
—— File Folder 106
— Letter, First National Bank of Denver to T.A. Schomburg, October 27, 1917.
— Letter, Natural Food Operating Company Inc. to T.A. Schomburg, July 27, 1920.
—— File Folder 107, Letter, Walter R. Sheldon to T.A. Schomburg, April 15, 1920.
—— File Folder 108, Letter, Z.J. Fort to T.A. Schomburg, March 18, 1925.
—— File Folder 109, Letter, Feather River Lumber Company to all shareholders, received by Thomas W. Schomburg, November 26, 1946.
—— File Folder 115, Incorporation of the Pagosa Lumber Company, 1920.
—— File Folder 119, Box Estimator, 1904 and 1928.
—— File Folder 178, Pagosa Lumber Company photographs.
PH.605. T.A. Schomburg Photograph Study Prints Collection.

Government Publications

Barnett, James P., Lueck, Everett W. 2020. Sawmill Towns: Work, Community Life, and Industrial Development in the Pineywoods of Louisiana and the New South. Gen. Tech. Rep. SRS-257. Asheville, NC: U.S. Department of Agriculture Forest Service, Southern Research Station.

Department of Commerce and Labor, Bureau of the Census. *Thirteenth Census of the United States: 1910 – Population*. Ponil Precinct 26, Colfax County, New Mexico.

Department of the Interior, National Park Service, National Register of Historic Places. The Ring Place National Register of Historic Places Continuation Sheet. NRIS # 88001054. July 19, 1988.

Department of the Interior, US Geological Survey.
—— Topographic map, Koehler Quadrangle, 1915. New Mexico Historical Topographic Maps, Perry-Castañeda Library Map Collection, University of Texas at Austin.
—— Topographic Map, "Raton, New Mexico; Colorado." 1954.

Interstate Commerce Commission.
—— *Annual Report on the Statistics of Railways in the United States.* 1916; 1920; 1921; 1923; 1924; 1925; 1926; 1927; 1928; 1929; 1930.
—— *Decisions of the Interstate Commerce Commission of the United States of America.* Vol. 82, Finance Reports. July – December 1923. Accessed via Google Books.
—— *Decisions of the Interstate Commerce Commission of the United States of America.* Vol. 106, Valuation Reports. October 1925 – February 1926. Accessed via Google Books.
—— *Decisions of the Interstate Commerce Commission of the United States of America.* Vol. 166, Finance Reports. June – December 1930. Accessed via Google Books.

Maps

"Map of the Maxwell Land Grant situated in the territories of Colorado and New Mexico. USA. Showing the Project Railways, 1870." Fray Angelico Chavez History Library, New Mexico History Museum. 78.9 F1870.

Palmes, Guy H. "Right of Way and Track Map Cimarron and Northwestern Railway." May 20,1917. United States National Archives and Records Administration, College Park, MD.

Newspapers

Albuquerque Daily Citizen. (Albuquerque, New Mexico). Chronicling America: Historic American Newspapers, Library of Congress. 22 March 1902, 29 March 1909.

Albuquerque Morning Journal (Albuquerque, New Mexico). Chronicling America: Historic American Newspapers, Library of Congress. 03 Jan. 1908, 31 July 1910, 12 July 1917, 16 Dec. 1917, 08 Feb. 1920, 7 March 1920.

Albuquerque Journal (Albuquerque, New Mexico). Journal Publishing Company. 19 Dec. 1909.
—— Dunn, Scott. "Bountiful Valley." 2 Nov. 2000.

Chronicle-News. (Trinidad, Colorado), 10 Nov. 1915. Colorado Historic Newspapers Collection, Colorado State Library.

Cimarron Citizen. (Cimarron, New Mexico). Chronicling America: Historic American Newspapers, Library of Congress. 15 April 1908, 03 June 1908, 17 June 1908, 18 March 1911, 27 May 1911, 15 Jan. 1914, 16 April 1914, 30 July 1914, 15 Oct. 1914, 31 Dec. 1914, 24 Feb. 1915.

Cimarron Citizen. Village of Cimarron. No. 47, Wednesday, February 10, 1909.

Cimarron News-Citizen. (Cimarron, New Mexico). University of New Mexico Digital Repository, New Mexico Historical Newspapers. 06-24-1911, 03-05-1914, 07-02-1914, 07-23-1914, 09-17-1914.

Cimarron News and Press (Cimarron, New Mexico). Chronicling America: Historic American Newspapers, Library Of Congress. 28 Feb. 1907, 21 March 1907, 4 April 1907, 11 April 1907, 14 March 1907, 23 May 1907, 30 May 1907, 13 June 1907, 20 June 1907, 11 July 1907, 8 August 1907, 5 September 1907, 24 October 1907.

Denver Post (Denver, Colorado). 20 Jan. 1929. Denver Public Library.

Las Vegas Gazette. (Las Vegas, New Mexico), Chronicling America: Historic American Newspapers. Library of Congress. 26 Oct. 1878.

Las Vegas Optic. (East Las Vegas, New Mexico). Chronicling America: Historic American Newspapers. Library of Congress. 05 Nov. 1909, 29 March 1909, 09 Dec. 1909.

La Revista de Taos. (Taos, Nuevo México), 14 Jan. 1921. Chronicling America: Historic American Newspapers. Library of Congress.

La Voz del Pueblo. (Santa Fe, Nuevo México), 26 April 1919. Chronicling America: Historic American Newspapers. Library of Congress.

Meeker Herald. (Meeker, Colorado). 01 Sept. 1894. Chronicling America: Historic American Newspapers. Library of Congress.

New Mexico State Record. (Santa Fe, New Mexico). 08 June 1917. Chronicling America: Historic American Newspapers. Library of Congress.

The Pagosa Springs Sun. (Pagosa Springs, Colorado), 9 Feb. 2017.

"Pagosa Lumbers into the 20th Century," by John Motter.

Raton Range (Raton, New Mexico). Microfilm. Arthur Johnson Memorial Library. 30 March 1907, 6 April 1907, 4 May 1907, 15 June 1907, 14 September 1907, 21 September 1907, 19 October 1907, 2 November 1907.

Rocky Mountain News (Denver, Colorado). 20 Jan. 1929. Denver Public Library.

Santa Fe New Mexican. (Santa Fe, New Mexico). Chronicling America: Historic American Newspapers. Library of Congress. 19 April 1890, 22 Aug. 1891, 25 Oct. 1905, 1 June 1907, 4 June 1907, 16 July 1907, 26 Dec. 1907, 15 January 1908, 02 April 1909, 12 April 1909, 20 Dec. 1909, 26 August 1913, 15 Dec. 1913.

The Silver Lance. (Crystal, Colorado). Chronicling America: Historic American Newspapers. Library of Congress. 6 Oct. 1899, 13 Oct. 1899.

Times-Promoter. (Hernando, DeSoto County, Miss.), 08 April 1909. Chronicling America: Historic American Newspapers. Library of Congress.

Online Databases and Websites

"Eagle Nest Dam," *Sidetracked Charley*, Blogspot, by Jacqui Binford-Bell. June 14, 2014. http://sidetracked-charley.blogspot.com/2014/06/eagle-nest-dam.html

"Fire Burns Sawmill in Cimarron, Smoke Forces Dozens of Families to Evacuate." KAOT Action News. April 15, 2001. https://www.koat.com/article/fire-burns-sawmill-in-cimarron/5010875

Kirkland, Jacqlyn. "New Mexico Gains New Sawmill Venture." Timber Harvester and Forest Operations. December 13, 2019. http://www.timberharvesting.com/new-mexico-gains-new-sawmill-venture/

Krasnow, Bruce. "NMEDD Awards $350,000 LEDA Grant to Resurrect Cimarron Sawmill." KRTN Radio, Raton, NM. December 11, 2019. https://krtnradio.com/2019/12/11/nmedd-awards-350000-leda-grant-to-resurrect-cimarron-sawmill/

"Living History: BNSF Helps Philmont Scout Ranch take Campers on an Unforgettable Adventure." Rail Talk, BNSF Railway. August 12, 2020. https://www.bnsf.com/news-media/railtalk/community/philmont.html

"Philmont Metcalf Station Project." The Santa Fe Railway Historical and Modeling Society. https://sfrhms.org/philmont-metcalf-station-project/

Steam Locomotive Dot Com.

—— PRR: Allegheny Valley / Buffalo, New York & Philadelphia / Cleveland, Akron & Columbus / Cornwall & Lebanon / Cumberland Valley / Grand Rapids & Indiana / Pennsylvania / Pennsylvania & Northwestern / Pittsburg, Cincinnati, Chicago & St. Louis / Western New York & Pennsylvania 2-8-0 "Consolidation" Locomotives in the USA. Class 163/H odd (Locobase 11648). https://www.steamlocomotive.com/locobase.php?country=USA&wheel=2-8-0&railroad=prr

—— The Pennsy Modeler. Keystone Crossings Databases. All Time Steam Locomotive Roster. Class H. http://pennsyrr.com/databases/steam/detail.php?q=11317

Written and Personal Correspondence

Lamm, Gene. Aztec Mill Museum, Cimarron, New Mexico. Email to Tucker Baker, May 6, 2020.

Leven, Carrie. Assistant East Zone Archaeologist, Questa Ranger District, Carson National Forest. Email to Tucker Baker, July 16, 2020.

Lueck, Everett. Certified Professional Geologist, The Woodlands, Texas. Letter and email to Tucker Baker with Google Earth KMZ file. April 25, 2020.

Van Dreese, John. General Manager, Northern Tier High Adventure Base, Boy Scouts of America. Ely, Minnesota. Phone Conversation with Tucker Baker, May 20, 2020.

Werhane, David. Director, National Scouting Museum, Philmont Scout Ranch, Boy Scouts of America. Cimarron, NM. Email to Tucker Baker, August 10, 2020.

Acknowledgments

The research and writing of this book were made possible through the kind support of our friends and family and prior historical research by many who preserved and shared the history of northeastern New Mexico and railroading in the American Southwest. This book would not have included the wealth of primary sources and knowledge contained in it were it not for the writing and investigative efforts of Lawrence R. Murphy, Ronald E. Bromley, Jim Berry Pearson, David Myrick, Samuel D. Bogan, Stephen Zimmer, and Steve Lewis. We are inspired by all these prior efforts, and we are deeply grateful for them.

Additionally, many Colfax County citizens that shared an appreciation for history made invaluable contributions to historical preservation and promotion, such as Audrey and Frank Alpers, Gene Lamm, the Cimarron Historical Society, the Aztec Mill Museum, and many others in the past whose names we do not know, but we know their contribution through preserved artifacts, maps, and photographs.

Lawrence Murphy deserves special credit for his research and writing on the Cimarron and Northwestern Railway and the Continental Tie and Lumber Company, including correspondence in the 1960s with company managers still living, recording an interview with Thomas W. Schomburg in 1964, and denoting the first authoritative series of works on the history of these two companies.

We are thankful for the Boy Scouts of America and Philmont Scout Ranch. Not only did these organizations have a positive impact on our lives, but they are also partially responsible for the writing of this book. Working at Philmont brought together three young men from North Carolina, Colorado, and Louisiana to work on a reconstruction of the Cimarron and Northwestern at Metcalf Station, and this was the first step toward this book. Metcalf Station holds a very dear spot in each of our hearts and we continue to contribute however we can to its ongoing success.

We are deeply grateful to the people and organizations that made Metcalf Station happen, including Bill Glavin, Mike Marler, Darwin Desen, David Witt, Sid Covington, David O'Neill, John Van Dreese, Mark Anderson, Herzog Railroad Services Inc., the Texas Department of Transportation Rail Division, the New Mexico Department of Transportation, the Union Pacific Foundation, and BNSF Railway.

John Van Dreese was the originator of the Metcalf Station concept and laid the foundation for the camp's future success. We are also thankful for his time to share his background, thoughts, and documents with us regarding the proposal and formation of Metcalf Station. Bill Glavin and Mike Marler also have our thanks for teaching us a skill that has served us well for many years: how to be safe working on railroads.

We are very thankful to two gentlemen that have been tremendous mentors and supporters, not just of our writing, but as great friends in life. David O'Neill has poured his heart into making Metcalf Station succeed and the camp is a shining testament to his hard work. He supported us both while we worked the summers at Philmont and during our research for this book. Sid Covington has supported our research and writing at each step, provided feedback on our initial draft, coordinated logistics for our research trip to New Mexico in June 2021, and has been a marvelous friend to each one of us. His support helped push this book across the finish line.

Thank you to David Werhane and Harold White at the National Scouting Museum at Philmont Scout Ranch. Harold transferred the old reel-to-reel tapes of the Lawrence Murphy interview of Thomas Schomburg to MP3 files, provided a transcript of the interview, and greatly assisted our in-person research while at the museum. David continually supported our research and writing through email correspondence, providing scans of historical documents and photographs, pointing us to other institutions housing valuable historical information, and allowing behind-the-scenes access to pertinent artifacts and photographs for our research. Deep appreciation is expressed to Gene Lamm for his writing advice, feedback of our draft, and providing numerous digitized historical photographs.

Thank you to Dennie Gum at the Raton Library, Roger Sanchez and Kathy at the Raton Museum, Catie Carl at the New Mexico History Museum, Tomas Jaehn at the Center for Southwest Research, Kellen Cutsforth, Katie Rudolph, and Sarah Ganderup at the Denver Public Library, Wes Pfarner at the Friends of the Cumbres and Toltec Scenic Railroad, Elizabeth Villa at New Mexico State University Library, Kay Peterson at the Smithsonian Institution, and Jori Johnson, Katie Bush, and Bethany Williams at the History Colorado Center.

Thank you to Everett Lueck who researched the geography and geology of the Cimarron and Northwestern Railway and provided research results of his LIDAR 1-meter review, along with numerous maps. Thank you to Dennis Hogan, Stephen Zimmer, David Caffey, and Carrie Leven who graciously provided background on the local area, valuable insight on historical writing, and correspondence that helped keep our research and writing on track. Gratitude is extended to those who provided copies of historic artifacts and photographs in their personal collections, including Dennis Hogan, Tim Gneier, David O'Neill, Stephen Zimmer, Steve Lewis, and Alex Moushey. A lasting gratitude is extended to our publisher, Steve Lewis.

Finally, thank you kindly to our family and close friends who supported us in this great historical endeavor. We could not have done this without you.

About the Authors

Tucker Baker

Transportation has always fascinated Tucker Baker. From spending time with his maternal grandparents who met working for the Southern Pacific Railroad in Louisiana or with his forester parents watching timber loading onto log trucks, he was always interested in the transporters of the world. His first taste of transportation was swinging spike hammers for the Boy Scouts of America as part of a living history program recreating the Cimarron and Northwestern Railway at Philmont Scout Ranch near Cimarron, New Mexico. His professional experience began as a dispatcher and later terminal manager for Miller Transporters, Inc. in New Orleans, Louisiana, handling bulk-liquids, largely hazardous chemicals. He graduated from Tulane University in 2016 with a degree in economics, lives in New Orleans, Louisiana, and currently works at the Port of New Orleans Napoleon Avenue Container Terminal. He serves as a volunteer and a member of the board of trustees at the Southern Forest Heritage Museum in Longleaf, Louisiana, which preserves and promotes history of forestry, railroading, and community life in the southern United States.

Matthew Hauser

Ever since riding behind a narrow-gauge steam locomotive at a young age, trains and railroads has been one of Matthew Hauser's greatest lifelong passions. In 2012 he began living that passion by volunteering in the Rail Operations Division at the North Carolina Transportation Museum in Spencer, North Carolina. Two years later Matthew enjoyed the unique opportunity of teaching participants how to build standard gauge railroad track by hand while interpreting the history of the Cimarron & Northwestern Railway at Metcalf Station at Philmont Scout Ranch. He would serve as a program counselor for two summers at Metcalf. He graduated from Western Carolina University in 2015 with a bachelor's degree in Engineering Technology. At the time of this project, Matthew works as a manufacturing engineer at Arneg USA in Lexington, North Carolina and continues volunteering as the Assistant Road Foreman of Engines at the North Carolina Transportation Museum.

Trevor Lombardi

Railroads came into Trevor Lombardi's life at the age of 3 on a visit to his grandparents' house in Wibaux, Montana. His room would shake whenever the Burlington Northern trains would pass on the line adjacent to the house. Waking up to those green diesels in the middle of the night was thrilling and as his childhood years went on, standing next to the driving wheel of a Union Pacific *Big Boy*, riding on the Durango & Silverton Narrow Gauge Railroad, and riding in a Galloping Goose solidified a fascination with railroading that is still present today. His cousin Jacob, a rail fan who formerly worked security for Union Pacific, used to take him around Colorado to watch freight trains go by before putting the passion to the wayside for being outcast by classmates for liking trains. It was not until getting the opportunity to work five summers at Metcalf Station at Philmont Scout Ranch which brought that passion front and center. The years spent at Metcalf gave him the opportunity to preserve and interpret railroad history to participants and staff with the desire to ignite or rekindle an interest in railroading in others. Trevor's passion also includes photography, similar to that of Theodore Schomburg, one of his railroading heroes. He currently works as a photo lab technician working with analog film and photo sublimation at Mike's Camera in Boulder and volunteers at the Colorado Railroad Museum as a Brakeman-In-Training.

Index

www.ingramcontent.com/pod-product-compliance
Lightning Source LLC
LaVergne TN
LVHW052351100826
845147LV00013B/813
* 9 7 8 0 9 9 7 4 2 6 7 5 5 *